Facts and Fictions About Coins

Facts & Fictions
about
COINS

Leon Lindheim

FUNK & WAGNALLS • NEW YORK

Library of Congress Catalog Card Number: 66-25885

First paperbound edition published 1968 by Funk & Wagnalls,
A *Division of* Reader's Digest Books, Inc.
Published by arrangement with The World Publishing Company

Printed in the United States of America

✑ Preface

In 1949 or 1950 I came across a copy of *The Numismatist*, the monthly publication of the American Numismatic Association. Although I had accumulated coins since childhood, I knew no collectors, never knew that coin clubs existed or that there was a national organization for numismatists.

Because I enjoyed reading *The Numismatist*, I wrote the A.N.A. asking how I might subscribe. Their answer was "join and receive the magazine gratis." This I did and to my surprise found myself flooded with auction catalogues and fixed price lists from firms that I never knew existed. My education was beginning.

About this time I met Mike Kolman, proprietor of the Federal Coin Exchange. He was then operating his business from his home. On my first visit he informed me that he had a basement stacked full of old copies of *The Numismatist*. We made a deal and I acquired most of the back issues from 1912 to date.

Evenings spent reading these back issues opened a whole new world to me. I became intimately acquainted with Farran Zerbe, Waldo Moore, Charles Steigerwalt, Lyman Low, the Chapman brothers, Captain William Hazeltine, B. Max Mehl, William Idler, Wayte Raymond, Robert McLachlan, and David Bullowa.

Next I discovered *Numismatic Scrapbook Magazine, Seaby's Coin and Medal Bulletin,* and *Spink's Numismatic Circular.* The latter two are house organs of London, England, coin firms and from them I acquired a taste for foreign proof sets.

My numismatic browsing eventually led to the acquisition of bound volumes of Scott's *Coin Collector's Journal* (1875–1885), Wayte Raymond's *Coin Collector's Journal* (1934–1950), and *Spink's Numismatic Circular* (1899–1930). Finally, with the purchase of most of the back issues of the *American Journal of Numismatics* (1866–1915), my library became fairly complete.

In time I found myself quoting the odd and interesting facts that I had so recently discovered. One of the patient individuals who listened to my numismatic ramblings informed me that he had been publishing a men's fashions monthly newspaper for two years. He suggested that I write down some of these facts and he would print them. After my writings appeared in six issues he decided to abandon the enterprise for a more profitable business that he had developed. Now the problem was what to do with all the material that I had written.

The ex-publisher was good enough to suggest that I submit this material to Phil Porter, who at that time was Sunday and Feature Editor of *The Plain Dealer*. The rest is history. "Coin-Wise" has appeared each Sunday in *The Plain Dealer* since December, 1960. This volume has drawn on the column for much of its basic material. However, I have had the happy experience of expanding much of this information, since the newspaper limited me to some five hundred words a week, and I tried to cover at least three different subjects each week in order that readers with varied interests would find some part of it to their liking.

It is my hope that you, too, will be stimulated into delving further into the fascinating subject of numismatics. My advice to the would-be collector is *"Read first, buy later."* The bibliography of this volume makes an excellent checklist.

Most of the photographs were obtained from the extensive files maintained by the American Numismatic Society. My thanks to this, the finest numismatic organization in the world, for their assistance.

Also my thanks go to Dave Rimmel, the present Sunday and Feature Editor of *The Plain Dealer*, for his help and encouragement; to Ralph and Terry Kovel, authors of the syndicated column "Know Your Antiques," for their words of wisdom over the past five years; to my dear wife, Isabelle, for her assistance in preparing the manuscript; and to Wallace Exman, my editor, for his patience in handling a neophyte author.

L. L.

Shaker Heights, Ohio
February, 1966

Facts and Fictions About Coins

Is numismatics concerned solely with money and money substitutes?

Questions of this nature are frequently asked. If you add medals and tokens, the answer today is yes. Eighty to ninety years ago this was not true.

A glance at the *Coin Collector's Journal* from 1875 to 1885 reveals that the numismatist of that day had many divergent interests. In fact, the American Numismatic Society was then known as the American Numismatic and Archaeological Society. The coin collector also collected and studied Indian arrowheads, mummies, autographs, and rare books.

An extremely interesting article in the *Coin Collector's Journal* of March, 1881, told of the celebration in New York City on February 22, 1881, when the famed Obelisk, known as Cleopatra's Needle, "presented to the United States by Ismail Khedive of Egypt," was erected in Central Park. For the benefit of the readers the hieroglyphics on two of the four sides were interpreted.

In another issue of the *Journal,* in May, 1881, a story told of a rare book sale in New York. Here a Gutenberg Bible realized the tremendous price of $8,000. (According to the Cleveland Public Library, an article in the February, 1962, issue of *Hobbies Magazine* mentioned that the last available copy was appraised in 1930 at $600,000.) In the same article prices realized for famous autographs were mentioned. A letter from Admiral Coligny to the Queen of Navarre was sold for $180.

Technically, these other fields are not numismatics, but there is nothing wrong with the inquisitive mind, from time to time, taking off on a tangent.

*Why were French coins used to produce
the first United States silver coins?*

James Ross Snowden, Director of the Mint, wrote a 400-page volume in 1860 entitled *A Description of Ancient and Modern Coins, in the Cabinet at the Mint of the United States.* In presenting the history of U.S. coinage he recounted that the first silver made into coins was from a deposit made by the Bank of Maryland on July 18, 1794, and that the deposit consisted of "coins of France" in the sum of $80,715.735.

It was not until October 15, 1794, that the Chief Coiner delivered the first silver dollars, amounting to 1,758 pieces. And not until December 1 was the second and last delivery of the year made, this being 5,300 half dollars. Mr. Snowden failed to mention that some half dimes were also struck in 1794, but the number coined is not known since they were delivered in 1795 along with pieces dated 1795. We do know that 86,416 half dimes were struck in the years 1794–1795. And assuming that 50 per cent were the earlier year, we come to the arithmetic conclusion that less than $6,600 worth of the more than $80,000 silver received on deposit was used.

We can now further conclude that at least part of the 1796 silver coinage of the United States could have been struck from "French" silver.

 Does Canada issue commemorative coins?

Yes, and all have been silver dollars except for the five-cent nickel struck in 1951 to honor the two-hundredth anniversary of the successful isolation of nickel by the Swedish chemist Cronstedt in 1751.

As far back as 1911 Canada was authorized to strike silver dollars, but not until 1935 did she strike her first one. This coin was minted to honor the silver jubilee of George V as King of

England. This fact was noted on the face of the coin with the words "GEORGIUS V REX. IMPERATOR ANNO REGNI XXV" (George V King, Emperor, the 25th Year of His Reign). Regular issues followed in 1936, 1937, and 1938.

Again, in 1939, to celebrate the visit of King George VI and Queen Elizabeth, Canada chose to strike a special silver dollar. For this occasion the reverse pictured the Parliament building at Ottawa.

With the advent of the war, silver dollars were not struck from 1940 until 1945. They have been struck each year since then. But not until 1949 was another commemorative dollar struck. This time the event honored was the entry of Newfoundland as a province. For this occasion the reverse carried a picture of the sailing ship *Matthew*, which brought John Cabot to North America and led to England's claims in the New World.

Nine years later, in 1958, the dollar honoring the one-hundredth anniversary of British Columbia as a Crown Colony was minted. This coin pictured a totem pole as the main design.

Finally, in 1964, the dollar commemorating the one-hundredth anniversary of the Charlottetown Conference, which paved the way to Confederation three years later, was struck.

Each piece is a representative work of art, making the collecting of the coins of Canada a pleasure.

✒ *What is Simon's Petition crown?*

During the time of Oliver Cromwell in England, in about 1650, the Mint decided to experiment with a new method of striking coins, which had been perfected in France by Pierre Blondeau. In place of the hammer and punch, the "mill and screw" method, which had been tried in England some ninety years earlier, was again introduced. With the older method the coin blank was placed between two dies and the blow of a hammer forced the design into the coin. The new, sophisticated "mill and screw" method employed the principle of slowly increasing the pressure by tightening a screw that forced the two dies closer together. The even pressure exerted by the latter method resulted in a better-struck coin. Some patterns were struck for Cromwell, but no regular issue used this improved technique.

When Charles II took the throne in 1660 he hired Blondeau to install his improved equipment in London. He then ordered that pattern coins of five-shilling (silver dollar) size be prepared by John Roettier of Antwerp and Thomas Simon, both engravers at

the Mint. The engraver whose pattern piece he preferred was to remain as Chief Engraver.

Experts today agree that Simon was the finer engraver, and produced a superior pattern piece. But Simon's effort was not as flattering a bust of Charles II, and the vain monarch chose Roettier as his Chief Engraver.

In desperation Simon sought to appeal to the king. His petition took the form of a struck copy of the pattern coin that he had submitted. Engraved around the edge in two lines was his petition, which read: "THOMAS. SIMON. MOST. HUMBLY. PRAYS. YOUR. MAJESTY. TO. COMPARE. THIS. HIS. TRY-ALL. PIECE. WITH. THE. DUTCH. AND. IF. MORE. TRULY. DRAWN. &. EMBOSS'D. MORE. GRACEFULLY. ORDER'D. AND. MORE. ACCURATELY. ENGRAVEN. TO. RELIEVE. HIM."

This Petition crown is one of the rarities of the British series, with only twenty copies reportedly struck. The petition failed. Roettier got the job and Thomas Simon won everlasting fame.

How did the Bureau of Engraving and Printing start?

A Treasury Department bulletin says: "The beginning of the Bureau of Engraving and Printing may be traced as far back as August 29, 1862, when a force of two men and four women working in a single room in the attic of the main Treasury building began to separate, seal and sign $1 and $2 notes which had been printed by private contractors."

United States currency had its birth with the advent of the Civil War. A financially hard-pressed country found it necessary to print money that could not be redeemed for gold or silver. By an Act of Congress of July 17, 1861, sixty million dollars of "legal tender" money was authorized. This paper money was printed by private bank note companies in New York City and hand signed by government officials. This process was slow and cumbersome.

A young government worker named S. M. Clark is credited with suggesting the use of facsimile signatures, a completely new concept. Salmon P. Chase, Secretary of the Treasury, approved the idea, which has been in continuous use since 1862. Young Mr Clark was not to be denied. He next invented a machine to cut the notes, eliminating another hand operation. Clark was one of the two men referred to in the first paragraph.

Although in 1864 it was recommended that The Engraving and Printing Bureau of the Treasury Department be established, pressure from private bank note companies caused delays. Official recognition of this department was not received until 1876. And only after October 1, 1877, were all obligations of the United States centralized in this division of the Treasury Department.

What was the first Congressional Medal?

The Continental Congress was convened in 1774. But it was not until March 25, 1776, that it authorized its first medal.

General George Washington had, with his troops, forced the British to evacuate the city of Boston on March 17, 1776. Eight days later the grateful Congress authorized that a special gold medal be struck and presented to the General.

Congress appointed John Adams, a delegate from Boston (and later the second President of the United States), to head a commission to arrange for the execution of the medal. They commissioned Pierre Duvivier of France to design the medal.

The face shows a strong head of Washington, surrounded with words in Latin that translate to: "The American Congress to George Washington, Commander-in-Chief of its Armies, Protector of Liberty." The reverse pictures Washington and four other soldiers, all on horseback, watching from a hilltop the British vessels sailing out of Boston harbor.

The presentation was made in Philadelphia with a resolution that read in part ". . . that the thanks of the body, whom they represent, be presented to Gen. Washington and the officers and soldiers under his command, for their wise and spirited conduct of the siege and acquisition of Boston."

Copies in bronze may still be obtained from the United States Mint at Philadelphia.

Why are so many old coins inexpensive and so many new coins expensive?

Hoards of ancient coins, Roman and Greek, are continually being uncovered. In those early days, the threat of a foreign invasion was the signal to get out the shovel and bury the family wealth. One hoard was discovered in 1936 in Dorchester, England, that contained 22,121 Roman pieces, all minted between A.D. 211 and 257, with many in uncirculated condition. Thus the great number of coins available for collectors has tended to keep their individual price within a modest range.

However, until 1935, relatively few uncirculated specimens of modern coinage were set aside for the future collector. Since then, a group of investors has come into being who specialize in buying and selling uncirculated coins by the roll. Their number has grown tremendously since 1960, and the amount of coins available for collectors has thus decreased considerably.

A prime example of this matter of supply and demand is a Roman silver denarius, obtained in Europe in 1958 by a member of my family. This beautiful uncirculated coin, minted about 200 B.C., cost less than $2. At the same time, an uncirculated 1921 United States dime, almost identical in size and design (both show a winged, helmeted god) sold for about $100. No rolls of dimes were being set aside for investment in 1921. What a shame!

✒ What English adjective originally referred to a coin?

The word is "picayune," which will be found in any modern English dictionary. Its English meaning is "little," "worthless," "mean," or "cheap." Originally it was of French origin, referring to a small French coin called a "picaillon." The Creoles of early Louisiana and New Orleans, being of French descent, used the term, but corrupted it to picayune. They used this picturesque word when referring to the Spanish-American (Mexican) half-real coin that circulated in that part of the country. Later, when this territory became part of the United States, the small silver United States half dimes were also called picayunes. Today this word is accepted as a good English adjective and almost never is used as a noun referring to a coin.

✒ *Who is V. D. B.?*

Every schoolboy (or schoolgirl) who has collected Lincoln pennies knows to look on back of the 1909 (first year of issue) to see if these famous initials appear. If they do, the young collector knows that he has one of the early strikes of the 1909 one-cent piece. The designer of the Lincoln cent, Victor David Brenner, placed his initials on the bottom of the reverse side in small letters, but not small enough to go unnoticed. Public indignation caused Mint officials to fill in on the reverse die and thus eliminate the initials.

This famous sculptor and medalist was born Viktoras Bamavskas in 1871 in Lithuania. His training started at the age of thirteen when he assisted his father engrave seals and work at stone cutting. From the ages of sixteen to nineteen he worked as a jewelry engraver. In 1890 he came to America and anglicized his name. He continued his formal schooling in New York, attending the Cooper Union and the School of the National Academy of Design. At the age of twenty-seven he moved to Paris to become a pupil of Louis Roty, who designed many of France's coins. After two years he returned to New York and opened his own studio.

Brenner gained renown through award-winning works in the Paris Exposition in 1901 and the Louisiana Purchase Exposition in 1904. By 1908 he had thirty-nine pieces in the Metropolitan Museum of Art in New York City. This same year he produced an outstanding plaque of Abraham Lincoln in honor of the one-hundredth anniversary of the Emancipator's birth. The plaque was followed by a medal that was enthusiastically received by the public. Of the latter, the New York *Tribune* wrote: "It bears an excellent

BRENNER'S 1908 PLAQUE
OF LINCOLN

likeness of Lincoln . . . it has simplicity and dignity."

When it was decided to honor Lincoln on the one-cent piece, it was only natural that he was given the commission to execute the design.

V. D. B. died in 1924 at the early age of 52.

 Is topical collecting popular with coin collectors?

This is the type of question often asked by the philatelist. Topical collecting has been very popular with stamp collectors. The topical collector is not interested in any particular country, or type of coin (such as dollars of the world, commemorative pieces, pioneer gold) He searches for items that relate to a particular subject, as flags, birds, animals, transportation, heroes. Of course, it can be done, but it is a little more difficult and quite a bit costlier. After all, stamps are merely printed paper and after cancellation have no exchange value. But a used coin will buy as much as a new coin.

I suggest, as a starter, a topical collection showing ships on coins. Here are a few to look for: In the United States, commemorative half-dollar series are 1936 Delaware, 1892 or 1893 Columbian, 1920 or 1921 Pilgrim, 1924 Huguenot-Walloon, 1935 Hudson, N.Y., 1936 Norfolk, Va.; foreign examples are 1953 Bermuda crown, 1932 Brazil 200 reis, current Canadian 10 cents, 1949 Canadian silver dollar, 1932 or 1936 Chinese silver dollar.

Now, after you have a representative collection, it is time to search out the historical significance of each ship, vessel, boat, or craft. And of course you will want to identify each type of ship.

When you get tired of modern coins it is time to look back in history. A multi-oared galley is shown on a Phoenician coin of about 200 B.C. A ship's prow is pictured on some of the earliest Roman bronzes. Ships are scarce on medieval coins, but we do have the fourteenth-century British golden angel showing a beautiful sailing vessel.

☙ Who was the first living American to be pictured on a United States coin?

In early 1920, there was a concerted effort by various groups to have commemorative half dollars struck to honor events that were dear to their hearts. Congress was in a generous mood and on May 10, 1920, authorized the striking of 100,000 half dollars in honor of the one-hundredth anniversary of the admission of the State of Maine to the Union and a like number for the one-hundredth anniversary of the admission of the State of Alabama.

That two commemorative coins were authorized on one day was most unusual since from the time of the establishment of the Mint in 1792 only three other commemorative half dollars had ever been approved. These were the Columbian in 1892, the Panama-Pacific in 1915, and the Illinois Centennial in 1918.

Precedent was broken with the execution of the design for the Alabama Centennial coin. The obverse pictures busts of William Wyatt Bibb, the first governor of Alabama, and Thomas E. Kilby, her governor in 1920.

Laura Gardin Fraser, the designer of the coin, broke with tradition in portraying a living person on a coin of the United States. Although no laws or statutes prohibited the action, it was understood that George Washington had requested that his face not appear on a United States coin and this was enough to establish a precedent that lasted for one hundred and twenty-seven years.

The coin is dated 1921, but because Alabama was admitted to statehood in 1819, the dates 1819 and 1919 appear on the reverse.

This half dollar also initiated a new idea, used by later issues to generate additional sales. This was to show an incused (cut in) design on the field on a limited number of coins, then remove this

special design and thus create a second variety. This was relatively simple to do, as an incused design is made by a raised portion of the die. Buffing off this raised portion eliminates the incused design. In this particular case a "2 × 2," calling attention to the fact that Alabama was the twenty-second state admitted to the Union, appeared on the first 6,000 coins. Then the "2 × 2" was buffed off the die and an additional 64,000 (of which 5,000 were remelted) were struck.

Until 1950 the "2 × 2" variety enjoyed a much higher retail price in uncirculated condition. After that date the price differential virtually disappeared. This indicates that most of the common variety were not treasured highly, with the result that many became pocket pieces and could no longer be classed as uncirculated. And the series of commemorative half dollars is almost always collected in strictly uncirculated condition.

What is a toughra?

The toughra (or toghra or tughra) is the name of a device that at times looks like a triple G clef. It was used, since the fourteenth century, by the Turkish Ottoman Empire on her documents and later on her stamps and coins.

According to some histories it had its beginning with Murad I (1319–1389), who was Sultan of the Ottoman Empire from 1359 until his death. He was illiterate and, when asked to sign a treaty, he was said to have placed the first three fingers and thumb of his right hand in an ink pot and made a flourish. This created an interesting monogram that was used with variations by future sultans.

The finger flourishes of Murad I led to a refinement in which the names of the ruling sultan and of his father were woven into the lines. This was a usual practice, since in those days people in the Middle East were known as So-and-So son of So-and-So. The script might even be more elaborate and say, for example, Sultan Murad, son of Ali the Illustrious.

With the death of the Otto-man Empire in 1923 and the birth of the Turkish Republic, the toughra no longer appears on coins. Since it was definitely associated with the Ottoman sultans, it probably never will be seen again on documents, stamps, or coins.

Is it true that Caruso was a coin collector?

Enrico Caruso was more than a coin collector; he was a true numismatist, collecting the finest both in objects of art and medals and coins.

It was not generally known until after his death in 1921 that the great operatic star enjoyed this hobby. Henry Chapman of Philadelphia, a well-known coin dealer of that time, cataloged some three hundred coins from the Caruso estate that were sold on March 5, 1923, along with other of Caruso's art objects at the gallery of the American Art Association, 30 E. 57th St., New York City.

This collection was known to be only a small part of his total holdings, the bulk being retained in Italy pending the outcome of certain court rulings. To illustrate the quality of the pieces sold in New York we can point out three United States gold pieces, all uncirculated. The first was a 1795 eagle, which realized $90. The second was a 1915 Panama-Pacific fifty-dollar round piece that brought $160. The third was the 1915 Panama-Pacific fifty-dollar octagonal piece that sold for $170. (The 1966 catalog lists them at $2,500, $6,000, and $4,750 respectively.)

Two months later it was announced that in June, 1923, the firm of C. & E. Canessa of Naples, Italy, would sell the balance of his collection. Besides a group of fine medals, this accumulation included rarities of ancient Greece, Roman, Byzantine, and medieval, as well as modern Italian, European, and American coinage.

Only after the sale was it generally known that the whole collection of over 1,700 pieces were all gold coins or medals. Truly, Caruso collected only the finest.

✌ *How much is a gold talent?*

Those of you who either read General Lew Wallace's historical novel *Ben Hur* or saw the movie adapted from the book may remember the betting on the chariot race. The wealthy Romans wagered one or more gold talents.

At a time when coinage was in its infancy, many of the commercial transactions were completed in gold or silver by weight. The dictionary defines a talent as a unit of weight with a minimum of fifty-eight pounds. The United States government buys gold at $35 an ounce. At this government buying price, one talent of gold is worth a minimum of $32,480, quite a fortune.

ᥦ Does the United States have a coin collection?

On March 3, 1839, Congress appropriated $1,000 for specimens of ore and coins to be preserved at the Mint. Thereafter, for more than twenty years, an annual appropriation of $300 was requested and received in order to increase the collection.

But even before 1839, unusual foreign coins that were redeemed at their intrinsic value at the Mint were saved toward the day that a coin cabinet would be authorized by Congress. This foresight allowed for the acquisition of fine pieces at a relatively low cost.

This collection was housed at the Philadelphia Mint until March, 1923. In that year Secretary of the Treasury Andrew Mellon authorized its removal to the Smithsonian Institution in Washington, D.C. Although there was a public outcry from the citizens of Philadelphia on the loss of this tourist attraction, it had to be conceded that the collection would receive far greater exposure in the nation's capital.

By 1923 the collection, which included medals, decorations, tokens, and paper money, as well as coins from around the world, exceeded fifty thousand pieces. At that time it was admitted that this collection was only the second largest in the United States, the largest being that of the museum of the American Numismatic Society in New York City.

Aside from outright purchases, foreign governments have made gifts of their new issues to this coin cabinet. An outright bequest of some 1,300 medals and tokens of Abraham Lincoln was received from the estate of Robert Hewitt of New York. In 1954 the Bureau of Engraving and Printing presented a specially prepared set in duplicate of all current United States currency from one-dollar to ten-thousand-dollar bills. By 1954 the collection had grown to over sixty thousand specimens.

Since the Mint collection includes all major types of coins of the world since the first coinage of about 700 B.C. to the present, it is recommended that a trip to Washington should include a visit to the coin room of the Smithsonian Institution.

What are "star" notes?

In the series of small-size United States currency that has been in use since 1929, these are the bills used to replace notes that have been rejected.

Rejections occur because of improper printing, defects in the paper, and errors in cutting. Since notes are numbered and are packaged in numerical sequence, there must be some special series that can be used so that each package of one hundred notes can begin with "01" and end with "00."

United States currency begins and ends with a letter of the alphabet, with eight digits between. Federal Reserve notes begin with the letter that designates the district (A for Boston, B for New York, C for Philadelphia, D for Cleveland, E for Richmond, F for Atlanta, G for Chicago, H for St. Louis, I for Minneapolis, J for Kansas City, K for Dallas, and L for San Francisco), while all other series start with A-A and, after completing A-Z, switch to B-A.

The "star" replaces the first letter in all series except the Federal Reserve notes. In this series the "star" replaces the final letter.

Do people collect imperfectly printed paper money, and if so, what?

There are some paper money collectors who specialize in misprints, just as there are many who collect coins that have been misstruck.

Paper money errors are far scarcer than coinage errors. The work at the Mint is highly automated, as it must necessarily be in order to produce the tremendous quantities needed by a nation with a continually expanding population and economy. Until a mint-sealed bag of coins is opened at the Federal Reserve Bank, at another bank, or by a bank customer, the individual coins have probably not been seen by human eyes.

Quite the contrary is true at the Bureau of Engraving and Printing. Each bill is inspected many times during the printing operation. These inspections take place both before and after the sheets of eighteen and thirty-two notes are cut into individual notes. When a misprint is noted a red-and-white-striped rejection sticker is placed on the note.

But every so often printing errors are overlooked and even notes with the rejection sticker intact sometimes reach the public. To understand how errors may occur, it will be helpful to know how notes are printed. First the green reverse is printed on the sheets, followed after a day or so, when the sheets are dry, with the printing of the black obverse. Finally the obverse is over-printed with signatures, seal, series, and numbers. The sheets are then cut into individual notes and these are packaged in numerical order. At this point "star" notes are used to replace any rejected notes.

With all these steps in production, it is understandable that errors occur. For example, a fold in the paper prior to printing can result in a white unprinted line when the paper is later smoothed out. An extra piece of paper, lying over part of the sheet when it is in the press, can cause part of a note to be unprinted. Failure in the mechanism of the numbering machine can cause different numbers to appear on the lower left and upper right. A fold in the sheet after it has gone through the first two processes can cause missing or partially missing seals, signatures, or numbers. Misalignment of the sheet after one side has been printed can cause parts of two or more bills to appear on the reverse. (It could happen the other way around, but this is not likely since the face gets more inspections than the back.) Ink smudges are considered errors, but these are fairly common. Mirror reverses may show on the obverse, because of improperly cleaned rollers. Then there is the ultimate and most sought-after error, the double denomination note, in the printing of which plates of different value bills were used—for example, a ten-dollar face and a twenty-dollar back.

This is an exciting series to collect, but the pickings are slim.

ॐ When did Australian coinage start?

The Commonwealth Coinage Act of 1908 provided for the establishment of a separate and distinct type of coins for Australia. Until then, only the coins of England served this sparsely populated country. The denominations were to be similar to the English coins that circulated there at the time and the British duodecimal system was to continue.

In 1910 the first truly Australian coins were struck at the Tower Mint in London. These were the silver three pence, six pence, shilling, and florin (2 shillings). In 1911 the bronze half penny and penny were added. In the years prior to 1916 all the coins of Australia were struck either at the Tower Mint or at Heaton's Mint in Birmingham, England. These latter pieces had the mint mark "H" on the coin.

By 1916 the Melbourne Mint had been completed and for at least the next four years all of Australia's silver coins were minted there. The Sydney Mint opened in 1919, first coining half pennies. Until it closed in 1926 it struck some of each coin denomination used "down under."

The Perth Mint opened in 1921, striking pennies dated 1922, but struck no other coins until 1940. Only in 1946 did Perth strike a silver coin—a sixpence piece.

Had Australia been able to foresee the necessity for a changeover to a decimal system and arranged for it in 1908, she would literally have saved millions of dollars. As of February, 1966, a mass changeover took place. Not only did all transactions, credits, debits, notes, bank balances, and the like have to be converted to dollars and cents, but also bookkeeping machines, computers, cash registers, and other mechanical devices.

Because of a well-executed program of education, begun more than a year prior to the changeover, the transition took place without undue confusion.

What commemorative coins has Australia struck?

The Commonwealth of Australia has been very stingy in her output of commemorative coins. To date only four such issues have been minted. All of these are florins or two-shilling pieces.

It was seventeen years after Australia began her own coinage —in 1910—that she struck her first commemorative coin. This florin of 1927 had a mintage of 2,000,000 pieces and was ordered to honor the first session of Parliament in its new building in Canberra, the federal capital. For the occasion, on May 7, 1927, the Duke of York came from England to represent his father, King George V, at the opening ceremonies.

The second commemorative florin was dated 1934–1935. The double date was used because the coin was to honor two events. The first was the one-hundredth anniversary of the founding of the city of Victoria in 1834; the second was the one-hundredth anniversary of the founding of Melbourne the following year. Melbourne, which had its modest beginnings in 1835 with the erection of a few huts on the banks of the Yarra River, grew to become the capital when the Commonwealth was founded in 1901 and remained the seat of government until the opening of the new Parliament buildings in Canberra in 1927. This coin is rare. Only 75,000 were minted and of these 21,000 were remelted, leaving a net mintage of only 54,000 pieces.

In 1951, to celebrate the fiftieth anniversary of the Commonwealth, the third commemorative florin was struck. Two million pieces were minted, making it fairly common.

The last of the series was in 1954, when a florin was struck to honor the visit of Queen Elizabeth II. This piece had a mintage of 4,000,000 coins. Much unfavorable comment was received when it was struck. There was nothing on the coin to indicate why it was struck. The reverse merely showed a kangaroo and lion side by side, and critics felt that mention of the historic occasion should have been made on the coin.

The earlier issues left no doubt as to why they were struck. In 1927, the reverse read "PARLIAMENT HOUSE AUSTRALIA" and pictured the new edifice. In 1934–1935 the reverse pictured a man on horseback holding up a flaming torch and the words "CENTENARY–VICTORIA–MELBOURNE–1934–35." And the 1951 issue showed six stars, representing New South Wales, Victoria, South Australia, Queensland, Tasmania, and Western Australia, which joined together to form the Commonwealth, and the dates "1901–1951."

The florin commemorative issues are finished. There will be no more than four, for Australia has now changed to a decimal coinage of dollars and cents.

🎕 How are proof coins made?

A proof coin is meant to be as perfect a coin as can be made, in other words a "flawless gem." To start with, the blanks (planchets) that are to be used are carefully chosen. Blanks free of heavy scratches are selected and then chemically washed to remove dirt or grease. The dies used are highly polished and during all stages of production are kept clean of any imperfections that might be in the air. In order that all details show up to the fullest, the regular coining machines are not used. Instead, the hydraulic presses generally used to strike medals are employed. The blanks are individually hand-fed into the coining machine and care is taken that the coins are not mishandled. The result is a gem coin with a mirrorlike finish and a high square edge. The mirrorlike finish is obtained because a clean blank and a clean die result in coins with no rough surfaces to break up light and therefore light is perfectly or almost perfectly reflected. The high square edge is produced by the coin's being struck with a great deal of pressure, causing the metal to be pressed firmly against the collar in the coining press.

Proof coins that have a matte finish, not generally seen today, are either the result of the dies' being pickled in acid to give them a rough surface or of the coin's being sand-blasted after being struck. Either method produces a coin with a dull surface instead of a smooth mirrorlike one.

✒ What is a "frosted head proof"?

United States proof coins of the period from 1858 to 1915 generally showed the main design, whether Seated Liberty, Liberty Head, or Indian Head, with a frosty or satinlike appearance, while the field (background) had a mirrorlike appearance, causing the main design to show up to good advantage. This was done by intentional polishing of the part of the die that struck the field and not polishing the part that struck up the design.

The proofs of 1936 and later were generally mirrorlike in all details because the whole die and not just the field was highly polished. When one of these late proofs was similar in appearance to the early proofs, special note was made in referring to it as a "frosted head proof."

Originally a set of proof or specimen coins was made at the direction of the Head of State (king, president, dictator) to be presented as a gift, generally through an ambassador, to the head of another state. These perfect gem coins were presented in a special ornate case. The demand from collectors resulted in similar sets being struck in limited numbers to fill the numismatist's desire for as near perfect specimens as possible. In the United States, before 1858 only the favored few were allowed to obtain proof coins or sets. After 1858 collectors could order sets directly from the Treasury Department, but, sad to say, they were not struck during each year since then. From 1858 to 1915 sets were struck each year. During many of these years it took pressure from the collecting public to get the Treasury Department to make these "gems." The Mint tended to balk at producing the perfect or near-perfect coins because of the extra time and trouble it took to make them, and because these coins were being requested in increasingly smaller numbers each year. From a high of 1,355 sets in 1880 the numbers ordered each year gradually decreased until in 1914 only 380 sets were ordered and in 1915 only 450 sets. The advent of World War I gave mint officials the needed excuse to discontinue the production of proof sets, because now the U.S. Treasury Department had requests to manufacture coins and medals for foreign governments. Not until 1936 was sufficient pressure put on the Treasury Department to produce this press release: "Secretary Morgenthau has announced he had authorized the Mint to resume the practice of issuing 'proof' coins—pieces stamped from polished discs, which are regarded as near perfection." The striking of these coins continued for only seven years, this time interrupted by World War II, and again the Mint found it necessary to strike coins and medals for foreign governments. But unlike the conditions that existed in 1914 and 1915, by now the demand had increased yearly and 21,120 sets were struck in 1942. And finally, after another seven years, President Truman signed a bill on May 10, 1950, to resume the manufacture of proof coins. They have continued to be minted each year since, through 1964.

In England, the early proof sets such as those of 1826, 1839, and 1854 were sold by the Mint officials for their personal gain. But beginning in 1887, with the set issued to commemorate Queen Victoria's golden jubilee, the public was allowed to purchase sets at will. Within recent years, some of the newly formed African nations have struck large numbers of proof coins, far out of proportion to their size and regular coinage. In these cases it must be assumed that the coins were struck to create additional revenue for these newly created nations.

✺ Why are early U.S. proof sets so expensive?

Have you heard of the population explosion? It has been nothing compared to the proof set explosion.

Between 1863, when records were first kept, and 1915 the demand was comparatively small. The maximum number struck was 1,355 sets in 1880 and the minimum number was 380 sets in 1914.

When proofs were again made in 1936, 3,837 sets were ordered, and each year more were made until, by 1942, 21,120 sets were made. Provided the facilities were available, the Mint produced as many sets as the public requested. In these early years, the demand caused no production problems.

After the end of World War II there was a great public demand that the Mint again strike proof sets. Fearing an avalanche of orders, the Treasury Department announced in 1950 that proofs would again be struck, but with a limit of five sets per person. Thereafter, the number allowed per person varied, and at times orders were even cut back—but the explosion was on. The annual production from 1950 to 1964 tells the story:

1950——51,386	1954——233,300
1951——57,500	1955——378,200
1952——81,980	1956——669,384
1953——128,800	1957——1,247,952

1958——875,652	1962——3,218,019
1959——1,149,291	1963——3,075,645
1960——1,691,602	1964——3,950,762
1961——3,028,244	

Even assuming that 90 per cent of the sets sold in the period of 1961–1964 were purchased for speculation and only 10 per cent by collectors, this means that some 300,000 or more collectors might wish to own early proof sets. But even if only 1 per cent of that number (3,000) were in the market vying for sets struck prior to 1916, it is small wonder that a 1914 half dollar in proof sells for over $500.

🐟 Why did American collectors become interested in foreign proof sets?

A few collectors have always been interested in this series, but the average numismatist did not "discover" these beautiful sets until 1964.

When the United States Treasury Department placed a "freeze" on the date 1964, continuing to date coins minted in 1965 with the date 1964, and discontinuing to issue proof sets, the American collector started to look elsewhere to satisfy his appetite for more and different types of coins.

Almost overnight the proof sets of South Africa, Australia, and Great Britain, to name a few, started to spiral upward in value. Seeing a "good thing," other nations started to issue sets. These included Austria, Germany, Malta, Malawi, Sierra Leone, and Zambia, all looking toward the American market.

The striking of proof sets is not a new idea. In the English series, proof sets have been struck intermittently since 1826. South Africa struck her first proofs in 1892. Bolivian sets are known from as far back as 1884. These early sets are rare, with few struck. This is only because there was little demand for them, not because there was any idea to create a rarity.

🎐 *What is a puffin?*

First, a puffin is a sea or marine bird, a member of the auk family; but, second, and more important (except to the puffin), it is a coin value.

The puffin and half-puffin coins in bronze were the creation of one Martin Coles Harmon who, in 1925, purchased the Isle of Lundy, off the English coast. He then declared his island to be independent and proceeded in 1929 to have coins struck in Birmingham, England, for his "empire."

A news dispatch from Bideford, Devonshire, England, date-lined April 15, 1930, announced the beginning of Mr. Harmon's problems:

Martin Coles Harmon, London businessman and owner of Lundy Island, in the Bristol Channel, off the north coast of Devonshire, today was fined £5 with 15 guineas cost, on a charge of issuing special coins in his island kingdom. Mr. Harmon bought the island in 1925 and has been more or less of an uncrowned king over the forty residents since the island's position regarding the sovereignty of the British empire has been the subject of dispute.

The London financier refused to acknowledge the jurisdiction of the Devonshire court and declined to plead the case, but the court held that issuing the coins was contrary to the coinage act. Mr. Harmon's attorney declared that the island was "outside world," that no taxes were paid and there was no register of births, deaths, or marriages. He cited various legal cases in which he contended the British courts had held the Island of Lundy was outside of the United Kingdom.

This was not the end of "King" Harmon's troubles. In 1933 he was arrested along with three other financiers and charged with conspiracy to defraud. A special cable dispatch from London to *The New York Times* in March, 1934, reported:

Martin Coles Harmon, uncrowned "King" of Lundy Island and a picturesque figure in the London financial world, was sentenced to eighteen months imprisonment for conspiracy to defraud. After a sixteen-day trial at Old Bailey the jury found Mr. Harmon guilty of having misapplied funds of the Chosen Corporation, of which he was a director.

R. S. Yeoman's *A Catalog of Modern World Coins* lists the coins with a notation that "these 'unlawful coins' have created considerable interest among collectors and for that reason have been included in this volume."

The face of both coins shows the head of Harmon and the inscription "MARTIN COLES HARMON 1929." The reverse shows the head of the puffin bird on the half puffin and the complete bird on the puffin. At least Mr. Harmon had the good grace not to use the word "king," "emperor," or "ruler" on his coinage.

✒ What qualities originally made money acceptable in place of goods?

The office of Director of the Mint, Treasury Department, issued a release a number of years ago that probably does the finest job of defining the qualifications. Its definition reads in part: "Of course, you know that years ago the barter system was in effect instead of money. At another time, laborers were paid in the commodity that they manufactured rather than money. We can easily see the inconvenience of these customs. It sometimes worked out all right for the man who was a baker—he could take his pay in bread—but the poor fellow who made wheelbarrows and windmills had a difficult time trying to trade his wares for food and clothing for the family. After all, the butcher may already have 25 or 30 wheelbarrows!" (The release then goes on to list the six special qualities needed to do the job properly.)

Cognizability—The word "recognize" comes from the same root—it means the quality the commodity has that makes it readily distinguishable. In short, the butcher and baker will not have to examine it at great length to recognize what it is.

Divisibility—The quality a commodity has that lets it be readily divided so that the several parts will have the same value as the whole. This quality is not prevalent in many substances. Take diamonds, for instance. A large diamond may be of very great value, but if it is cut into smaller stones the sum of their values would not nearly equal the value of the one larger stone.

Durability—The quality of not wearing out. Cloth and food do not possess this quality and it is a most desirable one, particularly if you want to save.

Portability—The quality of being easy to carry. Lack of portability was the trouble with the windmills!

Homogeneity—Remember homogenized milk? That is milk with the same amount of cream throughout the entire bottle. For a metal to have this quality it must be capable of being divided into hundreds of parts and still retain value. For an illustration, take a block of gold about the size of a box of safety matches. This gold is worth about $35.00 an ounce. It is also homogeneous, so that if you chipped a little piece of it off—about the size of a pencil point—that chip would also be worth $35.00 an ounce.

Stability—The quality of retaining its value. It must be scarce enough to make it valuable and yet plentiful enough to meet the demand for it.

If we examine copper (bronze), silver, and gold, we discover that they meet the requirements necessary to change a barter system into an acceptable monetary system.

✒ Why is the Russian ruble of 1883 so common?

A report of the occasion was given in the *Coin Collector's Journal* of October, 1883. Alexander III (1845–1894) became Czar of Russia following the assassination of his father, Alexander II, in 1881.

His coronation took place on May 27, 1883. For this historic event a special coronation ruble was struck. On its face appears a bust of the Czar with the words in Russian translating to: "By the Grace of God Alexander III Emperor and Autocrat of all the Russias Crowned in Moscow 1883." The reverse pictures the royal crown and scepter.

At the time it was believed that the whole issue was passed out to guests attending the regal event, but later official figures indicate a coinage of 279,000 pieces. So now we assume that not all were passed out in 1883 and that some are released from time to time from an undisclosed hoard. This reasoning is based on the fact that more coronation rubles become available to collectors with the passing of time.

How can you recognize a die break?

A working die is used until it is noticed that the die is cracking as a result of the tremendous force needed to stamp the design on the coin. Metal can and does enter such a crack when it appears. This causes a raised area at that point on the coin.

Die breaks can appear anywhere on a coin. They cannot be faked, since it would be most unlikely that a person would or could add a piece of raised metal to a coin.

For purposes of identification, one die break serves a most useful function. It authenticates a Grant "with star" variety of this 1922 U.S. commemorative half dollar. Since the star is incused, it could be punched into the "no star" variety (the "star" variety sells for over five times the "no star"). Most "star" varieties have a die break extending out from Grant's chin. This break proves the authenticity of the coin.

It was because of a die break on an 1803 one-cent obverse die that Howard Newcomb was able to prove that the 1804 restrike actually used a retooled 1803 die.

Collecting of coins with die breaks need not be limited to the older, more expensive coins. They are just as likely to appear on modern-day coins, for dies are not discarded until they

DIE BREAK
ON EARLY
AMERICAN CENT

show wear and this is usually accompanied by a crack or cracks appearing on the die. It is possible to follow the progression of deterioration of a die by noting the lengthening and deepening of the break. All that is needed is a good magnifying glass.

When was a die break interpreted as an omen of disaster?

Ferdinand Maximilian (1832–1867), Archduke of Austria and younger brother of Emperor Francis Joseph of the Holy Roman Empire, was invited by Mexican conservatives to become Emperor of Mexico. In 1864 he and his ambitious wife, Carlota, sailed from Europe to Mexico to accept the honors.

Only through the aid of French soldiers, acting under orders from Napoleon III, was the new emperor able to hold his throne. The majority of the Mexican people were republicans at heart and supported the rebellious patriot, Juárez.

When the first pesos were struck at the Mexico City Mint for the new emperor, a die break started near the forehead of the emperor, getting progressively larger with each strike. On the thirty-sixth strike the die shattered completely.

Superstitious workers at the Mint immediately took this occurrence as an omen of disaster and predicted that Maximilian would not live to celebrate his thirty-sixth birthday anniversary.

It is a matter of history that Maximilian and his troops were defeated in May, 1867, and on June 19, 1867, he was executed by a firing squad. Whether the die break indicated the exact spot that one of the bullets struck him is a matter of conjecture. But the prophecy was fulfilled in that he did not live to celebrate his thirty-ninth birthday.

The pesos still extant from this first die can be easily recognized because the lettering is smaller than on those produced from later dies.

The story of the 1866 Maximilian peso led Horace Hayden of Brownsville, Pa., in 1879, to write the editors of the *American Journal of Numismatics* a letter concerning another coincidence, part of which read:

I have in my collection one of Paquet's "North Western Sanitary Fair" Medals of the late President Lincoln. When I obtained this medal, I was told that when fifty-five of the medals had been struck, the die cracked on the fifty-sixth medal. And as Mr. Lincoln was just fifty-six years of age when he died, the cracking of the die on this particular medal was very remarkable. . . .

When Mr. Lincoln was assassinated, he was sitting in his box at the theatre, looking toward the stage, so that his head was slightly inclined forward and downward. Hence the ball of the assassin struck him in the back of the neck, at the base of the brain, remaining imbedded in the skull; the line of direction which the ball followed being from the *right mastoid process toward the centre of the nasal bone.* The Paquet Medal before me shows the crack in the die very plainly. It runs across the head of the President and the line of direction of the crack is *precisely* that which the ball of the assassin took. . . .

The only difference of note between this coincidence and that of the Maximilian Dollar is that the crack in the Mexican die occurred *before* the death of the Emperor, while in the Lincoln die the crack occurred *after* the death of the President.

When were playing cards used as currency?

According to the *Columbia Encyclopedia,* playing cards were introduced into Europe in the fourteenth century. An expense account of King Charles VI of France in 1392 mentioned them. The fifty-two card deck of four suits was said to have originated in France in the sixteenth century.

Canada was first settled by the French in 1604, and as time went on she found it necessary to defend her new colonial possession from the British colonists to the south. At first privately chartered companies attempted to rule this New World settlement, but by 1663 they turned control over to the French royal government and France sent large contingents of soldiers to defend her territory. French soldiers were avid card players. Many carried their own deck of cards with them, playing when possible to break the monotony of military duty.

When funds from France failed to arrive on time to pay the troops, means had to be found to issue notes or "promises to pay." Since a shortage of good paper also existed, the acting governor,

Jacques de Meulles, requisitioned playing cards and used their reverse sides as notes.

The first playing-card money was issued by M. de Meulles on June 1, 1685, after he posted a proclamation announcing their use and making it mandatory for all to accept them in lieu of money, and made them subject to a fine if they should not give full value for them. This type of money substitute by the local colonial government continued until 1721.

Again in 1729 it became necessary to use playing-card money, and now those issued were by royal sanction, since France found herself unable to pay her own troops. Their use continued until the English won possession of Canada in 1763.

Few examples of this unique money substitute exist today.

🕮 *When were U.S. half cents coined?*

Half cents were coined intermittently from 1793 through 1857, the same years that the large copper one-cent pieces were coined.

This series of coins can be considered the most underrated and undervalued of all United States coins. In all the years that they were struck, less than eight million were made. In only two years, 1804 and 1809, were more than a million coined.

The half cent makes a wonderful companion piece for the one cent, since the designs of both are the same, and when a design change was made in one, it was also made in the other. But while one-cent pieces were struck every year from 1793 to date, except for 1815, the half cent skipped a number of years. The reason for this was the lack of demand at the mint for additional pieces for commercial transactions.

During the sixty-five-year period that half cents were struck there were five basic design changes. (Compare this to the Lincoln cent, which retained the same design from 1909 to 1959.) Type one was struck only in 1793 and showed Miss Liberty facing left. Type two, the following year, showed her facing right, and pieces of this type were struck in 1794, 1795, 1796, and 1797.

For the next two years no half cents were coined. Type three, referred to as the "draped bust," was used from 1800 through 1808, except that none were coined in 1801. Type four, the "turban head" variety, was struck intermittently from 1809 to 1836. The final type, the "braided hair" variety, was struck only in proof from 1840 to 1849 and for circulation from 1849 through 1857, except for 1852, in which year the coin was struck only in proof.

Walter Breen, in his monograph "The United States Minor Coinage 1793–1916," aptly states: "This denomination has always been a poor relation of the large cent, a sort of Cinderella coin, unduly neglected from the Mint's infancy." Someday "Cinderella" will come into her own.

❧ Is there a 1913 Liberty Head five-cent piece?

Yes, five or six are known to exist. They were struck at the mint in Philadelphia without official sanction. Since the proposed design for the Buffalo–Indian Head nickel had not been approved in January, 1913, it became necessary to have dies of the Liberty Head type ready for use in the event that Treasury Department approval was withheld for the Buffalo–Indian Head design. Approval was received in February, 1913, but in the interim a mint official struck off a few coins before the dies were destroyed. Rumors about these coins flourished, but they were not offered for sale until ten years later. In the December, 1923, issue of *The Numismatist* an advertisement appeared that read "FOR SALE/ Five (5) Five-Cent Liberty/ Head 1913 Coins. Proof./ The only Five-Cent Liberty Head/ Coins of this design and year in/ existence/ AUGUST WAGNER,/ 31st and York Sts./ Philadelphia, Pa." It is believed that the widow of the mint official who struck the coins was the seller and that Wagner was only the agent. I believe that the original asking price was $600 per coin or $3,000 for the set. The last one I recall offered for sale was when the Egyptian government disposed of the King Farouk collection in 1954. In that sale Lot No. 1,695 was a complete collection of United States five-cent pieces from 1866 to 1948-D plus the 1913 Liberty Head and also the 1937-D three-legged nickel. The complete lot sold for only 1,575 Egyptian pounds or about $4,500. Today the 1913 Liberty Head alone would realize in excess of $15,000.

What is a "five-shilling dollar"?

Over a period of years, during the reign of George III, a coin shortage had been developing in England. As the shortage increased, the people started to panic and took every opportunity to hoard any "good money" (gold or silver) that they could rightfully claim. This, of course, only made the situation worse. By 1798 it was so acute that the British government, through the Bank of England, bought Spanish and Spanish American eight-real pieces (silver-dollar size) which pictured the Spanish king, counterstamped them with a small head of George III, and announced that these counterstamped coins had a value of four shilling nine pence. By 1800 the price of silver rose and the coins had to be revalued to five shillings. Using coins of an ofttimes enemy was repugnant to the citizenry, who composed the following ditty:

> To make the dollar of Spain for five shillings to pass,
> Stamp the head of a fool on the neck of an ass.

Whether or not this ridicule of the king had any effect, complete dies were prepared, dated 1804, and the Spanish pieces were completely overstruck with an obverse design showing the bust of George III and the reverse design reading in part, "Bank of England Five Shilling Dollar." On most pieces some details of the original Spanish coin can be seen.

How many 1856 flying eagle cents were struck?

Contrary to the belief of many collectors, the flying eagle cent of 1856 was merely a pattern coin and not legal tender when issued. The act that legalized the small-sized copper-nickel cent was not approved until February 21, 1857. That they did circulate is evidenced by the number that are known in good to fine condition.

According to most authorities, a sufficient quantity was struck so that each member of Congress as well as officials of the Treasury Department could be given one or more. All efforts to obtain an official statement as to the exact number has proved futile. Records indicate that the coins were also restruck in the 1860's.

Estimates vary from 960 to 10,000. The latter figure is attributed to a Chicago numismatist, William Evans. The 960 figure was given by Wesley R. Hauptman of Los Angeles, in an article that appeared in *The Numismatist* of September, 1938. Considering the rarity of the piece today, this writer would tend to agree with Mr. Hauptman.

Although in earlier days the coin showed up with great regularity both at auction and fixed-price sales, no one was ever able to accumulate a tremendous hoard. In 1906 Henry Chapman sold the collection of R. B. Leeds. The catalog of the Leeds collection read in part:

For many years he was an ardent collector, turning his attention to accumulating all the examples he could of certain dates, his especial hobby being 1856 Eagle Cents of which he had 109 specimens.

In 1911 George W. Rice of Detroit, Michigan, is said to have sold a hoard of 1856 cents that he had acquired over many years. This group was said to consist of 756 pieces.

Today the accumulation of this coin by John A. Beck of Pittsburgh, Pa. (he died in the early 1920's), reputed to be 531 pieces, is said to be intact in the vaults of a Pittsburgh bank.

Considering the fact that no one collector ever succeeded in acquiring more than 756 pieces, it seems reasonable to assume that less than a thousand 1856 flying eagles, originals and restrikes, were minted.

⬧⬧ Why is the 1856 flying eagle cent such a popular coin?

They say that it pays to advertise. And this pattern one-cent piece has been the most publicized of any of the United States series of pattern coins.

Most other patterns are far rarer, with generally only some ten to seventy five struck. This coin had a mintage of close to one thousand pieces, making it easily collectible in earlier days when there were far fewer coin collectors. Its extremely high selling price as compared to the truly rare patterns is attributable to the fact that it is collected not only by the few collectors of U.S. pattern coins, but by the large group of numismatists who collect U.S. small-size cents (1856 to date).

In 1886 *The American Exchange and Mart* called attention to the coin in an article that said:

One of the most remarkable instances of the increase in fictitious value, in the United States, of a single coin, applies to the little nickel-cent of the year 1856. When the old copper cents were about to be dispensed with, as a legal tender, experiments were made to introduce a smaller and more convenient one-cent coin; hence, in 1855 experiments were made in nickel, and after repeated trials with large and small Eagles (so-called "Buzzards" and "Crooked Necks"), the nickel-cent, with flying eagle of date 1856, was produced and sent on its course in small sums throughout the United States. At that time any person could walk into the mint and get a hundred of the new coins. Now comes the sequel, showing fluctuations.

```
1856——$ .01
1860——   .50
1870——  2.00
1880——  3.00
1885——  4.00
```

We can continue, showing the tremendous price rise in the past forty years:

```
1927——$  12.00
1937——     35.00
1947——    175.00
1958——    600.00
1966——   2700.00
```

Strange, but true, had there been but one hundred struck, it is safe to assume that the coin would sell for a lesser amount, since it would be sought only by pattern collectors.

✎ *Did the Kingdom of Hawaii ever have*
its own coinage?

  Hawaii had never had her own coinage until King Kalakaua I ascended the throne in February, 1874. Foreign currency and coins, especially of the United States, had been used as legal tender.

After visiting Europe in 1881 the king ordered patterns struck to help him determine the design for a new national coinage. These patterns were not accepted or approved by the Hawaiians, and only the persuasion of Claus Spreckels, a close friend and advisor to the king, caused him to ask the United States government to enter into a contract for one million dollars worth of a new silver coin in 1883.

The coins were designed by Charles Barber, Engraver of the Mint. The obverse showed the head of King Kalakaua I facing right, the words "KALAKAUA I KING OF HAWAII" and the date "1883." The reverse of the dollar, half dollar, and quarter, besides showing the denomination, pictured the royal coat of arms and the words "UA MAU KE EA O KA AINA I KA PONO" (the life of the land is in righteousness). Only the dime was different in that it showed a crown instead of the coat of arms.

In November, 1883, coinage was begun at the San Francisco Mint, with delivery completed in June, 1884. A total of 1,950,000 pieces were struck as follows: dollars, 500,000 pieces; half dollars, 700,000 pieces; quarter dollars, 500,000 pieces; dimes, 250,000 pieces.

We must assume that this issue of 1883, the only national coinage of this island kingdom, was not well received, because in July, 1884, the Hawaiian government passed the following act:

From and after December 1, 1884, the gold coins of the United States of America shall be standard and legal tender at their nominal value in payment of all debts, public and private, within the Kingdom of Hawaii. Further, the standard silver coins of the United States of America and the silver coins of the Kingdom of Hawaii shall be from and after December 1, 1884, a legal tender at their nominal values for any amount not exceeding $10 in any one payment. . . . Chapter 37 of Session Laws of 1880, being an act to provide for a national coinage, is hereby repealed, this repeal to take effect on the 1st day of December, 1884.

As recently as 1947 a set of these four silver coins in uncirculated condition could be acquired for less than $15. Today they sell for more than $400.

Is there any United States coin for which a single date makes up a distinct type?

There are quite a number, probably more than most people realize.

There is the 1793 half cent. On this first year of issue Miss Liberty is facing left, while on the years that follow until 1809 she faces right.

There is the 1793 one cent. Here the reverse must be considered. For although in 1793 the wreath-type reverse was used, two other reverses also appeared. Both had the words "ONE CENT" encircled with a chain made up of thirteen links, but one had "UNITED STATES OF AMERICA" around the perimeter, while the other had "UNITED STATES OF AMERI."

Next is the 1859 Indian Head cent. Here again, the difference is on the reverse. On this first year of the Indian Head the wreath wholly encircled the words "ONE CENT," while from 1860 to 1909 the wreath was broken by a shield that appeared above the "ONE CENT."

The first single-date variety in the five-cent series appears in the first issue of the V nickels in 1883, on which the word "CENTS" is omitted but was added later in the year and kept on until the design change in 1913.

There is no single-date variety in the dime series, but the quarter dollar of 1796 is a variety unto itself, probably only because none were struck in 1797, 1798, 1799, 1800, 1801, 1802, or 1803. When they were again issued in 1804 a new reverse design was used.

Next we move to the gold-dollar series. The first year of minting, 1849, had reverses with open wreaths and with closed wreaths. The open-wreath design was used only on the 1849 dollars.

Continuing in the gold series, the first year of the quarter eagle ($2.50) came with the face of the coin starless and with stars. The starless variety was used only in 1796.

You will notice that in each case the single-date variety occurred in the first year of issue. Sometimes a change was made the same year, at other times in the following year. In either event, the change was made because Treasury Department officials felt that the design could be improved, either artistically or to prevent chicanery, as in the case of the 1883 "no cents" nickel.

✒️ Why are there so many 1883 five-cent pieces around?

Actually, there were three types of nickels minted in 1883. First, there was the "shield" type, which had been minted each year from 1866. Second, there was the new "V" nickel, which pictured Miss Liberty on the obverse, had the "V" for "5" on the reverse, but made no mention of "cents." Third, there was the new Liberty Head type, but with the word "CENTS" under the "V."

The third type was made necessary because confidence men were gold-plating the second type and passing them off as five-dollar gold pieces. A favorite trick of one of these rogues was to act the part of a deaf mute, make a purchase, and tender the gold-plated coin as payment. If the coin was accepted, change for five dollars was received. One arrest was reported, but the con artist was released because, as a deaf mute, he had not implied by a spoken word that the coin was a half eagle.

Naturally, as soon as the public became aware that the "no cents" types were being withdrawn and replaced by the "with cents" type, everyone wanted to save one or more of the former.

So today the second type is relatively common, and the third type relatively scarce even though almost three times as many of the "with cents" variety were struck as were the "no cents" variety.

✒ *What are Conder tokens?*

During the eighteenth century in England minor copper coins were in extremely short supply except for the years between 1770 and 1775. A copper-mining firm known as Pary's Mines Co. in 1787 illegally issued a one-penny token. This mining company was located in Anglesey, Wales, and its token became known as the "Anglesey penny."

ANGLESEY PENNY

It was received with such enthusiasm that George III issued a proclamation that permitted responsible firms to issue penny, half-penny, and farthing tokens made of copper. These eighteenth-century tokens, actually struck between 1787 and 1803, are sometimes called Conder tokens, taking the name of an early cataloguer of the many varieties that appeared in a relatively short time.

The earlier pieces were struck to fill a need, gave full value in the amount of copper used, and were well made. They were made in sufficient numbers so that they circulated freely. But as time went on, folks started to collect them for their beauty and a new group of token collectors came into being. This led to abuses through which limited issues were struck solely for collectors. In just ten years, in 1797, the British government ordered their discontinuance.

Although one-penny and farthing pieces are occasionally seen, the majority of the Conders are half-penny pieces. Pictured on them were famous Englishmen such as Sir Isaac Newton, Earl Howe, the Duke of Wellington, Admiral Horatio Nelson, Queen Elizabeth I, Thomas Johnson (a famous prizefighter), and William

Pitt. Another group showed famous landmarks such as Norwick Castle, Canterbury Cathedral, Abbey Church, East India House, and St. Paul's Cathedral. In fact, a series of articles appeared in the *Coin Collector's Journal* in 1940 called "Sightseeing in the British Isles via Conder Tokens."

Probably the best-known piece in the United States is the Coventry half-penny token, which shows Lady Godiva in the nude riding a horse. Max Mehl was responsible for its popularity by picturing it in his *Star Rare Coin Encyclopedia*, which was the most popular coin publication in the 1920's and 1930's. This token plus ninety-nine others was sold to hundreds of numismatists for only ten dollars.

Why did the United States coin a trade dollar?

After the conquest of Mexico by the Spaniards, not only were large quantities of already mined silver found, but large deposits waiting to be mined were discovered. It is said that until the middle of the nineteenth century, more than half of the world's silver was produced in Mexico. During this time she had the ability to mint and export millions of dollars' worth of the precious metal every year. Because the coins were almost pure silver they were accepted around the world and actually used as legal tender in China and other parts of the Far East.

The discovery of large silver deposits in the western part of the United States toward the middle of the century prompted congressmen from the states where silver was discovered to exert pressure for legislation authorizing the striking of trade dollars. The bill was finally passed on February 12, 1873. While the standard dollar was 412½ grains, 900/1000 pure, the trade dollar was 420 grains, 900/1000 pure. This fact was placed prominently on the coin. Our lawmakers had erred, though, since while the Mexican dollar that it was trying to compete with had only 418 grains, it was over 97/100 pure. Rightly, the wily Chinese merchants preferred the Mexican dollar to the U.S. trade dollar.

Although the trade coin was not intended for local use, it was nevertheless legal tender and as such was used to some degree in the United States. The public, for some reason, disliked the coin. The first year of issue was 1873. By 1876 Congress removed its legal tender status, making it mandatory for export use only. After 1878 none were struck for commercial use, but only for the collector of proof coins.

&%   *What is the true story of the rare 1884 and 1885 trade dollars?*

According to reputable coin catalogs there are ten coins dated 1884 and five coins dated 1885, all fifteen being proof struck.

Before 1908 their existence was not generally known. In that year Captain John W. Haseltine reported a "hoard" of them. This was as much as this writer knew of these rare coins until he read a publication in 1952 that caused him to write the following letter to the editor of *The Numismatist* in March, 1952:

Dear Sir:

In all the numismatic literature that I have read concerning U.S. Trade Dollars it has been stated that the proofs of 1884 and 1885 "were not generally known until recent years."

Chas. Steigerwalt in his "Coin Journal" of May–June, 1884, page 139, and of September, 1884, page 13, advertised at fixed price under U.S. Silver Dollars, "1884 Trade, Brilliant Proof $2.50," the same amount asked for the proof Trade Dollars of 1881, 1882 and 1883.

Mr. Steigerwalt lived in Lancaster, Penna., not too far from the Philadelphia Mint. Is it possible that he had first call on proof coins! Is it also possible that more than ten were minted!

Yours truly,

Leon T. Lindheim

This letter brought an immediate response from Walter H. Breen, who answered the letter via an article that appeared in the July, 1952, issue of *The Numismatist*. In essence, his scholarly reply stated that he believed that Mr. Steigerwalt advertised the 1884's in anticipation of receiving a quantity of these coins from the mint. To quote Mr. Breen, "It is very easy to prove that the 1884 and 1885 Trade Dollars were a result of private enterprise or chicanery in the Coiner's Department, and could not have been offered for sale through the Medal Department in those years." He goes on to mention that although the Mint Director's reports for 1884 and 1885 mention all other dies on hand, nowhere are the trade dollar dies mentioned. Since dies are the responsibility of the Coiner and Walter Breen's research in the Archives disclosed no mention of these dies, it must be assumed that the known coins were unofficially struck for the personal profit of certain Mint officials. He places these pieces in the same class as the 1913 Liberty Head nickels.

Why do arrowheads appear on either side of the date on certain U.S. coins?

The arrowheads, pointing outward toward the rim, were placed on the silver half dimes, dimes, quarters, and halves to indicate a change in weight in 1853. Stated in grains, the half dime was reduced from 20⅝ to 19.2, the dime from 41.25 to 38.4, the quarter from 103⅛ to 96, and the half from 206¼ to 192.

The arrows were retained in 1854 and 1855 and dropped in 1856, even though the silver content of the coins remained unchanged until 1873.

In 1873 the arrows again made their appearance, this time to indicate an increase in weight. The half dollar was increased by nine-tenths of a grain, the quarter by half that amount, and the dime by eighteen one-hundredths of a grain. The half dime was discontinued in 1873, so no change here was necessary.

Because of the Congressional action in changing the silver content of these various coins, certain years had both varieties. The half dime of 1853 comes both with and without arrows. The dimes of 1853 and 1873 come both ways. The quarter of 1853 comes both with and without, but the arrowless variety is extremely scarce. Conversely, the 1873 quarter without arrows is common while the type with arrows is scarce. Both types of 1853 halves are readily available, but only a few specimens of 1873 without arrows are known, these all being New Orleans Mint coins. The arrows were dropped on all denominations in 1875.

After 1873 there was no change made in the silver content of the dime, quarter, and half until 1965.

 Is medal collecting expensive?

Not necessarily. And there is a lot of fun in searching for them. In most cities there are pawn shops or antique stores that handle all sorts of medals. We must remember that thousands of types have been struck or cast. You don't need a license to make a medal.

The Philadelphia Mint sells copies of many of the medals that were presented to American heroes of the past. These were authorized by the United States Congress as a means of expressing the thanks of the nation to her patriots and good citizens. Bronze copies vary in price from $3.50 up to $15, although most sell for $3.75. It might be worthwhile to mention a few.

The first one authorized by Congress (on March 25, 1776) was to George Washington for the successful evacuation of Boston. This medal was discussed earlier in this volume.

The second medal was authorized on November 4, 1777, and presented to General Horatio Gates after his defeat of the British troops under the command of Sir John Burgoyne at Saratoga. The face shows a bust of the general while the reverse pictures Gates in the act of receiving the sword of General Burgoyne. In the background to the left are the British troops laying down their arms, while to the right can be seen a row of soldiers of the Revolutionary Army with muskets on their shoulders.

The first medal to a naval hero was presented by Congress to John Paul Jones for his sinking of the British vessel *Serapis* off the coast of Scotland on September 23, 1779. The face has a bust of the naval hero. The reverse shows Jones's ship, *Bonhomme Richard*, in the foreground and the burning *Serapis* in the background. The whole reverse is alive with action.

The list of Mint medals is large. Beautiful works of art honor Anthony Wayne, Andrew Jackson, Zachary Taylor, Winfield Scott, and "Lighthorse" Harry Lee. The Navy has its share, too, from Captain Decatur to Vice Admiral Hyman George Rickover, the father of the atomic submarine.

Civilians have also been honored. Here the list includes Cyrus W. Field, the Wright Brothers, Dr. Jonas Salk, Robert Frost, and Dr. Thomas A. Dooley III.

A list of medals available will be sent on request by the Superintendent of the U.S. Mint, Philadelphia, Pa.

What banker started his business career as a coin dealer?

Meyer Amschel Rothschild (1743–1812) of Frankfurt-am-Main, Germany, at the age of ten began helping his father, who was a moneychanger. This was a necessary profession in the days when no international banking was conducted. A merchant traveling to another country to transact business needed to be supplied with coins acceptable in the country where he was going to purchase goods.

After finishing his schooling, young Rothschild took a position with a firm in Hanover. Here he became friendly with a General von Estorff, who was a coin collector. His childhood knowledge led to his being commissioned by the General to find coins for his collection.

Discovering that numismatics offered a way to reach the influential noblemen of that time, Rothschild studied all the numismatic literature available to him. His wise selections for the General led to his introduction to William, Prince of Hesse-Hanau. Wisely, he is said to have sold coins and medals to William at cost or less, for in 1755 the Prince became Landgrave of Hesse-Cassel.

We know that by 1770, and possibly earlier, he became an established coin dealer in Frankfurt, since copies of his coin catalogs still exist. On the title page he introduces himself as "Factor of His Highness the Prince of Hesse-Hanau."

By supplying rare coins to the nobility (and most royalty at that time had coin cabinets) at reasonable prices, Rothschild endeared himself to the most powerful families in Germany. Naturally, when he expanded into the field of international banking, sending his sons to live in the various European capitals, these same noblemen championed his cause and gave him their patronage.

Who is the first Negro pictured on a United States coin?

This honor went to Booker Taliaferro Washington (1858–1915), who was born a slave in Franklin County, Virginia, and died as one of America's most distinguished educators and scholars. Probably more than any other Negro, he did most to aid his race in the development of scholarly pursuits. He organized Tuskegee Institute and the National Negro Business League. His whole life was devoted to gaining better education for the Negro.

The Booker T. Washington half dollar was authorized by Congress on August 7, 1946. Its purpose was to raise sufficient funds to erect a memorial building in his name near the site of his birthplace in Virginia.

The coin was designed by Isaac Scott Hathaway, a Negro sculptor. Mr. Hathaway was a native of Lexington, Kentucky. He obtained his formal training in the arts at the New England Conservatory, the Cincinnati Art Academy, and the New York College of Ceramics. During Washington's lifetime, Hathaway had been fortunate enough to persuade the educator to allow him to take a life mask of his head.

The bust of Washington on the face of the coin is modeled from the bust that resulted from the life mask. The reverse pictures the Hall of Fame at New York University and below it a log cabin. Between the two structures are the words: "FROM SLAVE CABIN TO HALL OF FAME."

Why is there a raised dot in the center on the reverse of certain large cents?

Most coin authorities agree that the dot is there through carelessness. When the early coins were produced, dies had to be handmade by a die cutter. The artist probably used a compass to help him lay out the large letters that appear in the form of a circle on the reverse. Failure to fill in the hole left by the compass point would cause a raised dot to appear on the coin.

Because the dies on these early American cents were hand cut, many other variations and differences are readily discernible. The spacing of letters often varies, as does the style of the lettering. The wreath may have long or short stem or be stemless, the size of berries fluctuates, and the fraction bar may be found long or short, high or low.

Many numismatists studied the die varieties of the early U.S. large cents. Probably the best known today is Dr. William H. Sheldon of New York City. His *Early American Cents,* written in 1948 and revised in 1958, with the collaboration of Dorothy I. Paschel and Walter Breen, under the title of *Penny Whimsy,* identifies and describes 195 varieties of large cents struck through 1814. This medical man has taken a completely scientific approach toward grading. His system takes into account both amount of wear and surface discoloration.

A lifetime could be devoted to a study of United States large cents from 1793 to 1814. And who knows, maybe you will discover a new variety.

50

*What United States coin pictures a
Dutchman and a Frenchman?*

The coin is the Huguenot–Walloon Tercentenary half dollar of 1924. On its face are the busts of Admiral Gaspard de Coligny of France and William the Silent, Prince of Orange.

Admiral Coligny (1519–1572) joined the Huguenots in 1559 and became the standard-bearer of the Protestants of France. He was among the first to die in the St. Bartholomew's Day massacre in Paris.

William the Silent (1533–1584), Prince of Orange, was born a Lutheran, became a Catholic, but returned to the religion of his birth in adulthood. He persuaded the Dutch provinces to revolt against Spain and form a league of United Provinces of the Netherlands in 1576. The Spanish king, Philip II, offered a reward for his death, bringing about his murder in 1584.

Thus two Protestant martyrs were chosen to be pictured on a coin struck to honor the three-hundredth anniversary of the founding of New Netherland, the Dutch colony that was largely settled by French-speaking Huguenot Walloons who came to America's shores to escape religious persecution. It possibly would have been more fitting to have pictured Peter Minuit on the coin. He was the leader of the colony in 1624 and arranged the purchase of Manhattan Island from the Indians in 1625, acquiring title to the land for gifts valued at a mere $24.

Congress authorized the minting of 300,000 coins, but wisely only 142,000 were struck. None were remelted, although the public did not buy up the whole issue at its original sale price of $1 per coin. With some 55,000 unsold, it was decided to pass these pieces out over the counter at the Fifth National Bank of

New York. Because so many ended up as "small change" and not numismatic treasures, the number of uncirculated specimens saved by collectors is considerably under 87,000. In fact, since it sells for more than the Cleveland Great Lakes Exposition half dollar with a net mintage of only 50,000, we can assume that less than 50,000 mint-condition coins are extant.

An interesting sidelight: William the Silent married—as his fourth wife, in 1583—the daughter of Admiral Coligny!

What is meant when a coin is called a "freak"?

A mint error causes a freak. Walter H. Breen, one of America's most qualified numismatists, breaks down the types of errors into six groups: one, metal error, when a coin is struck on a planchet (blank) of another metal (e.g., copper quarter or silver cent); two, rolling error, when the planchet is rolled too thick or too thin; three, cutting error, when the error causes imperfect planchet; four, edge error, when reeding is omitted or lettered edge is not properly applied; five, die error, when improper die cutting causes overdate or recutting of letters; six, striking error, when a mistake at the coining machine causes a misstrike such as a double strike or an off-center strike. These errors take many forms and make interesting displays.

One popular error, for example, is the clipped planchet, which causes a part of the coin to be missing. This type of error is most prevalent in the one-cent and dime series. It occurs when the blanks are cut from the strip of metal. Remember how Mother rolled and cut cookie dough? If she got careless the cutter might clip off the corner of a piece already cut. If the outside edge of another coin of the same denomination fits into the missing space, then we possibly have this type of error. On the other hand, if Mother carelessly got too close to the edge of the dough, she would end up with only part of a cookie. Similarly, if the machine got off center and stamped only part of the blank, the resulting planchet would strike up a coin with a part missing that has a straight edge. Both types are found very infrequently. The important thing to determine is whether or not the coin left the mint in the condition it is now in. Anyone could mutilate a coin, and this certainly would not make a common coin rare or valuable. But if the blank (planchet) was clipped before it reached the coining machine we have a premium item.

Another type of error is the off-center strike. This is what happens when the blank does not slip into the collar that is meant to hold it in position as it is being struck. As a result the  die makes contact with only part of the coin, leaving the rest blank.

Then there are "brokage" errors. Originally the term brokage was applied to any coin that was damaged or faulty and was therefore rejected. Today the term usually indicates a coin that has on one side an incused impression of what normally appears on the other side. This is caused by a coin failing to be ejected after being struck and means that the next coin will bear, on the underside, the incused design of the upper side while the normal raised design of the upper side will appear where it belongs. This incused design is a mirror image—in other words, the face of the coin that failed to eject acts as the reverse die.

Double or triple strikes are interesting oddities. In this case the coin fails to be ejected from the machine and is restruck. Sometimes this type of error takes place with the coin in the collar, in which case it merely shifts. At other times it jumps outside the collar, causing one or more impressions to be off center.

Interesting varieties occur when a die becomes clogged with foreign matter. This may result in a coin such as the three-legged 1937-D nickel, on which one leg never struck up. Other examples are coins that show only some of the numbers in the date, such as 194– or –964.

Recently, variety collectors have been searching for double-struck mintmarks. Many double D's have been discovered. This type of error happens because the mintmark is hand-punched into the die at the branch mint with less than precision workmanship. It takes more than one blow on the hand punch with the hammer to form the mintmark. Should the punch not be replaced in exactly the same position each time, a double mintmark may appear.

An early type of error was the overdate. In this case a die is prepared but not used when a new calendar year arrives. Rather than destroy the old die, a new date is engraved. Usually only the last number has to be changed. For example, in the one-cent series we had the 1811 over 10 and in the dime series the 1942 over 41 "error."

When a coin flips over in the machine instead of being ejected, we have an interesting error with the reverse showing on the obverse and vice versa.

Then there are off-metal errors, of which there are two types. The first type occurs when there is a metal change in a certain coin denomination. When the 1943 cents were struck, the metal used was zinc-coated steel, replacing the bronze that had been used since 1864. Thus a bronze 1943 cent is a mint error. Likewise, with the switch back to bronze in 1944, a steel 1944 cent would be an error. The second type of off-metal error occurs when a one-cent bronze blank is used to strike a quarter, half dollar, or nickel, or a dime blank creates a silver penny.

Assuming that the error was not intentional, there is a logical explanation for an "off-metal" coin. But first it must be understood that the coin is probably of a smaller size than the normal one-cent piece, because it is struck on a blank intended to be made into a ten-cent piece.

Let us say that a bag of dime planchets has been fed into the coining machine for dimes. The empty bag is then set aside for reuse at a later date. But, by mistake, a blank becomes caught in the bag, does not fall into the hopper, and so lies hidden in the discarded bag. At a later date the "empty" bag is filled with bronze blanks for the one-cent machine. This loosens the silver piece, which now becomes commingled with the bronze pieces. When the contents now go into the one-cent hopper, the silver blank goes through, too, and we have a silver "penny."

Five-cent pieces are known on one-cent bronze planchets. Quarters and halves on dime blanks and nickels on one-cent blanks are also known. All are extremely scarce and highly prized by collectors of oddities. A word of warning. At the time of this writing, it is ruled illegal by the U.S. Treasury Department to hold an off-metal coin.

✌ *What are bracteates?*

The bracteates were a true product of the Middle Ages, being thin, waferlike silver coins. Instead of being struck from two dies to make a front and back in different designs, only one die was used. The reason was that the metal was so thin that it could not stand the pressure of two dies. Naturally, the reverse design was merely the mirror image of the obverse.

The first bracteates were made in Germany, in the Harz Mountain region known as Thuringia, in the early part of the twelfth century. The earlier coins of this region included the silver penny, copied after the Roman denarius. These were small and thick, with both front and back designs. The bracteates were the result of the evolution of silver pennies becoming larger and at the same time thinner.

Strangely enough, these coins were well received. Soon other parts of Europe started to make similar coins. Before long they were being struck in Hungary, Poland, Switzerland, Denmark, and Sweden.

Although they lent themselves to more artistry, because of their size, they were not suited for commercial transactions, since they lacked the quality of durability.

Most were made by minor noblemen and ecclesiastics. They generally showed religious scenes, bishops, saints, and sometimes knights in armor.

Certainly those that circulated in the twelfth and thirteenth centuries have long since disappeared. We still have good examples, though, existing today only because hoards are still uncovered that include new or almost new pieces.

✌ *Do coins always increase in value?*

Not always. In an auction sale conducted by B. Max Mehl, numismatist, on June 22, 1920, a silver dollar of 1885 from the Carson City mint sold for $25. A similar coin in the March, 1960, issue of *The Numismatist* was offered for sale at $7.50.

This sort of thing has happened many times in the silver-dollar series, because until 1964 bags of uncirculated silver dollars were in Treasury Department vaults. They were struck to back the Silver Certificates in circulation, being payable in silver on demand. Today less than 3,000,000 remain on hand, and these are not being released to the public. But in earlier years a previously scarce date could become common overnight with the release of a bag of one thousand uncirculated dollars of that date.

The same can be said for the hoard of six hundred 1856 Flying Eagle cents that is said to repose in the Pittsburgh bank vault. Should this collection all be placed on the market simultaneously, the price of 1856 one-cent pieces would drop sharply.

But generally speaking, over a period of years, rare and scarce coins increase proportionately more in value than the common garden variety found in circulation. Then, too, popular coins, because of greater demand, increase at a faster rate than those collected by a few. Here is an example of two uncirculated coins, the popular 1909-S-VDB one-cent and the not-so-popular 1854 three-dollar gold piece. The following are retail catalog prices over a period of twenty-six years:

	1909-S-VDB Cent	1854 Three-Dollar Gold Piece
1940	$ 3.00	$ 10.00
1949	$ 15.00	$ 30.00
1958	$ 65.00	$ 67.50
1962	$115.00	$185.00
1966	$350.00	$275.00

There were 484,000 of the one-cent and only 138,618 of the three-dollar gold pieces. Should the three-dollar gold piece ever become as popular as the cent, you can watch for the gold piece's price to skyrocket!

When did the United States have a one-cent nickel?

We are so used to the slang word "nickel" when referring to the five-cent piece that we forget certain facts.

The United States had a one-cent piece of copper-nickel (88 per cent copper and 12 per cent nickel) nine years before it had a copper-nickel five-cent piece (75 per cent copper and 25 per cent nickel).

On February 21, 1857, a bill became law that (1) authorized the small-size one-cent piece of copper-nickel and (2) demonitized certain foreign gold and silver that up to this time had had legal tender status in the United States.

Harper's Weekly ran a cartoon entitled "Brother Jonathan's New Baby" (Uncle Sam was then called Brother Jonathan) picturing a mother Liberty holding the baby 1857 Flying Eagle one cent. Papa Jonathan is standing over them, gazing with admiration at his new "baby," while big sister "large cent" is standing to the side crying.

The nickel cent of 1857 with the Flying Eagle obverse caused quite a furor in its day. Its color when newly minted was silvery, causing objections because it might be mistaken for a silver coin.

57

Then the Albany *Journal* wrote, "The latest objection we have noticed is that children swallow it, with great consequent irritation of the stomach and bowels, from the corrosive nature of the metal of which it is composed." At this late day it is hard to tell if the author was enraged or making a bad joke.

Some of the criticism came about because people had a mistaken idea that all money should have a metallic value equal to its stated value. The pure copper one cent that was discontinued in 1857 had just that, approximately a penny's worth of copper. This idea was eventually dispelled with the first printing of United States paper money in 1861.

In spite of its unpopularity, the nickel cent persisted until 1864, when it was replaced with the bronze one-cent piece. The term "nickel" reappeared two years later, but then it meant the five-cent piece that we recognize as the good old-fashioned nickel worth five pennies.

🎀 What is a "champagne taler"?

In the days before the German Empire (1871), each German state had its own coinage, often using different units and silver of various degrees of fineness. Without attempting to become technical, let us say that the northern states used a unit of a taler, while the southern states chose the gulden as their unit.

PRUSSIAN DOUBLE TALER

Agreements arrived at in monetary conventions held in 1837 and 1838 established a ratio of two talers to three and a half gulden. The double talers of the 1840's and 1850's reflected this action by stating on their face both "2 Taler" and "3½ Gulden." Such pieces were issued by Anhalt, Baden, Bavaria, Brunswick, Frankfurt, Hannover, Hesse, Nassau, Prussia, Saxony, and many smaller duchies and principalities.

These coins, slightly larger than U.S. silver dollars, became known as "champagne talers," because at that time the cost of a magnum of champagne was approximately two talers.

⚜ *Did you know that the motion picture industry sponsored a commemorative coin?*

On December 5, 1922, a bill was introduced in the United States Senate by Senator Hiram Johnson of California. It called for the coining of not more than 300,000 half dollars in commemoration of the one-hundredth anniversary of the enunciation of the Monroe Doctrine. It further stated that the coins "shall be issued upon the request of the Los Angeles Clearing House and upon payment by such clearing houses to the United States of the par value of the amount of their face value." The bill was signed into law on January 24, 1923.

It seemed most unusual that the Los Angeles Clearing House and not a commission set up to arrange a centennial celebration should be the original recipients of the coins. Inquiry to the Los

Angeles Clearing House by the American Numismatic Association brought a response from a group whose letterhead read "Monroe Doctrine Centennial, First Annual American Historical Revue and Motion Picture Industry Exposition, Commemorating the One Hundredth Anniversary of the Monroe Doctrine, June 1, 1923 to June 30, 1923, Under the Direction and Supervision of the Motion Picture Industry." The letter read:

I take pleasure in stating that the object of the proposed issue of Monroe Centennial souvenir half dollars is that we may use same for the purpose of raising funds with which to justify the great cost of reproducing the highlights of American history, which reproduction is to be supervised by a historical commission composed of the heads of universities, colleges and secondary educational institutions in the State of California. Upon the presentation of these reproductions a series of educational films may be made as a contribution of civilization to be used in connection with our schools and other educational agencies.

We tend to agree with Arlie R. Slabaugh, who wrote in *United States Commemorative Coinage:* "I suspect that the underlying idea was not so much to obtain money as to obtain 'good' publicity. Even back then, there were people who thought motion pictures should be less entertaining and more educational and uplifting."

The coin pictures busts of James Monroe and John Quincy Adams, President and Secretary of State respectively, who jointly formulated the United States policy that European governments should not interfere in problems of the American hemisphere. The reverse pictures the Western Hemisphere, the dates 1823–1923, and the words "MONROE DOCTRINE CENTENNIAL LOS ANGELES."

There were 274,077 struck. Since many could not be sold at a premium by the Commission, they were released at face value, making the coin scarce in uncirculated condition.

*What founder of the Federal Reserve
System and the Federal Deposit
Insurance Corporation is pictured on a
United States coin?*

This renowned citizen was Carter Glass (1858–1946),
Virginia State Senator, Congressman, Secretary of the Treasury
under Woodrow Wilson, and later United States Senator. The
coin is the Lynchburg, Virginia, sesquicentennial half dollar of
1936.

Over Senator Glass's protest he was pictured on the coin, being
recognized as Lynchburg's leading citizen. Besides being considered father of the Federal Reserve System, since he was the
chairman of the House Committee on Banking and Currency that
designed the Federal Reserve Act in 1913, he was co-author of
the so-called Glass-Steagall Act that created the Federal Deposit
Insurance Corporation in 1933.

Carter Glass had the unique privilege of serving in the United
States Senate when the bill authorizing the striking of this coin
was presented to Congress. On May 28, 1936, a mintage of 20,000
coins was authorized, with the obverse design showing his bust,
facing left.

Should a coin ever be struck to honor the soundness of the
American banking system, Carter Glass's name, if not face,
should appear on that coin. The Federal Reserve System, his
brainchild, has stood the test of time for over half a century.

What U.S. Congressman had the privilege of voting to have his own picture on a coin?

In anticipation of celebrating the one-hundredth anniversary of Arkansas' statehood in 1936, a group of Arkansas citizens in 1934 petitioned Congress for a special commemorative half dollar. Enabling legislation was passed on May 14, 1934, authorizing a maximum of 500,000 pieces, but did not specify that all coins bear the date 1936. As a result limited quantities were issued each year from 1935 through 1939.

The obverse on all showed the dates "1836" and "1936," "ARKANSAS CENTENNIAL," and the profiles of Miss Liberty and an Indian warrior. The reverse bore the year of issue with a design featuring an eagle in flight.

Because of the demand for the 1935 coins the Arkansas Centennial Commission asked Congressional approval for a second issue of half dollars, using the same reverse, but with an obverse picturing her leading citizen, Senator Joseph T. Robinson. This new type, referred to as the Arkansas–Robinson half dollar, was approved by Congress in June, 1936, with a minimum of 25,000 and a maximum of 50,000 authorized. In reality, 25,265 coins were struck and sold.

Senator Robinson was only the second American privileged to vote on whether or not his face should appear on a United States coin. (Carter Glass was the first.) Whether he abstained or not is unimportant. What is important is that his state felt that he was worthy of this signal honor.

History will probably agree with his constituents. He served his state from 1903 to 1913 in the U.S. House of Representatives; he was elected Governor of Arkansas in 1913, serving only a short time, since his party sent him to the Senate, where he served until his death.

The Senator had only a short time to enjoy the unusual honor paid to him. The coins were struck in January, 1937, and on July 14, 1937, this able legislator died, at the age of sixty-four.

𝕾 *What is a "Becker"?*

A German by the name of Carl Wilhelm Becker (1772–1830) coined forgeries of ancient Greek and Roman gold coins. His workmanship was excellent, and many went into coin collections as authentic pieces.

In 1924 and 1925, Spink and Son of London published in two volumes *Becker the Counterfeiter,* by George F. Hill. The author was at the time Keeper of the Coins and Medals Department of the British Museum. The first volume dealt with forgeries of Greek coins, while the second dealt with Roman, medieval, and modern forgeries. Fine plates accompanied each volume, allowing comparison between a genuine coin and a Becker reproduction.

This misguided artist was tried for his crimes, and his defense was that he was enabling collectors to obtain an inexpensive copy of a rare coin. Nevertheless, he was convicted and jailed as a common criminal.

Today a recognized forgery of an ancient gold coin of good workmanship is referred to as a "Becker," regardless of whether or not it can be attributed to Carl Becker.

✍ *What country never issued any coins?*

This writer is aware of only one such country (in modern times). Its name was "The Republic of Texas."

From 1836, when Texans defeated Santa Anna in the battle of San Jacinto on April 21, until she joined the United States in 1845 as the twenty-eighth state, the only money issued by this short-lived republic was paper. For small change she used the reals of Mexico or the cents of the United States.

The paper money was issued without metallic backing and, because of the uncertainty of Texas' future, was traded at a discount. The fears of the holders of these notes were unfounded. For when Texas was admitted into the Union she had some boundary problems to settle with the federal government. In consideration of giving up all claims to the territory of New Mexico, the United States paid her $10,000,000.

With this sum the new state paid all its debts. The holders of all notes of "The Republic of Texas" or "The Government of Texas" were paid in full on demand. In 1898 the accounts were closed and funds remaining for this purpose reverted to the general fund. Any redemption after that date was done by a special act of Congress.

✍ *Why was a silver three-cent piece issued?*

In 1851 the rate of postage needed for mailing a letter by ordinary post was reduced from five cents to three cents. Since copper one-cent pieces did not circulate freely in certain states, Congress authorized a silver three-cent piece in order that people would have a coin that would pay for a postage stamp. It must be remembered that in 1851 letter writing was quite limited and most people bought one stamp at a time, not a sheet or a roll.

The Act of March 3, 1851, did two unusual things. It authorized that the coin be 75 per cent silver and limited it to being legal

tender up to only thirty cents.
During its first few years it
proved to be extremely popular,
but after that it fell into disfavor.
The biggest complaint was its size. Being so small, it was often
lost or mislaid. In 1851, 1852, and 1853 more than 36,000,000 were
struck. During the next nine years less than 6,500,000 were
requested even though the silver content was increased to 90
per cent. And in the last eleven years that it was coined only
77,790 were minted.

It would be misleading if it were not mentioned here that a
copper-nickel three-cent piece was introduced in 1865. It was
easier to handle, being larger, and so it better served the needs of
those who used small change and was more often requested than
the small silver coin. By 1873, the silver three-cent piece died a
natural death.

🐟 *Why did Canada issue a commemorative five-cent piece?*

Although in the past gold and silver mining had been
honored by special coins, the first instance of the metal nickel
being so honored was in 1951.

This date marked the two-hundredth anniversary of the first
isolation of the pure metal from ore by the Swedish scientist
Baron Axel Frederik Cronstedt.
Canada chose to honor the metal
since it is one of her most important mineral exports. Oddly
enough, later in the year a shortage of the metal occurred and
the mint discontinued the coinage, replacing the pure-nickel five-
cent piece with a chromium-plated steel coin.

The reverse design on the pure-nickel commemorative piece
pictured a typical nickel-smelting plant, the word "NICKEL," and

the dates "1751–1951." The steel "nickel" reverted to the beaver design that had been in use from 1937 to date, except for the years 1943, 1944, and 1945.

Strangely enough, the steel regular issue has a higher premium value than the special commemorative coin. It is this writer's belief that as more Canadian collectors compete for type coins, the commemorative nickel will eventually have the higher premium.

✎ Who was Ephraim Brasher?

According to Ralph and Terry Kovel, authors of *A Directory of American Silver, Pewter and Silver-Plate*, Brasher was a resident of New York City, born there in 1744. He ran a firm known as E. Brasher & Co. about 1790. His hallmark was generally his initials, E. B., enclosed in a square or circle.

In the New York City Directory of 1787 he was listed as a silversmith residing at No. 1 Cherry Street. We also know that he worked for the United States Mint in 1792, assaying gold and silver coins. Earlier he had unsuccessfully sought permission of the New York legislature for a license to strike copper cents for the state.

He is best remembered as the creator of the famous Brasher doubloon, which has been popularized in fiction and in the movies. Actually, the dies for these gold doubloons were probably prepared by him for the New York cent that he proposed to manufacture, since one side pictured his artistic conception of the New York State Seal.

Writing in the "Centennial Publication of the American Numismatic Society" in 1958, Walter H. Breen said that "through the aid of John J. Ford it has been possible to establish the provenance of all Brasher gold now known." Six doubloons are listed. One is in the U.S. Mint Collection, on loan to the Smithsonian Institution; one is in a "mid-west collection"; one is owned by Yale University; one is owned by F. C. C. Boyd; and two are the property of Johns Hopkins University. With none having been sold in recent years at public auction, it is difficult to place a value on these rare items. I believe that if any of the six were offered for sale today, it would bring more than $50,000.

In 1914, Waldo Newcomber, a Baltimore, Maryland, numismatist, made an unusual discovery. In an accumulation of foreign gold that he had purchased was a counterfeit eight-escudo coin dated 1742. Near the bottom of the coin was the word "BRASHER" and below that the letters "NY." Further, a similar hallmark—a counterstamp of "EB," such as appeared on the Brasher doubloons—also was on this coin. A study of the coin revealed that "BRASHER" and "NY" had been cut into the dies before the coin was struck and that the counterstamp had been added later.

Very possibly more coins of Ephraim Brasher will show up in the future.

What is Clark, Gruber & Co. gold?

In the 1850's three enterprising businessmen of Denver, Colorado, started a private bank known as Clark, Gruber & Co. These men were E. H. Gruber, A. M. Clark, and M. E. Clark. One phase of private banks was to exchange cash for gold dust.

Mr. Guber explained the firm's decision to coin gold pieces in a published interview that appeared in the Denver *Times* in 1904. The following are direct quotes from that article:

My firm was one of the heaviest purchasers of gold dust in the early days. And when we bought a large quantity of dust we had to ship it to the States to have it coined into money. This was a rather expensive proceeding, as there were only stage coaches and pony expresses reaching the city in those days, and we had to pay 5 per cent. of the value of the dust as an insurance against the loss in transit and another 5 per cent. expressage. Our dust was

out of our hands any where from three weeks to three months, and often times the cash we would have in transit would total nearly $300,000. This was considerable money to have and yet not be able to use for months at a time, so one day the idea struck me that the firm of Clark, Gruber & Co., bankers, should also become coiners. I spoke to one of my partners, Austin M. Clark, who with his brother, Milton E. Clark, was interested in all my enterprises in those days, about the matter. He was a lawyer, and after spending several days looking up the authorities, gave it as his opinion that there was no law of the United States which could be construed as against the coining of money by individuals, provided it was made of full weight.

We went ahead then and ordered the machinery required in the coining of gold, and in 1860 built the old Mint building . . . and having installed our machinery set to work to turn the dust of the miners into coins of our company.

Our first gold pieces differed from those of Uncle Sam. We had the Goddess of Liberty on the face of them, but on the fillet that bound her hair, instead of the word "Liberty" we placed the words "Pike's Peak," and on the obverse side, instead of the words "United States of America," we stamped "Clark, Gruber & Co."

The first coins struck were two-and-a-half-dollar and five-dollar gold pieces, as described by Mr. Gruber. They also struck ten-dollar and twenty-dollar gold pieces, also dated 1860, but with a different design. The face showed a mountain, the words "PIKE'S PEAK GOLD DENVER," and the amount. The reverse showed an eagle, the date, and the firm name.

The following year the design was identical to the United States quarter eagle, eagle, and double eagle, except that where "UNITED STATES OF AMERICA" appeared, the firm name and "DENVER" was substituted.

No coins were minted after 1861. In 1863 the United States government purchased both the machinery and the mint property from Clark, Gruber & Co. and Congress passed laws prohibiting the private manufacturing of coins.

Today a fine specimen of the ten-dollar piece of 1860 sells for about $750, while that of 1861 brings about half that amount. The ten-dollar piece of 1861 now has hit the $1,000 mark, while the 1860 coin, being excessively rare and seldom seen, would bring possibly ten times that amount. Fine copies of the two-and-a-half-dollar and five-dollar gold pieces, being more prevalent, sell in the $300–$400 range. All of these figures attest the rarity of Clark, Gruber & Co. gold.

Are you aware that the United States has changed the metallic content of its one-cent piece many times?

The first one-cent pieces, issued from 1793 to 1857, were made of pure copper. The coins were made of approximately one cent's worth of copper.

From 1857 to 1864 a smaller-size cent, made of 88 per cent copper and 12 per cent nickel, was introduced. The addition of the nickel made the coin better able to stand wear. It also gave it a light golden hue. This was a fine alloy and would have been continued except for the increase in the price of nickel in 1863.

Since a further price rise would have made the cost of producing a cent more than one cent, a substitute had to be found.

Testing revealed that the answer lay in changing to bronze, using an alloy of 95 per cent copper and 5 per cent tin and zinc. This alloy was used until 1943.

The zinc-coated steel cent was born and died in 1943. It was unpopular from the start. It was followed in 1944 and 1945 by the "shell case" copper alloy, in which discarded bronze shell cases were mixed with pure copper to make a most acceptable alloy.

With the end of World War II, in 1946 the Mint again struck the prewar bronze cents, using the same alloy until 1962.

Now a new problem developed . . . tin was in short supply. So with no fanfare (and no noticeable difference in the appearance of the coin), since 1962 the alloy has been 95 per cent copper and 5 per cent zinc.

What two coins, although of different size and metal, are identical except for a single word?

The Grant Memorial one-dollar gold piece and silver half dollar, both authorized by the United States Congress on February 2, 1922, have the identical obverse and reverse designs. The only difference is the word "ONE" appearing before "DOLLAR" on the gold coin and "HALF" before "DOLLAR" on the silver piece.

These interesting coins were struck to commemorate the one-hundredth anniversary of the birth of Ulysses S. Grant. Both show the head of Grant, facing right, on the obverse, and his birthplace, a simple frame house, on the reverse. The designer of this beautiful coin was Laura Gardin Fraser, who also designed the Alabama Centennial and Fort Vancouver Centennial half dollars and the Charles Lindbergh Congressional Medal.

There were approximately 100,000 of the silver halves and only 10,000 of the gold dollars struck in 1922. The committee in charge

of their sale found that the gold
pieces sold quickly, but that interest in the half dollars lagged.
To counter this, the committee at first required the purchase
of fifteen silver coins as a
prerequisite to the sale of a
gold coin. Public discontentment
made them reduce the ratio to
10 to 1. When all the gold dollars were sold out, there still
remained over 28,000 halves that
were returned to the Mint and
melted down.

🙈 *What is a "Kettle"?*

These are brass tokens that were struck to look like
United States and British gold coins. We do not consider them to
be counterfeits because the artist plainly placed his name,
"KETTLE," on each piece. The commonest varieties are copies of
U.S. two-and-a-half-dollar and five-dollar gold pieces of 1803 and
British spade guineas of George III.

The general belief today is that
the discs were manufactured as
"Spiel Munze" (play money), or,
in the popular jargon, poker
chips. According to L. Forrer,
in his *Biographical Dictionary*

of Medallists, the firm of Kettle & Son were die sinkers and counter manufacturers located in Birmingham, England, in the early
part of the nineteenth century.

Other gambling tokens or jettons were also made by this firm,
identified with the initials K & S or H. K. These pieces generally
commemorated an event or a person associated with events of

historical interest to the people of Great Britain. Many bore flowery sentiments such as "England & Ireland United, Prosperity to the United Kingdoms," "God Protects the Just," or "We Conquour to Set Free" and cover events that occurred from about 1800 to the coronation of Victoria in 1837.

✍ *When were coins first counterfeited?*

You have undoubtedly heard it said of a man, "He'd rather make a nickel dishonestly than a dollar honestly." Schemers, tricksters, thieves, and counterfeiters have always existed, since man learned to walk on two feet.

Counterfeit Hebrew shekels and Roman sesterces are in the writer's collection. These could have been copies cast more than nineteen hundred years ago. Early English history tells us that Canute (994?–1035), King of England, Norway, and Denmark, punished convicted counterfeiters by having their hands cut off. Earlier in history, Romans burned the felons alive or threw them to the wild animals in the arena. In colonial America we know that certain unscrupulous colonists even counterfeited wampum; a law making this act a criminal offense was passed by the Dutch in New Amsterdam. Still later, notes of the United Colonies bore the slogan "'Tis Death to Counterfeit." In fact, it was so widespread that The American Numismatic Society, New York, in 1957 published a book of more than 200 pages called *Counterfeiting in Colonial Connecticut* by Kenneth Scott. Mr. Scott stated that "the first recorded case of counterfeiting in Connecticut is that of Robert Fenton in 1699."

Probably the only reason that "Thou Shalt Not Counterfeit" was not one of the Commandments was that money as we know it had not been invented when Moses received the Law from God.

Why is the 1799 one cent so rare?

Mint records state that 904,585 pieces were coined. After more than a century and half, this coin remains rare. We therefore have a perfect right to believe that the Mint records were in error.

But there are a number of "old witches' tales" concerning this hard-to-find coin. It is fun to quote them because they make such interesting reading.

My favorite tale appeared in the January, 1918, issue of *The Numismatist,* and quoted a writeup in the Philadelphia *Ledger:*

The rarest cent is that of the series of 1799. It is said that the scarcity of this issue is due to the fact that a firm in Salem, Mass., which was then engaged in the slave trade, procured a large quantity of them from the mint, and after drilling holes in each one, shipped them to Africa, where they were given as ornaments to the chiefs in exchange for slaves. The veracity of this story cannot be vouched for, but, if it is true, coin collectors are much more likely to find specimens of this issue in Africa than in the United States.

Another variation of the above story failed to mention that the coins were holed. It did, though, end on a sad note, for it told that the vessel carrying the cents to Africa sank in a storm before reaching its destination.

*Did Canada strike proof coins in years
other than 1908, 1911, and 1937?*

The years mentioned are those in which proof sets were openly sold to the public, and in sufficient quantities to satisfy the collectors of the day.

Canadian proof coins, in limited numbers, were struck in other years. They do not come "on the market" very often in either the United States or Canada. Most seem to have found their way back to the "mother country," England. Of course, if they were dated prior to 1908, they were minted in London or Birmingham, and so possibly never left England.

In *Spink's Numismatic Circular* (the house organ of the firm of Spink & Son, Ltd., who have been coin and medal dealers since 1772) from 1901 to 1930, many Canadian proofs were offered for sale.

The 1858 set of silver five cents, ten cents, and twenty cents were available with either grained or plain edge. A set of ten cents, twenty-five cents, and fifty cents of 1870 was offered, as was a set of five cents, ten cents, and twenty-five cents of 1903. Individual one-cent pieces of 1859, 1881-H, and 1882-H were also on the list. In 1914 a proof specimen of the rare 1908 sovereign was placed for sale at £2 10s ($12.50). This coin is rare in any condition, as only 636 pieces were struck.

Issues of Newfoundland were also available in proof. These included the gold two-dollar coins of 1865 and 1880, the fifty-cent piece of 1870 (with plain edge), and the five-, ten-, and twenty-cent pieces of 1865. New Brunswick coins of 1862 were also represented with proof of the five-, ten-, and twenty-cent pieces. For about $9 you could have purchased the complete set of Newfoundland coins of either 1917 or 1919.

All of the above are truly mouth-watering, but the best is yet to come. The April, 1927, issue offered a set of Canadian five-cent, ten-cent, twenty-five-cent, and fifty-cent pieces in proof for the year 1921. The price was six shillings ($1.50). For those of you who are uninformed, the *1966 Standard Catalogue of Canadian Coins, Tokens and Paper Money* prices the five-cent piece in uncirculated condition at $4,000 and the fifty-cent piece at $12,000. And proofs are much rarer!

Why were there three types of U.S. five-cent pieces in 1883?

Prior to 1866 the United States had no nickel (copper-nickel) five-cent coin, only the silver half dime. In 1866 the so-called shield type made its appearance. Although it was criticized for its lack of beauty, its design remained virtually unchanged for eighteen years.

Congressional approval is needed to change the design of a coin if it has not been used for twenty-five years. Before such approval was received in 1883 for the change to the Liberty Head type, almost one and a half million of the shield-type nickels were struck.

The new Liberty Head five-cent pieces were applauded for their classic appearance, but in a very short time the Mint discovered that it had made an error. The designers had used a Roman "V" for five, surrounding it with a beautiful ornamental wreath, but they had left off the word "CENTS." Since the coin was almost identical in size to the five-dollar gold piece, clever operators immediately secured quantities of the new coins, gold-plated them, and passed them off as five-dollar gold pieces.

Immediately, the Treasury Department recalled the centless variety and redesigned the reverse. Where "E PLURIBUS UNUM" had appeared below the wreath, the word "CENTS" was placed. The motto was moved to a suitable space above the wreath.

Thus within a few months three varieties of five-cent pieces appeared. Oddly enough, the "no cent" variety, with a total mintage of about five and a half million—most of them recalled—is the common variety, while the "cents" variety with a coinage of over sixteen million is scarce. The explanation is simple—people tend to save, as a memento, any new type of coin. Since the third variety actually showed only a minor change, people disregarded them. As a result, most were used commercially and in time became worn, after which they were redeemed for newer coins. At best this series of Liberty Head nickels seemed to wear down quicker than most other coins.

A sampling of opinions today seems to indicate that the shield type would be preferred to the Liberty Head by a majority of folks. Tastes change, but if they did not there would only have been one variety of 1883 five-cent pieces.

♔ *How should coins be cleaned?*

This is a problem. What an expert can do well, a novice can botch up. Certainly dirt and grime should be removed. A mild soap and warm water can do no harm to a dirty coin. For copper or bronze, some mineral or olive oil applied with a soft rag can be used to remove any loose foreign matter, and will not disturb any natural patina that has formed. And when the coin is wiped clean, a thin film of oil will probably remain on the coin, which will act as a protective coating.

Nothing more is suggested. In most cases the natural tarnish or patina is superior to the bright shiny look.

If you are unhappy with the appearance of your coin after trying the above, consult an expert.

♔ *Whose head is on the Indian Head cent?*

We must all admit that the profile on the bronze United States one-cent pieces coined from 1859 to 1909 does not look like an American Indian. The only reason for referring to this cent as Indian Head is the fact that the head is wearing an Indian warrior's feathered bonnet.

According to Mrs. Sarah Peck, a distant relative of J. B. Longacre, designer of this coin, the following is stated as fact. Twelve-year-old Sarah Longacre, daughter of J. B., visited her father at the mint in Philadelphia at the same time that a delegation of American Indians was being shown through the plant. A chief placed his war bonnet on Sarah's head and the effect was so striking that Longacre made a sketch of his daughter wearing the headdress. It is said that a refined version of this drawing appears on the Indian Head one-cent pieces. The headdress is said to be that of the Sioux tribe. Little Sarah grew up to become Mrs. Keen, known in Philadelphia for having served thirty-five years as local secretary of the Philadelphia branch of the Methodist Women's Foreign Missionary Society.

What is a touch piece?

Just as the Caesars claimed to have descended from the gods of the Romans, so later kings claimed their thrones by "divine right." To this date British coins state "DEI GRATIA" (By the Grace of God).

As far back as A.D. 481, Clovis I, King of the Franks, claimed that a victim of scrofula (tuberculosis of the lymphatic glands, especially of the neck), known as the King's Evil, could be cured by being touched by his royal fingers.

This practice of "touching" came to England with Edward the Confessor in 1042. By this time the ceremony of "touching" was accompanied by the practice of presenting a coin to the ailing one. By the reign of Henry VII, King of England from 1485 to 1509, there developed what we know as the first touch pieces. It is believed that the coins were the angels, large gold pieces that pictured the Archangel Michael, spear in hand, slaying a dragon. The reverse showed a ship and bore the Latin motto that translated to "By Thy cross, O Christ, Redeemer, save us."

As can be imagined, the practice of giving each suspected victim of scrofula a gold coin became a royal luxury, then a royal burden, since we are told that many feigned illness to claim a gold piece.

Many touch pieces are found holed, leading to the assumption that they were worn about the neck on a chain or chord.

The practice of presenting these pieces discontinued with George I, the Elector of Hanover, who became King of England in 1714.

*Is there a market for your coin
collection if you wish to sell it?*

Certainly! But remember, if you formed a collection
from the small change that came into your hand, it is most
probable that it does not contain rarities. If you had a windfall
and found a rarity, you will be well rewarded when you sell it.

Too many people fail to realize that even a scarce coin may be
refused by a coin dealer. If he does not need the coin for stock,
because he already has similar ones, or because he is short of
cash, he may be unwilling to buy your coin.

Should you be unable to find a buyer, two alternatives remain.
The coins can be offered to a dealer on consignment or they can
be placed with a dealer who conducts auction sales. With the
former, you set the price and the dealer receives a percentage as
his commission. The weakness here is that it will take time to sell
the items. At auction you take your chances on the price that will
be realized for each coin, but you are assured of cash in a reasonable time. Should you wish to "protect" your selling price by
bidding, you may end up buying back your own coin.

In the past twenty years, with prices almost continually on the
increase, good coins have consistently over the long run brought
higher prices, whether sold at fixed price or at auction.

 *What is the history of the U.S. gold coin
of 1915 that shows a baseball player on
one side?*

I just had to sneak this question in someplace because
so many noncollectors have asked this question in some form or
other after seeing a copy of the gold dollar struck for the Panama-
Pacific Exposition. This was the World's Fair held in San Francisco in 1915 to celebrate the opening of the Panama Canal.

The head on the obverse is meant to represent labor and not a baseball player, although it must be admitted that the cap   on the workman's head does look like a baseball player's cap. Most folks fail to notice the design on the reverse, which is most artistic. It is a circle formed by two dolphins. Labor is shown on the face to honor the men who built the canal. The dolphins symbolize the joining of the Atlantic and Pacific oceans.

By Act of Congress the gold dollars were limited to 25,000 pieces. Although this number were struck, 10,000 unsold pieces were later remelted. So by today's standards this is a scarce coin, with a total mintage of only 15,000 pieces.

What is meant by "wartime cents"?

Because of the shortage of copper created by the entrance of the United States into World War II in December, 1941, the Treasury Department sought a substitute metal. Copper was a strategic material needed in the manufacturing of ammunition. The Mint conducted tests in its search for a substitute, for the one-cent piece had had a metallic content of 95 per cent copper and 5 per cent tin and zinc ever since 1864. The answer was found in the zinc-coated steel one-cent piece. Congress approved the change on December 18, 1942, in a bill that gave discretionary power concerning the minting of coins to the Secretary of the Treasury with the approval of the War Production Board. This power, though, was given him only until December 31, 1946.

The first "wartime cents," those of 1943, proved most unpopular. When new, they were often mistaken for dimes. When worn, they were a dirty gray and a most unattractive coin. Before the year was out metallurgists of the Mint found a more acceptable substitute. They discovered that the metal of used shell cases, being 70 per cent copper and 30 per cent zinc, to which a small amount of pure copper was added, bore a very close resemblance to the prewar cents. So the second type of "wartime cents" was created. When Mrs. Nellie Tayloe Ross, Director of the Mint, announced the change, she also added a plea: "Every one-cent piece resting in a coin bank, bureau drawer or other hiding place, whether copper or steel, calls for a replacement at the expense of war-necessary metals and manpower. Let us keep small change working, through our regular spending." These "shell-case" cents were minted in 1944 and 1945. By 1946 the supply of copper had increased and the war was over. So the Mint returned to the use of the pure copper plus 5 per cent tin and zinc as used during the preceding eighty years.

𝕾 What is a Stolen Kingdom dollar?

Legend has it that after Frederick the Great of Prussia conquered Silesia, he retained many officials of that country, including the mint master of Breslau.

When ordered to produce a taler with the head of Frederick in place of that of Maria Theresa, the mint master acted promptly, but after delivering the new coins he disappeared.

The reason was soon obvious. In place of "EIN REICH-THALER" (one imperial dollar), he had the coin re-engraved to read "EIN REICH STAHL ER" (he stole an empire).

All known specimens were immediately assigned to the melting pot and none are known to exist today.

Whose head has appeared on more coins than anyone else in all history?

This honor belongs to that grand old lady, Victoria, Queen of England and Empress of India. Her reign started in 1837, when she was only eighteen years old, and continued until her death in 1901. The greatest period of British colonial development took place in this period. With the help of the great statesman Benjamin Disraeli, who was her Prime Minister in 1867 and part of 1868 and from 1874 to 1880, her empire expanded. Historically, probably her greatest hour was when she was crowned Empress of India in 1876.

Her rule extended to every continent. Her profile appeared on coins of Australia, British Honduras, British Guiana, Canada, Newfoundland, New Brunswick, Nova Scotia, Prince Edward Island, Ceylon, Cyprus, East Africa, Great Britain, Hong Kong, India, the Indian States of Alwar, Bikanir, Dervas, and Dhar, Jamaica, Jersey, Malta, Mauritius, and the Straits Settlements.

As the good queen grew older, it became necessary to change the profile and gracefully show her first maturing from youth to young womanhood to middle age to old age. The designers of the coins of the British Empire did a masterful job, step by step.

*Who was the first man called
"The Father of His Country"?*

No, you are wrong. It was not George Washington!

Sawyer McA. Mosser, secretary of the American Numismatic Society, wrote a series of articles entitled "Roman Imperial Titles." In one of these he commented that in 2 B.C. the Senate and the Roman people granted to Augustus Caesar the honorary title of Pater Patriae (father of his country).

History tells us that he appreciated the honor so much that he used this title along with his name on coins struck during his rule.

But we must not be misled. Washington earned his title by his services to the new republic. Octavian, known as Augustus Caesar, ruled Rome from 31 B.C. to A.D.14 as the first of a long line of autocratic emperors. Even though his coinage bore the legend S. C.—with the consent of the Senate—he alone was ruler of Rome. There are all sorts of fathers.

 *Why are the coins of South Africa
popular in the United States?*

Only in the past twenty years have any large number of collectors in the United States and Canada shown an interest in the coins of South Africa.

It all started in 1947, when that country first decided to issue cased proof sets for collectors. A number of American dealers imported a supply. The nine-piece set included a silver five-shilling, two-and-a-half-shilling, two-shilling, one-shilling, sixpence, and three-pence pieces, and bronze farthing, half-penny and one-penny pieces. These beautifully struck proofs came in a velvet-lined leatherette case. Since they retailed for from $6 to $8, they were relatively inexpensive to purchase.

The South African government had issued very limited numbers of proof sets prior to 1947. In 1923 there were 747 sets, but after 1923, in no year did the number exceed 150 sets. In 1947 it was decided to strike a five-shilling piece for the first time since 1892. The occasion was to commemorate the visit of King George VI and Queen Elizabeth. The five-shilling or crown was then continued each year until South Africa switched to a decimal system of rands and cents in 1961.

A listing of the number of proof sets from 1947 to 1960 will show the present scarcity of this series.

Year	9-Piece Sets	11-Piece Sets (£1 and £½ gold added)
1947	2,600	
1948	1,120	
1949	800	
1950	500	
1951	2,000	
1952	3,500	12,000
1953	2,000	9,000
1954	2,275	875
1955	2,250	600
1956	1,350	350
1957	750	380
1958	625	360
1959	560	390
1960	1,860	1,600

After the changeover to the decimal coinage cased proof sets continued to be sold. The set is now composed of silver (which later was changed to copper-nickel) fifty-cent, twenty-cent, ten-cent, five-cent, and two-and-a-half-cent pieces, and brass one-cent and half-cent pieces. Gold one-rand and two-rand pieces were also struck.

As was true with other foreign proof sets, by 1965 the demand from American collectors was more than the South African Mint could handle, even though more than 20,000 were being struck annually. Since then the Pretoria Mint has refused all orders except from those on their mailing list of past subscribers. This condition could change overnight, so please do not take this writer's word that the South African Mint's policy is still in effect.

✍️ When is a gazette not a newspaper?

A gazette is not a newspaper when it is spelled *g-a-z-e-t*. A gazet or gazetta was a small copper coin of the city and province of Venice at the time it was the Venetian Republic in the sixteenth century.

It is stated that the first newspaper in Venice was published in 1556. It was called the *Notizie Scritte* and its cost was one gazetta. In turn a newspaper became known as a gazetta or gazette. Today in both the United States and Great Britain a newspaper is known as a gazette.

✍️ What is the origin of the Liberty Cap?

The United States half cents of 1793 through 1797 pictured a Liberty Cap, as did the large cents from 1794 through 1796 (and one variety of 1793 cents). Later U.S. silver, beginning in 1837, showed a seated goddess holding a pole upon which rested a Liberty Cap.

The symbolism has its roots back in the history of ancient Rome. When a slave was freed a ritual ceremony was followed. First, the slave's head was shaved. Then he was presented with a cap to cover the shaved head. This cap was his badge of freedom. In time the cap became a symbol of freedom for a group of people as well as a slave, and appeared on coins of the Roman Republic.

France, following the Revolution in 1789, used the Liberty Cap as a symbol of her newfound freedom from Bourbon tyranny. Undoubtedly the designers of United States coins believed that this symbol was also appropriate for her coins. In the New World, the Liberty Cap can also be found on coinage of Brazil, Chile, Colombia, Cuba, Ecuador, Guatemala, Honduras, and Mexico, to name a few countries.

Ordinarily the Roman went bareheaded at all times, making the wearer of the cap the exception and therefore easily recognized as one having recently attained freedom.

🪙 *Is there such a thing as "prison money"?*

Yes, there is. Many years ago I was shown a token of Sing Sing Prison. Investigation showed that in 1915 this prison issued tokens with a value of one, five, ten, twenty-five, and fifty cents, and notes with a value of one dollar, five dollars, and ten dollars as well. These metal and currency tokens all bore the slogan "Do Good—Make Good Sing Sing Prison" and the initials MWL for the Mutual Welfare League that issued them.

According to an article in *The Numismatist* of January, 1916, the prisoners were paid one dollar a day for their labor. They could use the token money to buy items at the Mutual Welfare League store in the prison. All items at the store had to be paid for with at least 50 per cent token money, while the balance could be paid for with real currency. The reason for this was to reduce discontentment among the poorer convicts, who resented those who were given cash by friends or relatives from the "outside."

This article mentioned: "A five-cent piece was recently found in the contribution box of the Greensburg Presbyterian Church, Dobbs Ferry, by the treasurer, when counting up the evening's offering." Since the donor realized that the token was valueless outside Sing Sing Prison, we can assume that he still pursued his corrupt ways.

🕸 *Why do some coins of George II have the word "LIMA"?*

Some of the gold five guineas, one guinea, and half guinea, as well as silver crowns, half crowns, shillings, and sixpence of George II of England have the word "LIMA" stamped in large letters below the bust of the king.

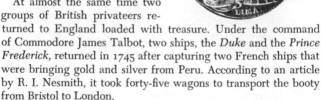

Although we know that Lima referred to Lima, Peru, and that the coins were said to have been struck from captured treasures that came from Peru, there are conflicting stories as to how this particular gold and silver was acquired.

At almost the same time two groups of British privateers returned to England loaded with treasure. Under the command of Commodore James Talbot, two ships, the *Duke* and the *Prince Frederick,* returned in 1745 after capturing two French ships that were bringing gold and silver from Peru. According to an article by R. I. Nesmith, it took forty-five wagons to transport the booty from Bristol to London.

The other enterprise was under the command of Commodore (later Admiral) George Anson. His ship, the *Centurion,* returned to England in 1744. His treasure was acquired from a Spanish galleon that had come from Acapulco, Mexico. Anson had started out in 1740 with six ships and about two thousand men. Although he returned with only one ship and fewer than two hundred men, he was acclaimed a hero, because his captured treasure was worth some six million dollars, a tremendous fortune in 1744.

Whether the gold and silver actually came from Lima is unimportant. It did come from the Spanish Main, and is a reminder of the immense treasures seized in America by the plunderers from Europe.

✍ Why was Moses Cleaveland pictured on a coin?

In 1936 and 1937 the Great Lakes Exposition was held in Cleveland, Ohio, to celebrate the centennial of the founding of that city. For the occasion Congress authorized the striking of up

to 50,000 half dollars. All were struck and none was remelted.

The obverse pictures Moses Cleaveland, the man who led a group of about fifty people from Schenectady, New York, to this wilderness in 1796. Cleaveland was born in 1754 in Canterbury, Connecticut. After attending Yale College he became an attorney. He was also trained as an engineer. When the Connecticut Land Company acquired title to a large tract of land in northeastern Ohio, he set out with his party to survey and possibly settle it. In his honor the settlement established on the shores of Lake Erie was named Cleaveland.

The village grew, especially after the opening of the system of canals that connected the Ohio River to Lake Erie. This promoted more freight traffic. In 1836 the city of Cleveland was incorporated. The name change had occurred earlier when the

Cleveland *Advertiser* found that by dropping the *a* its masthead fit the page without reverting to smaller type. The public seemed to relish the shortening of the name.

The coin that pictures Cleaveland has a reverse that shows a map of the Great Lakes area, with stars representing the principal cities: Cleveland, Duluth, Milwaukee, Chicago, Toledo, Detroit, Buffalo, Toronto, and Rochester.

✄ Will the U.S. Mint fill orders for foreign firms?

The usual policy of the United States Mint, an arm of the Treasury Department, is to supply coins for her citizens through the Federal Reserve Banks, which in turn distribute them to member commercial banks, from where they finally reach the individual or firm.

Exceptions undoubtedly are made, since *The Canadian Numismatic Journal* in February, 1957, reported an unusual occurrence. In December, 1956, a firm in Scarsborough, Ontario, ordered 35,000 silver dollars from the Royal Canadian Mint in Ottawa, to be given to its employees as part of a profit-sharing distribution. The Ottawa Mint refused the order, stating that a shortage of skilled labor and an increase in the demand for dimes and quarters would make it impossible to honor the request. The firm then turned to the United States Mint in Philadelphia for help. They not only received the 35,000 silver dollars (U.S., of course) requested, but a bonus of 1,500 more because of the favorable exchange rate.

The article concluded that the coins were all brilliant uncirculated pieces dated 1925. If the recipients saved them, they could more than double their money today.

Why do some coins have a smooth edge and others a milled edge?

Generally, only the minor coins, those of copper (or bronze), nickel (or copper-nickel), or brass have a smooth edge, while those coined of rarer metals such as gold or silver have the milled or reeded edge.

Coins of earlier years all had smooth edges, probably because until the advent of the steam press it was too costly and cumbersome to apply an ornate edge.

Because unscrupulous people pared or clipped the edge of a coin in order to acquire some of the coin's intrinsic value, a method had to be found to prevent this practice, or, if not prevent it, at least make the recipient aware that the coin was not whole. Thus a coin where part of the ornate edge was missing could properly be refused.

All of this presupposes that a coin is accepted because its intrinsic value is present in the metal of which it is composed. Actually today, with a shortage of silver, many countries have replaced their so-called silver coins with copper-nickel or other metals. In England this very thing was done in 1947. In the United States, it was not effected until 1965. But because of custom, the former silver coins, even though made of a metal that was not worth clipping or paring, still has the milled or serrated edge.

When did the United States strike "nickels" without any nickel?

Until 1866, the U.S. five-cent piece was made of silver and called (from 1837) a "half dime." When a five-cent coin of 75 per cent copper and 25 per cent nickel was introduced in 1866, this new type five-cent piece was called a nickel. This was perfectly logical because the silver half dime continued to be minted until 1873.

With the entry of the United States into World War II in December, 1941, a substitute had to be found for this strategic material. On March 27, 1942, Congress passed legislation that allowed the Treasury Department to make a five-cent coin of half silver and half copper or to use different proportions and add additional metals. The substitute finally selected was an alloy of 56 per cent copper, 35 per cent silver, and 9 per cent manganese. The law allowing this change in alloys specified that this "wartime" substitute could not be used after December 31, 1946. This fact, in itself, is interesting, because it was almost as if the legislators had psychic powers—with World War II ending in September, 1945.

In 1942 both copper-nickel "nickels" and silver "nickels" were struck at the Philadelphia Mint. In order to tell them apart it was decided to use a mintmark on coins from the Philadelphia Mint for the first time. Not only was the "P" used as a mintmark, but also the mintmark, whether "S" for San Francisco or "D" for Denver, was moved from the right of Monticello (on the reverse) to directly above the dome of Monticello. Further, the mintmark was enlarged many times, so that it could easily be seen.

With the reappearance of the copper-nickel five-cent piece in 1946 the mintmark was returned to its original location, its size was reduced, and the Philadelphia Mint coins dropped the mintmark completely. Few of the "silver" nickels are seen today. With each coin having approximately seven cents worth of silver, certain coin dealers are offering $255 for a $200 bag of "wartime nickels," culls included. More often than not, these end up in a furnace, being melted down in order to recapture the pure silver and thus generate a profit for the owner.

Why are there two sizes of gold dollars?

The gold dollar was first authorized in 1849. Until 1854 it was small and thick. Because of this thickness, it could be split.

It hardly seems worthwhile, considering the work involved, but certain unscrupulous individuals would split these coins, scrape out a quantity of gold, fill the void with lead and cement the two halves together.

To counteract this practice, the coins were made larger and thinner. In 1854 both types were minted, and from 1855 to 1889 only the larger-planchet coins were struck.

In order to clear the air, because we recognize three types of gold dollars, let us state that type one used the small, thick planchet, while types two and three both were struck on the larger, thin blank. The weight of all three was identical, being 25-⅞ grains of .900 fine gold.

Can a collection be built up of animals on coins?

Why not! Topical collections of minor foreign coins are relatively inexpensive. Start with Ireland. Her present coins are referred to as the "barnyard set." They picture on various denominations a pig, rabbit, bull, horse, and dog. Thailand (Siam) has coins that picture elephants. Australian coins show a kan-

garoo, Burmese the peacock, Ceylon the water buffalo, and the Union of South Africa the springbok. We could go on and on. Jamaican coins show an alligator, while coins of Greenland picture the polar bear.

Many species of animals appear on the United States commemorative half-dollar series, but possibly these should be bypassed, since those coins are quite high-priced.

Why does an automobile appear on a Chinese coin?

China has initiated many "firsts," even to picturing an automobile on a coin. This silver piece was struck in 1928 and is known as the automobile dollar, since it is silver dollar or crown size.

The striking of this unusual piece was ordered by Governor Chow Hsi-ch'en (Si-keng) following the completion of the first motor roads in Kweichow, a province in the Republic of China.

The coin first came to the attention of the general public through the following story, datelined Shanghai, that appeared in a December, 1933, issue of the New York *Herald Tribune:*

Chinese superstition attributes the violent death of General Chow Si-keng, Governor of Kweichow Province from 1926 to 1929, to the minting of a Kweichow silver dollar bearing the design of an automobile. Kweichow Province has no railways, and until Chow's administration had few motor highways. Gen-

eral Chow was an enthusiastic exponent of road building and a few months after his assumption of office compelled the virtual rebuilding of Kweiyang, the provincial capital, by arbitrarily widening all of the city streets and constructing an extensive system of automobile highways.

To popularize road building, the Kweichow chief executive ordered the minting of a provincial silver dollar stamped on one side with the picture of an automobile. The coin had a standard silver content and was equivalent to the Chinese yuan. But the general's passion for rapid communication was destined to be the indirect cause of his death. During a campaign against a military rival, General Li Shao-yen, the provincial chairman was riding in a motor car at the head of his troops. Too far ahead of his forces, the general's car was surrounded by an enemy advance guard and he was slain.

Chinese soothsayers, who attribute the death of the Chinese general to the minting of the "automobile dollar," have a different explanation of the executive's purpose in designing the new coin. They charge that the provincial chairman wished to have his own profile printed on the face of a new dollar in emulation of Yuan Shih-kai and Sun Yat-sen. Official modesty, however, forbade such a procedure, so the chief executive is said to have hit upon the clever subterfuge. General Chow gave instructions to design a new dollar featuring a motor car in bas-relief. That the implication might be unmistakable, the vegetation below the car were so arranged that they formed the characters "Si-chen," the personal name of Chow Si-keng.

It is said that the soothsayers predicted that the provincial chairman would die a violent death in a motor car accident as punishment for his pride and ostentation. General Chow's death was a misfortune to the province because at the time he was engaged in constructing two important truck-line motor roads.

Truth or fiction, it makes for wonderful conjecture.

✒ What was the public's reaction to the radical Indian-Buffalo five-cent piece?

United States coins up to 1913 had followed the classic style of design. The Lincoln cent of 1909 had broken tradition with regard to using an allegorical figure on the coin. Now, in 1913, a change in technique was employed. *The Numismatist* of March, 1913, wrote:

It is to be regretted that the new coin does not show much more finished die work, which could easily have been accomplished. We are inclined to think that the rough finish of the design will encourage counterfeiters, whose handicraft need not now fear the comparison which it has met in the past with the ordinarily delicate and finished mint issues. . . . We still prefer Miss Columbia as the proper representation of freedom.

Another opinion, quite contrary, was expressed by a Mr. A. H. Cooper-Prichard in the July, 1913, issue of *Spink's Numismatic Circular* (London):

That country is to be commended in having struck out in a new line of Liberty that hitherto have made her coinage so uninteresting, and again, in having done tardy justice to the unfortunate race of the so-called "Indians,"—the *real* Americans— in choosing the noble head of a chief, apparently of the once great Algonquin nation, as a coin type.

Mr. Cooper-Prichard, though, was quite critical when he said:

The incused field and raised edge are doubtless intended to prevent the coin from wearing away. Experienced numismatists may be pardoned however, in feeling somewhat sceptical of this "Yankee notion," particularly as the pieces which have found their way into circulation are by no means clear and sharp in their inscriptions or in the details of the type. Possibly this may be due to imperfect striking, which would only make matters worse, but the prominent relief in which the figure of the bison, as well as the ground he is supposed to be standing on, no less than the other extreme of the unnecessarily low relief of the Chief's bust, are not conducive to withstand a very great degree of friction.

How true. We know today that many of those still in circulation are "dateless," and that of all United States coins, the Indian Buffalo nickel has not withstood the wear and tear of normal handling.

🐟 *Do any coins picture Edward VIII of England?*

Edward VIII, now known as the Duke of Windsor, succeeded to the throne of England upon the death of his father, George V, on January 20, 1936.

As is custom, dies were prepared that would picture the new monarch on the coins of England, beginning in 1937, since 1936 coins, with the bust of George V, were already struck and circulating when the good king died.

The new king's love for a commoner, Mrs. Wallis Warfield Simpson, and Parliament's refusal to allow him to both marry her and retain the throne, caused him to abdicate on December 11, 1936.

According to an article by an anonymous British citizen that appeared in *The Numismatist* of March, 1937, the British authorities, seeking to obliterate Edward VIII from English history, sought to destroy all coins that may have been struck for 1937, and destroy all dies that pictured him.

We can say that they almost succeeded. A few brass three-pence pieces dated 1937, showing the bust of Edward VIII, facing left, were discovered in circulation. Whether these were trial or pattern pieces is hard to say. Up to this time the three-pence coin had been made of silver. The year 1937 was to introduce for the first time a larger twelve-sided brass three pence. Often with a design or metal change, trial and pattern pieces are used to test the new dies and the new metal. Now both were occurring, a design change and metal change. Since the threepence of George VI, which appeared later the same year, had a similar design to that of Edward VIII, it is most likely that the few that accidentally got into circulation were merely trial pieces used to test the new dies.

A few British colonial possessions issued coins that bore Edward's name, but none pictured the man who gave up his throne for love. Although none of these issues is scarce, they bring high prices. Since all are dated 1936, this one year is needed to complete a type set of British colonial coins. A Fiji Islands penny sells for $4, a New Guinea penny for $3.75, and a British West Africa set of ⅒, ½, and 1 penny for $4.

≈❧ *What is the largest coin ever made?*

Assuming that a coin need not be round, but must be made of metal, the honor of being the largest goes to the ten-daler copper coin of Sweden.

This rectangular copper piece is the largest of the series known as Swedish plate money. It weighs about forty-seven and one half pounds and is approximately 27½ inches by 12 inches. The ten-daler pieces were coined only in 1644.

Smaller pieces of plate money were also minted in amounts of one half, one, two, three, four, five, and eight dalers. They are all identified with a royal seal in each of the four corners and the value shown in a fifth seal in the center of the coin. All were struck between 1644 and 1776.

A shortage of silver and an abundance of copper led to the decision to manufacture this unique currency. When issued, the

8 DALER SWEDISH PLATE MONEY (*reduced*)

coins had as much intrinsic value in them as was stamped on them. At some period the intrinsic value must have exceeded the stated value, because plate money is rare today. In 1916 the Swedish government forbade its export, this at a time when most of Europe was engaged in World War I and copper was needed for the making of munitions.

While these pieces were cumbersome, it must be remembered that the buying power of ten dalers in 1644 was greater than a one-hundred-dollar bill would be today. Besides, it could not have been much worse to carry a piece of plate money than a sock full of coins. The convenience of using paper money was not appreciated, understood, or acceptable until the nineteenth century.

◈ Why did many early U.S. coins have lettered edges?

The custom of using a lettered edge was not unique with the United States, although generally the lettered edge was not for the purpose of showing the coin denomination, as with U.S. coins, but rather as a place to state a motto or slogan. (Possibly the best know is on the German Imperial pieces, reading "GOTT MIT UNS.")

Reason enough exists for stamping "FIFTY CENTS OR HALF A DOLLAR" on the fifty-cent piece and "HUNDRED CENTS, ONE DOLLAR OR UNIT" on the first silver dollars. These two denominations made no mention of their value on either the obverse or reverse of the coins. No reason, though, can be advanced for minting lettered-edge varieties of half cents and one cents, since the amounts were clearly stated on the coins.

And in case you did not know, the double eagles of 1907–1933, Saint-Gaudens' design, have a lettered edge. Unlike the early United States issues, which stated the value of the coin on the edge, these twenty-dollar gold pieces have around the edge the motto "E PLURIBUS UNUM."

◈ What is a Centennial Medal?

To the numismatist who collects U.S. medals, any medal struck to commemorate the one-hundredth anniversary of American independence is a Centennial Medal.

Of special interest are those medals authorized by Congress in June, 1874. The Mint was instructed to prepare and the Centennial Board of Finance to issue a large number of these historical items. Their sale helped defray the cost of the Centennial Exposition, held in Philadelphia in 1876.

More than 300 varieties have been described in white metal, silver, gold, bronze, rubber, and pressed wood. Besides those usually identified with the Fair, showing pictures of special buildings erected for the occasion and the like, various other interesting types were struck.

In the patriotic vein is one with the head of Washington on the obverse, while the reverse showed the famous autograph of John Hancock and the following: "WORDS SPOKEN BY JOHN HANCOCK AFTER SIGNING THE DECLARATION OF INDEPENDENCE. THERE! JOHN BULL CAN READ THAT NAME WITHOUT SPECTACLES, NOW LET HIM DOUBLE HIS REWARD."

A number appeared as souvenirs for special groups of visitors. For example, one medal pictured a bust of Pope Pius IX and said "IN HONOR OF THE CATHOLIC VISITORS TO THE INTERNATIONAL EXHIBITION/ PHILADELPHIA/ 1876." Another showed the head of Kaiser Wilhelm I and "DEN

DEUTSCHEN BESUCHERN DER WELTAUSSTELLUNG GEWIDMET/ PHILADELPIA/ 1876." For the French was one with the bust of President MacMahon and "A L'HONNEUR DES VISITEURS FRANÇAIS DE L'EXPOSITION INTERNATIONALE A PHILADELPHIA, 1876."

Another group, privately struck, had a patriotic obverse, such as the head of Washington or the face of the famous Libertas Americana medal, but with a store card on the reverse. For example, one read: "Good for 1 glass of soda water at Frederick's Pharmacy cor 60th & Second Ave. N.Y." Another pleaded: "Make your grocer get Dobbin's Electric Soap, the Best of All. J. L. Cragin & Co. Philada. Pa."

When attending an antique show, keep your eyes open; you may discover one of these interesting Centennial Medals.

Can numismatics be combined with autograph collecting?

A most enterprising young man came up with what is believed to be a unique way to combine numismatics with autograph collecting. He collected one-cent checks from famous people and well-known firms. Since a check is a substitute for money, it is a part of numismatics. And since a check is generally signed by the payer, it also has the signature of the maker.

A collection of this type was started by a well-known collector of the past half century, Waldo C. Moore. This energetic man was born in Verona, Ohio, in 1874, joining the Peoples Banking Company of Lewisburg, Ohio, in 1899, and remaining with the bank until his retirement. He joined the American Numismatic Association in 1904 and was its president in 1919 and 1920. His interests included membership in the National Geographic Society, the Indian Rights Association, the American Numismatic Society, the Ohio State Archaeological and Historical Society, and many other social and educational groups.

His collection of one-cent checks included items from President

Harding, Charles Evans Hughes, Henry Cabot Lodge, John Philip Sousa, Thomas Alva Edison, Luther Burbank, William Jennings Bryan, Irvin S. Cobb, and about 1,400 other celebrities.

One can imagine the vast amount of correspondence necessary to make a representative collection of checks.

✍ Who was Standish Barry?

Collectors of early American silver will recognize the name as belonging to an American silversmith of Baltimore, Maryland. According to Ralph and Terry Kovel's *A Directory of American Silver, Pewter and Silver Plate*, he used the following marks in the period from 1784 to 1810:

BARRY

Standish *Barry* S.B

Barry was born in Baltimore in 1763, growing up in an atmosphere of anti-British feeling and American patriotism. His claim to fame is a three-pence token that he designed in honor of Independence Day, 1790. Its face shows a bust of himself, with the words "BALTIMORE TOWN JULY 4–90" as a border. The reverse reads "THREE PENCE" with his name serving as the border. As early as 1862 one of these tokens sold for $22.

It is our belief that these three-penny pieces were not truly meant to circulate as money, but were merely Standish Barry's way of advertising his profession as a worker in silver.

✍ *What is a disme?*

It is merely an obsolete spelling for dime and the pronunciation is quite the same. The archaic spelling was in vogue at the time of the designing of the first United States coins. As a result the first five- and ten-cent coins were called half dismes and dismes.

The term disme means one tenth. When Congress set up the rules for coinage, it was resolved: "First; that the money unit of the United States of America be one dollar. Second; that the smallest coin be of copper, of which 200 shall pass for one dollar. Third; that the several pieces shall increase in a decimal ratio." Therefore the disme is one tenth of the unit or dollar.

The first coinage of the new United States was announced by President Washington in an address to Congress on November 6, 1792, thus:

In execution of the authority given by the legislature, measures have been taken for engaging some artists from abroad to aid in the establishment of our mint. Others have been employed at home. Provisions have been made for the requisite buildings, and these are now being put in proper condition for the purpose of the establishment. There has been a small coinage of half dismes, the want of small coins in circulation calling attention to them.

According to legend, Washington is said to have donated some of his own household silver for the purpose of supplying the silver necessary for the first dismes and half dismes.

Since the Mint was not formally opened until 1793, this first coinage is considered to be a pattern or trial issue, and not part of the regular series of United States coins.

✍ *Why is a quarter dollar called "two bits"?*

The Spanish milled dollar or eight-real piece, comparable in size to the U.S. silver dollar, was readily accepted in colonial America. In fact, most colonial currency, authorized by the various American colonies, was payable in Spanish milled dollars. These Spanish-American (most were minted in Mexico City) coins were actually legal tender in the United States until 1857.

Often these eight-real pieces were cut up into eighths, in order to make small change. This practice was more common on the various Caribbean islands than on the mainland, where one-half-, one-, two-, and four-real pieces were prevalent. These one-eighth pieces were called "bits." Their value was about twelve and a half cents, although they often traded in lieu of the dime.

Thus two pieces or two bits had the value of twenty-five cents and a new expression joined the American "slanguage."

✍ *Has England considered changing to a decimal coinage?*

England uses a duodecimal system, based on a unit of twelve rather than ten, which is used with a decimal system. The American standard of linear measure similarly uses a duodecimal system of twelve inches to the foot.

The British monetary unit is the pound, which is made up of twenty shillings. Each shilling is made up of twelve pennies. It is quite apparent that it can be complicated when adding, subtracting, multiplying, or dividing with columns of pounds, shillings, and pence.

Britishers have argued for centuries to make a change, and each year of procrastination makes the task of conversion that much harder, especially with the development of mechanical and electronic equipment. The British coin monthly, *Spink's Numis-*

matic Circular, discussed this problem almost annually between 1899 and 1911. In 1888 the *American Journal of Numismatics* reported:

The new British coin, the double florin, or dollar, is believed to be the beginning of the end of the old pounds, shillings, pence and farthings division of British money. For a long time the present pound has been regarded as an inconvenient unit of monetary value, and many schemes have been proposed to remedy the fault. The London Chamber of Commerce has now under consideration a plan making the four shilling (two florin) piece the unit of value or dollar, and dividing it into cents. By this plan nearly all the existing coins can be utilized without creating any confusion from having a double standard of unit value in force. The sovereign (pound) would become five dollars, two shillings (florin) a half a dollar, one shilling twenty-five cents, while the new coins would be ten and five cents, the one penny two cents and the half penny one cent.

Canada made the change way back in 1858. The Union of South Africa switched in 1961, while Australia made the change in 1966. England, at this writing, expects to convert to the decimal system by 1971.

*Why were only twenty-four dimes struck
at the San Francisco Mint in 1894?*

The story was told by Farran Zerbe, eminent numismatist and first curator of the Chase Manhattan Bank Money Museum in an article in *The Numismatist* in April, 1928.

The government's fiscal year ends June 30, at which time the "books are closed." On June 30, 1894, it was noted that 40 cents would round out to even dollars the bullion account at the San Francisco Mint. It was also noted that although dies were prepared, no dimes had been minted that year. So by striking any number of dollars' worth plus four, the bullion account could be closed showing an even dollar amount. It was therefore decided to strike twenty-four.

There was no thought at the time that these pieces might be rare, because it was expected that during the second six months of 1894 many would be minted. Only after the year ended did Mint officials realize that they had created a rarity. By 1928 only four of the pieces had been located, while today possibly twice that number exist. It is entirely possible that more will show up.

At "The Empire Sale" by Stack's, the well-known New York coin dealer, in November 1957 a specimen was sold at auction. It realized $4,750. The description in the catalog read as follows:

Lot 881 1894 "S" Dime. The second rarest silver coin from the San Francisco Mint, exceeded only by the 1870 "S" Dollar of which 6 or 7 are known to exist. The 1894 "S" Dime of which 7 or 8 are known, Stack's has had the pleasure of handling 5! At private sale we sold the Clapp specimen to Louis Eliasberg, another to James Stack. At auction we sold the H. R. Lee specimen in 1947, the Guggenheimer coin in 1953 and now we proudly offer this, the fifth specimen, in this great Empire Collection. Only when great and virtually complete collections are sold does the collecting fraternity have a chance to own or see such a rarity as this. To emphasize the rarity of this coin, even the great Anderson Dupont sale which we sold in 1954, considered one of the finest and most complete offerings of silver and copper coins in the last decade, lacked this coin.

If you think $4,750 is a high price, think of the specimen that sold for $13,000 in 1961!

✍ Why did the United States reduce the size of its paper money?

The old style note was 3⅛ by 7⅜ inches. Why that size was chosen back in 1861 is difficult to say, especially when so many of the private bank notes that circulated before 1861 were smaller in size.

Serious arguments were advanced as early as 1910 for a reduction in size. It was noted that the territorial currency of the United States for the Philippine Islands measured 2⅝ x 6¼ inches. This size had been used there since 1903 and had been found most acceptable.

In 1922 opponents to a reduction in size stated that because of the large amount of currency on hand in bank vaults, it could take fifty to seventy-five years before all the bills in circulation would be uniformly small size. (This writer worked as a bank teller in 1934 and never had a large-size bill offered over the counter.)

The main arguments for the change concerned a reduction in costs—less paper, less ink, more notes per sheet. Here there could be no argument, and it was this factor that finally led to the announcement in 1927 that preparations were under way for a reduction in size. The Treasury Department announcement stated in part:

From the standpoint of convenience to the public, the Treasury believes that the change in the size of the currency should be made. From the standpoint of the Government, the change is justified because the proposed reduction in size will create substantial savings in the expense of manufacturing, as well as in the cost of handling the currency.

At the annual meeting of the American Numismatic Society held on January 11, 1930, its Committee on United States Paper Money reported: "The year 1929 has been a notable one for United States paper money, for the long-talked-about small size money has been placed in circulation. Only the future can tell whether this radical change in our paper money will be a success." By 1931 the small-size note had become such a normal "way of life" that the Committee felt no need to even comment on the subject.

💠 *Why did Canada wait until 1935 to issue a silver dollar?*

        Canadians had attempted to introduce a silver dollar in 1911. Legislation authorizing the striking of these coins was passed in 1910 and dies had been ordered for the new coinage of 1911 which would bear the likeness of George V, who had just succeeded to the throne of England upon the death of his father, Edward VII, in 1910. After the dies had arrived, the new

Canadian minister of finance, W. T. White, decided that there was no need for a silver dollar.

The next opportunity to campaign for a silver dollar was twenty-four years later, when the British Commonwealth of

Nations was to celebrate the silver jubilee of George V's rule. By now public opinion was strongly in favor of a silver dollar, especially since England was striking a jubilee crown, as was New Zealand.

Initially it was planned to strike only 100,000 pieces, but the demand was so great that 428,707 were minted. The wording around the crowned head of the monarch read "GEORGIUS V REX IMPERATOR ANNO REGNI XXV" (George V, King and Emperor, in the 25th year of his reign).

The popularity of this first Canadian silver dollar led to its continued inclusion in the Canadian coin series, except for the war years of 1940 through 1944.

How were the unique Nova Constellatio patterns discovered?

The possible existence of certain silver patterns was known to numismatists because of a report by Robert Morris, Superintendent of Finances to the Continental Congress. In 1782 he reported a new coinage system developed by his assistant, Gouverneur Morris. He wrote: "The money unit will be equal to a quarter of a grain of fine silver in coined money. Proceeding thence in a decimal ratio, one hundred would be the lowest silver coin, and might be called a *Cent*. It would contain twenty-five grains of fine silver, to which may be added two grains of copper, and the whole would weigh one pennyweight and three grains. Five of these would make a *Quint* or five hundred units, weighing five pennyweight and fifteen grains; and ten would make a *Mark*, or one thousand units, weighing eleven pennyweight and six grains."

At the 1908 convention of the American Numismatic Association, held in Philadelphia from September 28 to October 1, the well-known coin dealer, Captain J. W. Haseltine, told of his discovery in 1872 of the unique pieces we call the "mark" and the "quint." We quote from *Mehl's Numismatic Monthly* of October, 1908:

It is well known to all numismatists the delight one experiences in finding a rare coin or a new variety, obtained sometimes for a trifle, or the discovery of a unique coin, but not always without considerable trouble.

The first designs for a U.S. dollar and half-dollar—the Nova Constellatio 1000 and 500 mill pieces—were obtained by me after one year's search. Mr. Elliott Woodward of Boston had in one of his sales two pieces described as 1000 and 500 mill pieces struck in some soft metal. They sold, I believe, for some $30 or $40 each. I saw them and was confident that they were molded in type metal, and I knew that the original must be somewhere, but not known to collectors. I inquired at the U.S. Mint about them, and all the information I could obtain was that Mr. Mickley had borrowed the originals, which were in silver, from the owner and had copies made of them, and that an article in reference to them had been published in a newspaper in Philadelphia some years ago. The paper was the *North American and U.S. Gazette*. That was all the information I could obtain, Mr. Mickley being dead. So whenever I had a spare moment I examined the back files of the *North American* for six or eight months, and finally found the article, which merely stated that they had been found in a secret drawer of Charles Thomson, the secretary of the first or continental congress. I then found out who were the descendants or heirs of Mr. Thomson and wrote to each one (not stating, of course, what I was after) but merely mentioning that I had heard they had a collection of coins they wished to dispose of, and that I was in the market to buy. The one favorable reply I received was from Mr. Rathmel Wilson of Wilmington, Del., from whom I finally purchased his collection, and you can imagine my delight when I found the said pieces struck in silver and in beautiful proof condition.

It is not inconceivable that others might show up since it is practically unheard of to prepare dies and then only strike a single specimen from each one.

Why were two types of gold dollars made for the Louisiana Purchase Exposition?

We can assume that the original intention was to coin a gold dollar with the bust of Thomas Jefferson on its face, but that the assassination of President William McKinley in September, 1901, caused the committee in charge of coinage to consider a second type, with the bust of the martyred President. On March 3, 1901, President McKinley had approved the original project by signing into law the bill that allocated five million dollars toward the cost of constructing the Exposition.

LOUISIANA PURCHASE JEFFERSON AND McKINLEY DOLLARS

There were 250,258 minted of both types. A price of $3 per coin was charged by the officials of the Exposition and it was hoped that a full half-million-dollar profit could be realized to further defray part of the cost of setting up the Fair. But the premium asked for was too high, and 215,250 of the coins had to be remelted since there were no buyers at $3 apiece, and all advance publicity had assured the public that the price would not be cut.

It is believed that approximately 17,500 of each type are extant, although no records were kept as to the exact number of each type minted or remelted.

*Why would an 1863 Indian Head cent
say "Not One Cent"?*

Because the piece is a token, not a coin. Close comparison with a United States Indian Head cent will disclose not only
a difference in design, but also that, unlike the U.S. coin, nowhere
on it does it say "United States of America."

It was not meant to be a counterfeit, but a substitute for the
elusive cent which was being hoarded by a jittery public during
the War Between the States.

Most had thirteen stars around the Indian head, but some few
varieties carried slogans such as "United We Stand" or "Union
and Liberty." Although most of the reverses merely had "Not One
Cent," there were variations that read "Not One Cent for Wid-
ows" or "I. O. U. One Cent."

The issuers of these tokens must have generated a nice profit
for themselves, since it had to cost less than half a cent a token
to produce and they were readily accepted at one cent apiece.
Nevertheless they were short-lived since the following year a new
federal law went on the books making it a penal offense for
anyone to manufacture this type of money substitute.

Two interesting books have been written by George and Mel
vin Fuld on various Civil War money substitutes, both published
by Whitman Publishing Company. They are *Patriotic Civil War
Tokens* and *A Guide to Civil War Store Card Tokens*.

 What is a restrike?

When a coin is struck bearing a date of an earlier year,
such a coin is a restrike. All the United States coins dated 1964
that were struck in 1965 or 1966 can be considered restrikes.

Until 1965, United States laws prohibited the manufacturing of
coins with any date other than the present date. To insure
compliance, the die bearing the date was defaced at year end.

In earlier years restrikes were not uncommon. The best-known examples were the famous (or infamous) 1804 silver dollars, none of which were made earlier than 1834.

Most restrikes of United States coins were made either for monetary gain or to use as trading material for coins needed for the Mint Collection.

Probably the best-known series is that of half-cent restrikes of coins dated 1840 to 1848. These pieces were all proof-struck. Interestingly enough, the restrikes command as high a price as the "originals."

A whole series of restrikes exist of silver type coins that were made from copper planchets. To list a few: 1864 three cent, silver; 1864 half dime; 1805 and 1827 quarters; 1813, 1823, 1833, 1834, and 1835 half dollars; 1801, 1802, and 1803 silver dollars.

Many of the restrikes used rusted dies, suggesting that these were made from dies discarded by the Mint which found their way into private hands. In this category is a variety of 1804 large cent which was muled to an 1820 type reverse die.

✄ *What does each of the Israel £5 pieces commemorate?*

This is the beautiful series of silver coins that are slightly larger than United States half dollars. These coins are dished on both sides, or (to use the scientific term) concavo-concave.

They have been issued by the Bank of Israel each year since 1958, the first being struck to commemorate the tenth anniversary of the founding of the State of Israel. Each subsequent issue was to honor some event on Israel's Independence Day. This first £5 has a stylized seven-branched candle holder or "Menorah" as its main design.

1958

The 1959 issue was dedicated to the "Ingathering of the Exiles," pointing up Israel's determination to leave her gates open for emigrants seeking a new homeland.

1959

1960

The silver coin of 1960 was struck to honor the one-hundredth anniversary of the birth of Theodor Herzl, the Austrian Jew who is recognized as the founder of modern political Zionism.

The £5 coin of 1961 is called the "Bar Mitzvah" coin. When a Jewish boy becomes thirteen years of age, he can become a member of the congregation after participating in a religious ceremony called "Bar Mitzvah." It was only fitting that this 1961 coin commemorate this event since it also ushered in the thirteenth year of independence.

1961

1962

The coin of 1962 was a drastic departure, honoring the industrial growth of the nation. Called the "Development" coin, it pictures parts of a steam shovel and an oil refinery.

Probably the most interesting and also the rarest of the series is the 1963 coin, called the "Seafaring." One side pictures an

1963

ancient galley with oars and sails, while the reverse shows the smokestack of a modern vessel.

The dedication in 1964 of the Israel Museum of Jerusalem became the theme for the issue of that year. The obverse pictures the capital (top) of an ancient pillar, while the reverse has an extremely stylized relief of the buildings making up the new museum.

1964   1965

In 1965 the government decided to honor its legislative body, known as the *Knesset* (Parliament). The face of this coin pictures the beautiful new building being erected to house the governing body of the nation.

As a set, these silver pieces are perfectly matched, yet each is distinctively different from any other.

What American did most to popularize numismatics?

Undoubtedly the most colorful figure in the coin world from 1904 to 1957 was B. Max Mehl, the Fort Worth, Texas, coin dealer.

He was born in Lithuania in 1884, and was brought to America as a child of nine. By the age of twenty he had become a professional coin dealer. By 1908 he was publishing a journal called *Mehl's Numismatic Monthly*. In the first issue he demonstrated his aggressive attitude and boldly stated:

As to the publisher I only wish to mention my success in the Numismatic Field. Within less than two years I have succeeded in obtaining a good share of the confidence and patronage of the numismatists of the country. My sales in 1907 aggregate $25,000. And the prospects of the future are very promising indeed.

Modesty was not one of his virtues and $25,000 in 1907, when there were possibly five hundred collectors as compared to ten million today, was a tremendous dollar volume. This publication ceased with World War I, but in the meantime he started a sales catalog called "The Star Rare Coin Encyclopedia and Premium Catalog."

Mehl advertised extensively in such popular magazines as *The American Weekly* and *The Saturday Evening Post*. His best-known ad was his standing offer to pay $50 for each 1913 Liberty Head nickel offered to him. This alone got many a youngster looking through his change, the first step in becoming a collector. Each ad of this type recommended the purchase of his *Star Rare Coin Book*, which listed his high buying prices. Over one hundred thousand copies of this volume reached American homes.

His auction sales boasted the finest catalogs, which attracted the highest type of clientele. King Farouk used his services when wishing to dispose of any of his coins or medals. The sale of the William F. Dunham collection in 1941 will illustrate the type of auction sales that he conducted. This sale included the famous Dexter 1804 proof silver dollar; the king of gold rarities, the 1822 half eagle (3 known); an 1875 three-dollar gold piece in proof (20 minted); a proof 1852 half cent (2 known); a proof 1841 quarter eagle (so rare that it is unpriced in current catalogs); an uncirculated 1829 half eagle (one sold in 1963 for $21,500). A total of $83,364.08 was realized at this sale, a record amount up to that time for any coin sale held in the United States.

B. Max Mehl was also well loved by his professional associates. In 1950 his friends in the American Numismatic Association awarded him an Honorary Membership for his fifty years as a numismatist and because of his work in encouraging the hobby of numismatics.

The dean of American coin dealers died at the age of seventy-four in 1957. A decade later his name is better remembered than that of many living experts in the field of coin collecting.

🍃 Did you know that a coin was struck to honor a 2500th anniversary?

About the year 563 B.C., near Nepal in Central Asia, a child named Siddhartha Gautama was born, later to be revered as the Buddha (the Enlightened One). To celebrate the twenty-five-hundredth anniversary of Buddhism, Ceylon in 1957 issued a beautiful silver dollar-size coin.

This silver piece has a most unusual and interesting reverse design. In the center is a circle with "2500" on its field. This is surrounded with a circle of flower petals. Around the flower petals is a circle of animals native to Ceylon—the elephant, the horse, the lion, and the water buffalo, one following the other. Finally there is an outer circle of walking geese carrying lotus buds.

A total of 500,000 pieces were minted, of which 1,800 were proof-struck, making the proof coin a rare and desirable piece.

Why did the United States coin a twenty-cent piece?

The Spanish influence still existed in the Southwest in the 1870's. This even extended to the coinage that was in use. Under Spanish rule the coin of the realm was the eight reals, equivalent to the U.S. dollar. Thus the one real was worth twelve and a half cents and the two reals a quarter. (As pointed out earlier, a real was commonly called a "bit," and thus the quarter was expressed as "two bits.")

Retail prices in this section of the United States were quoted in "bits," and merchants were known to take advantage of shoppers by shortchanging them two and a half cents on a purchase. For example, an item purchased is priced at "one bit." The customer pays with a quarter and receives in change a dime.

Senator John P. Jones of Nevada in 1874 sponsored a bill in the Senate that authorized the twenty-cent piece. His feeling was that this would help bring merchants around to pricing their goods in dollars and cents. His bill became law in 1875 and coinage was started the same year.

The twenty-cent piece was slightly smaller than the quarter. It had an identical obverse to the quarter, while its reverse showed the American eagle similar to that on the quarter, but facing right instead of left. Naturally the coin was often mistaken for the quarter and thus proved most unpopular. The Treasury Department recognized the public's dissatisfaction almost immediately, as shown by the following statistics:

Year	Mint	Struck
1875	Philadelphia	39,700
1875	Carson City	132,290
1875	San Francisco	1,155,000
1876	Philadelphia	15,900
1876	Carson City	10,000
1877	Philadelphia	510
1878	Philadelphia	600

The Mint figures clearly indicate the lack of public acceptance. The 1877 and 1878 coins were only proof-struck for the proof sets of those two years.

Finally, in 1878 Congress conceded that it had made an error and passed legislation to prohibit its further coinage.

Needless to say, the issuing of this double dime had no effect on how merchants priced their merchandise.

How many 1881 gold dollar proofs were minted?

Most collectors of United States coins own a copy of *A Guide Book of United States Coins*, by R. S. Yeoman. In this writer's opinion it is the finest volume giving retail values of coins of the United States in varying conditions. It contains much other valuable information for the collector, and each new edition is better than the previous one.

Mr. Yeoman states that forty gold dollars were proof-struck in 1881. I disagree with that figure. In 1952, after acquiring nineteen of these gems I wrote to Walter H. Breen, who was doing research on proof coins in the Archives. We had previously corresponded concerning restrikes at the Philadelphia Mint. I offered my coins for study to determine if there might be any die varieties that could indicate possible restrikes. I told Mr. Breen that I had already acquired nineteen of the forty minted. In his reply he said: "I regret to inform you that my records give the quantity cointed as 87 pieces. This breaks up as follows: March 16——— 60; Sept. 30——— 10; Dec. 31——— 17. The 40 referred to in the Mint Director's report were apparently those issued in sets. The rarest proofs of 1881 in the gold denomination are the $5 and $10 . . . only 42 were struck of each."

The following year the *Coin Collector's Journal* published "Proof Coins Struck by the United States Mint 1817–1921," by Walter H. Breen. Here, for the first time, the corrected number for 1881 and other dates were published. Mr. Breen's figures were also published in *The Standard Catalogue of United States Coins—1953*, by Wayte Raymond. Following Mr. Raymond's death in 1956, this publication also died. Its last edition was copyrighted in 1957.

There are other differences between Mr. Breen's and Mr. Yeoman's figures, but only this one issue has been pointed up. This is because I own what I believe to be fifty-four of the proofs. Should even 25 per cent prove to be "first strikes" instead of true proofs, I must contend that more than forty had to have been struck in 1881.

✍ When was a billion-dollar coin proposed?

The *American Journal of Numismatics* of April, 1903, quoted an article from *The New York World* that tells the tale:

A famous numismatist proposes the coinage of a billion-dollar gold piece for exhibition at the St. Louis Fair. It is to contain $1,000,000,000 worth of gold, according to the plan; will be forty feet in diameter, thirty inches thick and will weigh 4,480,000 pounds. Each milled edge will be six inches across the face, the milling being four and three-fourth inches deep. The 1904 date will be four and a half feet high, and the other letters thirty inches in height, each star measuring three feet across. Were this giant pocket-piece of Uncle Sam's re-coined into $1 gold pieces it would make a pile of gold dollars 700 miles high. The committee still has the unique plan under consideration, where it will doubt-less remain.

One favorable thing can be said for this press agent's night-mare. The first United States commemorative gold coins were authorized by Congress for the Louisiana Purchase Exposition, known as the St. Louis Fair. But they were merely gold one-dollar pieces!

What is the story of the 1848 "CAL" quarter eagle?

Richard S. Yeoman, author of *A Guide Book of United States Coins, Handbook of United States Coins, A Catalog of Modern World Coins,* and vice-president of Whitman Publishing Company, wrote a paper for the 1952 Oklahoma–Kansas Numismatic Association annual convention held in Wichita, Kansas, October 18–19, 1952. The title was "The 1848 Quarter Eagle with Cal." It was printed in the July, 1953, issue of *The Numismatist* for the benefit of the members of the American Numismatic Association. The following are highlights from this excellent paper.

Colonel Richard B. Mason, Military Governor of California, sent some 230 ounces of gold in 1848 to his superior, General Jones, in Washington, D.C. The purpose was to prove that a large gold strike had been made and that the story was not just a rumor. The gold in turn was delivered to Secretary of War W. L. Marcy.

It was at Mr. Marcy's suggestion that part of the gold "be made into quarter eagles with a distinguishing mark on each. . . ." This quote was part of a letter to the director of the Philadelphia Mint dated December 8, 1848. On January 5, 1849, a letter from the Mint Director to the Secretary of War stated that the coins had been minted, using $3,474.64 worth of gold. From this amount we conclude that 1,389 coins were struck, with $2.14 left over. Catalogs today use this figure as the number minted.

As to how "CAL" was put on the coins, all authorities agree that the letters were hand-punched into the coins individ-

ually while the coins rested on the obverse die. This accounts for the fact that no obliteration occurs on the opposite side, as is common with counterstamped coins.

Genuine specimens can be readily recognized since the California gold contained silver, giving the coins a brassy appearance. The other U.S. gold pieces all have a reddish color due to a copper alloy.

A conservative guess would be that not more than 20 per cent of the 1,389 pieces are known today, making this quarter eagle one of the rarities in the United States series.

Who was Admiral Vernon?

It is doubtful that any Englishman not of royal blood had more medals struck in his honor than Admiral Edward Vernon (1684–1757).

He started his naval career at the age of sixteen. His presence became known publicly in 1722, when, as a member of Parliament, he was most vocal in his opposition to the party of Robert Walpole, First Lord of the Treasury and Chancellor of the Exchequer.

In 1726 Admiral Hosier, with twenty ships, made an unsuccessful attempt to capture Porto Bello, a Spanish stronghold on the east coast of Panama. In 1739 in London, Vernon publicly stated that he could do the job with only six ships. In a short time he was given the opportunity to prove his words, for on July 20, 1739, he sailed to the West Indies as commander of nine ships of the line. Leaving three behind in Jamaica, he took his six ships and made good his boast.

When word reached England, Admiral Vernon became a public idol. Probably every medalist in England saw an opportunity to cash in on his success and struck medals for sale to the jubilant public. Literally hundreds of different medals were struck. The

October, 1894, issue of the *American Journal of Numismatics* puts it most aptly:

Of the execution of these pieces, struck to catch the favor of the populace, and more for the profit of the manufacturer, there is little to be said. The device they bear, and especially their legend and mottoes extolling the exploits of Admiral Vernon, and the revival of "British glory," appeals to the patriotism and national pride of the British people, as no other medals seem to have done.

The medals have such wording on them as "ADMIRAL VERNON TOOK PORTO BELLO WITH SIX SHIPS ONLY"; "THE BRITISH GLORY REVIVED BY ADMIRAL VERNON"; "ADMIRAL VERNON, THE PRESERVOR OF HIS COUNTRY."

George Washington's half-brother Lawrence served under the famous admiral, and in his honor named his American estate (later inherited by the first President) Mount Vernon.

✍ *Why was the Isabella quarter struck?*

The striking of the Columbian half dollars of 1892 and 1893 was conceived as a money-making business venture to help defray part of the costs of the World's Columbian Exposition, held in Chicago in 1893. Naturally there were other considerations, such as the publicity resulting from a commemorative coin, but the main concern was financial.

When the fair was organized, control was centered in a Board of Gentlemen Managers. This stirred the ire of Susan B. Anthony, who in 1890 had been instrumental in forming the National American Suffrage Association and was its president from 1892 to 1900. Wanting the ladies to have a say in this great fair, with the help of the organization and many Congressmen's wives, she convinced Congress to include a Board of Lady Managers in the World's Fair Bill.

Since Congress, on August 5, 1892, had approved the striking of the Columbian half dollars, Miss Anthony next petitioned for a Columbian quarter dollar to be sold by the Board of Lady Managers. This would help the fair financially and also further the cause of women's rights. Congress obliged by passing the enabling legislation on March 3, 1893, which authorized the minting of 40,000 pieces.

This unique coin, the only commemorative quarter dollar issued in limited quantity, pictured Queen Isabella of Spain on its face, while the reverse showed a kneeling woman spinning yarn with a distaff and spindle and the words "BOARD OF LADY MANAGERS COLUMBIAN QUAR. DOL."

The coin was not popular and after the Fair closed there were 15,786 returned to the Mint and remelted. In the October, 1893, issue of the *American Journal of Numismatics,* dissatisfaction was noted concerning the design of the coin. The *Journal* article said in part:

Of its artistic merit, as of the harmony which is reported to have prevailed at the meeting of those Managers, perhaps the less said the better. . . . The figure on the reverse is mournfully suggestive of the old anti-slavery token, "Am I not a woman and a sister?"

It originally sold for $1 at the Fair. By 1940 it still sold for only $2, by 1953 it advanced to $10, by 1958 to $32, and by 1966 to close to $100.

Isabella may not be pretty, but she certainly is popular.

Why are there only about fifty 1921 Canadian half dollars known?

You will note that no Canadian fifty-cent pieces were made in the years 1922 through 1928. This was because there was a sufficient supply on hand to meet all needs.

Since there was no demand for additional halves in 1921, the 206,398 struck never left the Royal Canadian Mint. By 1929 it was found necessary to supply halves to the banks. It is believed then that the decision was reached to release coins with a current date and remelt the earlier dated coins on hand. No official announcement was made when the 1921 coins were remelted into bullion.

Most collectors were unaware of the rarity of this coin until an article appeared in the *Coin Collector's Journal* of May–June, 1947, by J. Douglas Ferguson. His reason for writing the article was that a current catalog had routinely assigned a price of $2 for the coin in fine condition and $3 for the piece in uncirculated condition.

Earlier, in the March, 1947, issue of *The Numismatist,* a lengthy article called "The Decimal Coinage of Canada and Newfoundland," by F. Bowman, had appeared. It listed mintage figures of all of the coins discussed, along with a scholarly explanation of unusual facts of any of the series. Concerning this coin he stated:

The rarity of the fifty cent pieces . . . also requires explanation. The mint report shows 206,398 of these coins executed but it was found that the demand for them was very small. They were carried over and issued in subsequent years as necessitated by the demand, until 1928 when the balance remaining on hand were melted and recoined in the new strikings of 1929. Only twenty-four thousand, presumably all of the 1921 date, were issued for circulation during these years.

Mr. Ferguson, aware of Mr. Bowman's article, made further inquiry at the Mint. He was informed that all of the 1921 issue was remelted. He explained the few known pieces by informing us that it was Mint policy to allow a V.I.P. to exchange a coin in his pocket for one of the bright shiny newly minted coins, and in addition to allow Mint employees to purchase a new issue as a souvenir.

It is entirely possible that more may show up in the future, but should the number extant even double, the 1921 fifty cent will remain one of Canada's rarest coins.

🪙 Is it true that the Washington Head quarter is a commemorative coin?

Certainly the first year of issue of this quarter dollar can be considered commemorative. Plans had been made in advance for its introduction, and it was hoped that the first distribution of the new coins could take place on February 22, 1932, the two-hundredth anniversary of the birth of George Washington.

In order to take advantage of the talent available, a contest was announced for the most suitable design. Among the restrictions were that the picture of Washington on the coin should be modeled after a bust of Washington executed by Jean Antoine Houdon in Washington, D.C., in 1785. Ninety-nine artists were said to have competed and John Flanagan, American sculptor and medalist, was declared the winner.

The coin's appearance broke normal precedence, as the designs on United States coins remain unchanged for twenty-five years except by an act of Congress. Since the Standing Liberty type was only introduced in 1916 and normally would have remained unchanged until at least 1941, Congressional approval was asked for and received in March, 1931. But unlike other commemorative issues that called for a limited coinage, this act of Congress approved a design change without coinage limitations.

In its way it was comparable to the Lincoln one-cent piece, which was initially struck to honor the one-hundredth anniversary of the birth of this famous man in 1909.

ᵔᵊᵕ Was leather ever used as money?

Definitely. I am informed that Plato in his writings told of leather money being used by the Carthaginians. We know that Emperor Frederick II (1215–1250) of the Holy Roman Empire used leather money in 1241 when besieging Faenza in central Italy. He later redeemed the leather money for gold. In 1574, when the city of Leyden in Holland was laid siege to by the Spaniards, the citizens used leather money. The Russians at various times were said to use leather money. In fact the word "ruble," their monetary unit, is reputed to be derived from the verb *roobet,* meaning "cut." (Early coins were cut from a strip of leather.) Also, the word *pouly,* which referred to Russian copper money, was said to have had its genesis in the word *poul,* which in Russian means leather. Further, in Sweden in 1710, a copper-mining company that manufactured "plate money" switched to leather during a copper shortage. A 4¼ by 4½ inch sole leather piece still exists, imprinted with the same seals found on the copper two-daler plate money. As recently as 1920 in Austria, sole leather was used as money. One piece is known stamped "I K" for one kronen. And a story is told that in the town of Mattighofen, where 10-heller leather coins were issued, the townsfolk found it cheaper to use the sole leather for the purpose that it was originally intended—rather than buy sole leather with the "coins."

ᵔᵊᵕ What is the difference (except for the date) between a *1911* and *1912* double eagle?

There is a difference, which is generally overlooked by even the standard catalogs on United States coins.

From 1907 through 1911 the Saint-Gaudens type twenty-dollar gold piece had a border of forty-six stars on the obverse, one for each state of the Union. With the admission of New Mexico and

Arizona to statehood in 1912 the obverse was redesigned to show forty-eight stars. All double eagles from 1912 through 1932 have the forty-eight-star border.

Too bad that double eagles are not currently being struck—we would have a forty-nine- and a fifty-star variety.

What is the origin of the Victoria Cross?

It is believed that the Victoria Cross was thought of as a military honor by Henry Pelham Clinton, Duke of Newcastle, when he was Secretary of State for War. He is said to have suggested it to Albert, the Prince Consort, who in turn passed the suggestion on to his wife, Victoria, Queen of England. This was in January, 1855.

The original idea was for a medal bearing the words "FOR THE BRAVE," but Victoria is said to have changed this to "FOR VALOUR." The medal itself is of bronze obtained from cannon captured by the British during the Crimean War at Sevastopol in September, 1855.

It is given only to an individual who performs an act of bravery at the risk of his own life. The recipient is awarded an annual pension of £10. His name is published in the *London Gazette* and is also inscribed on the register of the Secretary of State for War. The holder is also allowed to use the initials "V.C." following his name.

There is a catch, however. Should the holder "be convicted or reasonably suspected of treason, cowardice, felony or any infamous crime," the cross must be returned, the pension stopped, and the culprit's name erased from the record book.

✒ Why are there "Grant with star" and "Grant without star" half dollars?

The Grant Memorial half dollar, which was authorized by Congress in 1922, called for a maximum mintage of 250,000 pieces. This was many more than could possibly be sold at a premium to collectors. The Ulysses S. Grant Centenary Memorial Commission, which was in charge of their sale, came up with an unusual plan to create two varieties. On the original die they requested that a single star appear above the N in GRANT. The star was to be raised on the die and after 5,000 strikes was to be ground off. This caused the star to be incused on the coin. The commission then requested 95,000 strikes without the star, thus creating a second variety. Naturally the type "with star" became the rare variety. But even the 5,000 "with" and 95,000, "without" proved too many for the public to absorb, and 750 of the former and 27,650 of the latter were remelted.

A similar procedure was followed when minting the Grant Memorial gold dollars, but here there were 5,000 of each variety minted. The creation of two varieties proved to be a wise move, because they both sold well and none were returned to the Mint unsold.

The only problem with the half dollar is that it is not difficult to counterfeit the "with star" variety. All that is needed is to purchase a "no star" half and punch a star in the proper place. This may fool the layman, but a coin expert can readily detect a tampered coin.

✒ What is PW money?

This refers to prisoner of war token money that was used in many countries. The concepts of fair treatment for captured soldiers were discussed at the Hague International Peace Conferences of 1899 and 1907. As a result, prisoner of war camps in World War I provided the inmates with more than bare necessities. Nominal pay was given, not in cash, but in scrip or tokens that could be exchanged for items at the prison store.

The reason for PW money was obvious. No country would want an escaped prisoner to have good currency or coin on his person. This would only increase the possibilities of a successful escape.

During World War I Germany, Austria, France, England, Belgium, Russia, and Italy all issued special money for their prison camps.

World War II brought, for the first time, "prison" camps for other than military personnel. Now PW money also included that issued for the unfortunates in concentration camps and refugee camps.

The refugee camps, properly called camps for displaced persons, were the only type run by other than an established government. Just as the International Red Cross has always helped the refugee, now some new organizations were established for this purpose. Under the sponsorship of some thirty-nine nations, the United Nations Relief and Rehabilitation Administration (UNRRA) and later the International Refugee Organization (IRO) set up camps and issued scrip. So also did the American Jewish Joint Distribution Committee, which took over the task of resettling many of the Jews who had been uprooted by Hitler all over central and eastern Europe.

If you wish to read further on the subject, an excellent series of articles appeared in 1964 and 1965 in the *Numismatic Scrapbook Magazine*.

🎨 Is a 1946 Booker T. Washington half dollar valuable?

I am afraid that it is not valuable and probably never will be valuable. More than a million were struck in Philadelphia, 200,000 in Denver, and 500,000 in San Francisco. This is a larger number than the 1892 and 1893 Columbian half dollars, which after more than half a century still sell for only a small premium.

But this only tells part of the story. Even if more than 1,700,000 were desired as type coins, regardless of date or mint, the supply would far exceed the demand. An additional 300,000 were struck in 1947, 24,000 in 1948, 18,000 in 1949, 512,000 in 1950, and 524,000 in 1951.

Congress authorized the striking of five million coins over a period of eight years. The great variance in numbers minted in different years is due to the fact that different schemes were tried to generate sales.

While an individual coin still is not valuable, the complete set of one from each mint, 1947 through 1951, bring good prices since there were only 100,000 full sets struck in 1947, 8,000 in 1948, 6,000 in 1949, 6,000 in 1950, and 12,000 in 1951.

🎨 Why are three-dollar gold pieces so expensive?

This coin is the scarcest of the United States gold series. In fact, most noncollectors do not know of its existence. It is an odd denomination and truly not compatible with the decimal system. As a result it was not popular, never in great demand, and so was produced only in limited numbers.

Congress authorized its striking on February 21, 1853, believing that it would make postal transactions easier since the rate charged to send an ordinary letter by first class was three cents.

(In 1853 Congress had authorized a silver three-cent coin to facilitate the purchase of a single stamp. We might now assume that Congress now felt that more people would buy sheets of one hundred instead of merely purchasing them one at a time.)

The three-dollar gold piece was minted only from 1854 to 1889. In all those years only 539,794 pieces were struck, while in only three of those years did the total coinage exceed 50,000. The largest number was minted in 1854, the first year of issue, and this was only 138,618 pieces.

The price of an uncirculated coin rose very slowly after they were no longer minted. By 1947 a choice specimen could still be obtained for about $30. By 1957 the price had doubled. Today it exceeds $200. This is a good example of the working of the economic theory that with a fixed supply and an increased demand there will be a rise in price.

🙞 *What is the history of the Charter Oak pictured on a U.S. half dollar?*

This commemorative half dollar was issued in 1935 to celebrate the three-hundredth anniversary of the founding of the colony that became the State of Connecticut.

Congress authorized the coinage of 25,000 pieces on June 21, 1934. All twenty-five thousand were coined and none were remelted, making it one of the smaller issues of commemorative half dollars.

The oak tree pictured on the face of the coin played an important part in the recognition of Connecticut as a colony. In the political byplay between 1635 and 1662 attempts were made to make this land part of the colony of New York. In 1662 a royal

charter was obtained from Charles II, the newly crowned king of England. This charter or grant made Connecticut a royal colony of England. But with the succession passing in 1685 to James II, this monarch ordered all charters of New England colonies confiscated, since he wished to form a Dominion of New England. To prevent this action the charter was taken and hidden in the old oak tree, where it remained until James II was overthrown and the people were again assured of their colonial freedom.

The now famous Charter Oak, believed to have been more than one thousand years old, survived until 1856, when, on August 21, it was uprooted in a storm and died. Its location in Hartford, Connecticut, is today marked with a monument of granite.

How many of each of Israel's commemorative coins were struck?

The State of Israel issued its first commemorative coins in 1958, ten years after the birth of the nation. Most had proof strikes as well as regular business strikes. As you will be able to tell from the figures, many of the issues are scarce and a few can be classified as rare.

Denomination	Year	Regular Coins	Proof Coins
£ 100	1962		6,000
£ 50	1962		6,000
£ 50	1964	5,500	500

£	20	1960	10,000	
£	5	1958	100,000	5,000
£	5	1959	70,000	5,000
£	5	1960	45,000	5,000
£	5	1961	20,000	5,000
£	5	1962	10,000	5,000
£	5	1963	6,000	4,000
£	5	1964	11,000	4,000
£	5	1965	25,000	7,500
£	1	1958	250,000	6,000
£	1	1960 (Deganya)	100,000	5,000
£	1	1960 (Szold)	17,000	3,000
£	1	1961	20,000	5,000
£	1	1962	12,000	5,000
£	1	1963	10,000	5,000
£	½	1961	20,000	5,000
£	½	1962	20,000	10,000

The £100, 50, and 20 are gold, the £5 are silver, and the others are copper-nickel. These coins are all beautifully executed. The £5 are especially interesting because they have no raised border and none is needed to prevent wear, since the coins are concavo-concave. This allows for relatively high relief in the design without the design being as high as the edge.

When did the Philippine Islands strike proof coins?

After the Spanish-American War in 1898, the Philippines became an American possession. United States policy was directed toward preparing the islands for eventual independence. One step in this direction was to establish a separate coinage for the Filipinos. In 1903 the American Congress established a coinage system compatible with that in the United States.

The Philippine coins were to be silver coins with a value of one peso, fifty centavos, twenty centavos, and ten centavos; a copper-

nickel coin of five centavos; bronze coins of one centavo and half centavo.

Full sets of proof coins were struck in only five years. The years and the number of sets are: 1903—2,558; 1904—1,355; 1905—471; 1906—500; 1908—500.

In December, 1906, the silver coins had to be reduced in weight and fineness because of the increased value of silver. As a result the set of 1908 has silver coins that are slightly smaller than those in the earlier proof sets.

✑ *What is numismatic about the word "Humbug"?*

The June, 1869, issue of the *American Journal of Numismatics* noted an interesting letter that had appeared in an English periodical called *Notes and Queries* in the issue of October 29, 1853:

Humbug—The real signification of the word *humbug* appears to me to be in the following derivation of it. Among the many issues of base coin which from time to time were made in Ireland, there was none to be compared in worthlessness to that made by James II from the Dublin Mint. It was composed of anything on which he could lay his hands, such as lead, pewter, copper and brass, and so low was its intrinsic value, that twenty shillings of it was only worth twopence sterling. William III, a few days after the battle of Boyne, ordered that the crown piece and half crown should be taken as one penny and one halfpenny respectively. The soft mixed metal, of which that worthless coining was composed, was known among the Irish as *Uim bog*, pronounced *Oombug*, i.e., soft copper, i.e., worthless money; and in the course of their dealings, the modern use of the word *humbug* took its rise, as in the phrases "that is a piece of uimbog (humbug)," "don't think to pass off your uimbog on me." Hence the word humbug came to be applied to anything that had a specious appearance, but which was in reality spurious. It is curious to note that the very opposite of *humbug*, i.e., false metal, is the word *sterling*, which is also taken from a term applied to the true coinage of the realm, as *sterling* coin, *sterling* truth, *sterling* worth, etc.

Fras. Crossley

This debased coinage of James II is the well-known "gun money," reputedly made from metal of discarded guns and cannons.

Even though etymologists consider the supposition of Francis Crossley to be pure fiction, this writer will always think of Irish "gun money" whenever the word *humbug* is mentioned.

Do pin holes in an otherwise crisp bill reduce its value?

With the present small-size bills the answer must be "Yes, they do." The bill must have been mishandled.

With regard to the large-size bills, there is a question of doubt. Naturally, a large hole will detract from the appearance of the bill, making it less desirable. But certain small pinholes, in evidence only when the bill is held up to the light, is another matter.

According to W. A. Philpott, Jr., an authority on paper money, many large-size bills issued before 1880 came with pinholes made by a needle and thread. In these earlier days currency was transported by private express companies and not subject to the safeguards used by the post office department today. It was then possible for a dishonest employee to steal a single bill unnoticed from the center of a package. This type of filching was proving costly to the express companies until someone came up with the idea of sewing the package together with needle and thread. Naturally, pin holes remained after the package was opened.

So if you come across an old "saddle blanket" with pin holes in it, do not deprecate the bill because of the pinholes, but rather remember the ingenuity of the man who found a way to overcome thievery among express company workmen.

✍ Why is a type set of 1873 U.S. coins so expensive?

There were more different coins struck in 1873 than in any other year. This was because some of the silver coins had two distinct types struck because of an increase in weight authorized by an Act of Congress of February 12, 1873. While silver coins had been struck prior to February 12, 1873, those struck after that date had arrowheads punched into the dies on either side of the date to inform the public that they were handling the heavier coins.

A type set of 1873 is made up of nineteen coins, which are one cent bronze, two cents bronze, three cents nickel, three cents silver (trime), five cents nickel, five cents silver (half dime), ten cents with arrows, ten cents without arrows, twenty-five cents with arrows, twenty-five cents without arrows, fifty cents with arrows, fifty cents without arrows, standard silver dollar, trade silver dollar, gold dollar, gold quarter eagle, gold half eagle, gold eagle, gold double eagle.

Assuming that you could acquire each coin without paying a premium, you would still have to invest $42.39. Then, if you look further into die varieties, you will find that many of these were

struck with dies that used differently designed "3's" in the date.
They are referred to as the "closed 3" and "open 3" varieties.

✍ *Why is the Canadian 1921 five-cent piece so rare?*

Most collectors will refer to Mint records, which disclose the number of coins of a certain denomination and date, to
tell them the rarity of coin. This method will usually be fairly
accurate. In the case of the Canadian 1921 five-cent silver piece it
is only misleading.

Mint records show that some 2,500,000 pieces were struck (one
source mentions 2,582,495, while another states 2,501,238). Early
Canadian catalogs gave a nominal value to the coin, in the
same range as the 1917, 1918, 1919, and 1920 pieces. No one, at
least publicly, advised the Canadian collectors that the 1921 issue
might be rare until 1928. In that year a collector attempted to
assemble a complete collection of five-cent silver pieces by date.
At that time coins were usually collected by types or sets. Being
unable to locate a 1921 coin, this collector, in desperation, wrote
to the Canadian Comptroller of Currency, inquiring whether
such a coin had been minted. This was in 1930. The reply he
received stated in part: "In the year 1921 five-cent silver pieces to
a value of $70,000.00 were struck." Six desperate years followed,
during which time fellow collectors were contacted and rolls by
the hundreds were examined, but none turned up. Finally in 1937
the searcher found one in a roll of used five-cent pieces. The
following spring our sleuth wrote to all Canadian members of the
American Numismatic Association to find out if any of them pos-
sessed this elusive coin. None did, but one took it upon himself to
inquire again at the Royal Canadian Mint. This time the reply
was far different, and said in part:

In 1921 there were actually struck 2,501,238 pieces of 5-cent
silver and counted into $100 bags ready for issue to the public

when the amendment to the Currency Act was passed in 1921 authorizing the 5-cent nickel coin.

On the introduction of this latter coin all stock of five-cent silver were returned to the melting pot and made into other denominations, so that as far as is known, there are no five-cent silver coins dated 1921 in existence.

Today there are some one hundred pieces known and possibly some more will show up in the future. Their existence is explained by the fact that it was common practice for a visitor to the Mint to request a coin of the new mintage and exchange a coin of like denomination for one of the newly struck pieces.

The persistent collector was Norman B. Mason, who told the story of his search to the annual convention of the American Numismatic Association, held in Columbus, Ohio, in August, 1938. Numismatics is indebted to men of the caliber of Mr. Mason.

What was the first money coined in the territory later to become the United States?

The Massachusetts Bay Colony was established in 1620. The earliest trade was carried on by barter, and later with the use of Indian wampum. Some small amounts of coins came from England, but by 1650 the colony's growth was such that more coins were needed than were being supplied by the mother country. In May, 1652, the General Court of Massachusetts Bay Colony, without royal approval, granted John Hull, a silversmith, the privilege of coining shillings, sixpence, and three pence. The silver was available, since limited quantities were reaching New England from the West Indies.

Hull was paid for his work by being allowed to retain one shilling of each twenty that he produced. In spite of being a skilled goldsmith and silversmith, the first coins were quite crude. A simple die was prepared for each denomination, with the ini-

tials N E (for New England) on one side and with the Roman
numerals III, VI, or XII on the other to designate three pence,
sixpence, or twelve pence (one shilling). The dies were punched
with the necessary letters, a simple process, which made them
appear raised on the coins.

Oddly enough, although all are rare, specimens of the shilling
are attainable, but copies of the three pence and sixpence are
almost never seen. I have been told that since it took as much
time to strike a three- or six-penny piece as a shilling, the wise
Mr. Hull chose to strike more of those that generated more profit
for him.

❧ *When was the Purple Heart decoration first used?*

The Order of the Purple Heart was originally authorized by General George Washington through an order issued on
August 7, 1782, which read:

The General, ever desirous to cherish a virtuous ambition in his
soldiers, as well as to foster and encourage every species of Military merit, directs that whenever any singularly meritorious action is performed, the author of it shall be permitted to wear on
his facing over the left breast, the figure of a heart in purple cloth
or silk, edged with narrow lace or binding. Not only instances of
unusual gallantry, but also of extraordinary fidelity and essential
service in any way shall meet with a due reward. Before this
favor can be conferred on any man, the particular fact or facts,

on which it is to be grounded must be set forth to the Commander-in-chief accompanied with certificates from the Commanding officers of the regiment and brigade to which the Candidate for reward belonged, or other incontestable proofs, and upon granting it, the name and regiment of the person with the action so certified are to be enrolled in the book of merit which will be kept at the orderly office. Men who have merited this last distinction to be suffered to pass all guards and sentinels which officers are permitted to do.

The road to glory in a patriot army and a free country is thus open to all—this order is also retrospect to the earliest stages of the war, and to be considered as a permanent one.

Records extant indicate only three purple hearts were given during the Revolutionary War. Until the early 1920's this award seems to have been forgotten.

In 1921, Mr. C. S. Gifford of Boston, a member of the American Numismatic Association, wrote to federal government officials, suggesting that the order be used again. Nothing came of this until 1932, when Mr. Gifford's persistent correspondence finally bore fruit. In honor of the two-hundredth anniversary of the birth of George Washington the order was revived by President Hoover for Army personnel. The Navy authorized its use in 1942. Since World War II it has been awarded to members of the Armed Forces who are wounded in action against the enemy.

🐚 *What is* fei?

Twenty-five hundred miles southwest of Honolulu is an island group called the Caroline Islands. This is made up of three smaller island groups known as Palau, Truk, and Yap. These names were in the news during World War II, as they were occupied by the American troops heading toward Japan. Most of the natives are Micronesians and very primitive in their ways.

Among numismatists the Yap Islands are the best known, for here an unusual type of stone money is used that is called *fei*.

These are varying-size discs of white limestone through which has been drilled a large hole. These discs resemble millstones. This round stone money varies in size from about six inches up to twelve feet in diameter. Limestone is not found on Yap, but is quarried at Palau, some four hundred miles southwest.

The Yap natives, excellent seamen, travel to Palau, quarry the fei, then transport it by open boat to their home. Once home it serves as money. Its exact value is hard to determine, but students of Micronesia report that a twenty-inch fei is worth in trade an 80- to 100-pound pig or 1,000 coconuts, and that a four-foot stone will buy a wife.

Another interesting feature is that a large fei may remain in one place for generations even though its ownership has changed hands many times. Though too unwieldy to move, it still serves its purpose as a medium of exchange.

The largest fei mentioned is twelve feet in diameter, eighteen inches thick, with a center hole two feet in diameter. It is beyond comprehension how this huge piece was ever transported the four hundred miles from Palau to Yap.

There is no way of determining how long fei has been used by the Yaps, but certainly for more than one thousand years.

✺ Why were National Gold Banks chartered?

The National Banking Act of 1863 allowed the federal government to grant charters to new or already existing state banks. The state banks lost their privilege of issuing notes and all federally chartered institutions given the right to issue notes up to 90 per cent of the face value of government bonds deposited with the U.S. government. In most parts of the country the new national bank notes were accepted without question at par. This was not true in California, where the populace was used to dealing in gold coin or bullion. Since the national bank notes were not redeemable in gold coin there was resistance to their accep-

tance. Congress in 1870 passed legislation authorizing the charter-
ing of national gold banks, who would be legally bound to
redeem their notes on demand in gold coin. The following banks
were chartered:

> First National Gold Bank of San Francisco
> National Gold Bank and Trust Co., San Francisco
> First National Gold Bank of Santa Barbara
> First National Gold Bank of Stockton
> Farmers National Gold Bank of San Jose
> National Gold Bank of D. O. Mills and Co., Sacramento
> First National Gold Bank of Petaluma
> First National Gold Bank of Oakland
> Union National Gold Bank of Oakland
> Kidder National Gold Bank of Boston

The first nine, all in California, issued notes, while the Boston bank did not.

The need for these gold banks is evidenced by the fact that most notes known today are quite worn, indicating extensive use in normal commercial transactions. In all some $3,500,000 worth were issued. By October 31, 1914, only $74,235 were reported unredeemed.

By 1879, the need of this special type of bank no longer existed and by Act of Congress of February 14, 1880, these banks' charters were amended so that they became regular national banks and they dropped the word "gold" from their name.

✍ *What is hogge money?*

This refers to the first coins struck for Bermuda. This group of about 300 coral islands lies about 650 miles southeast of North Carolina in the warm gulf stream waters of the Atlantic Ocean.

Juan Bermúdez, a Spaniard, discovered the islands in 1515. Preparatory to landing, supplies and a number of hogs were put ashore. A sudden gale forced Captain Bermúdez and his crew to set sail. Subsequently the swine, the island's only inhabitants, multiplied.

In 1593 a French warship was wrecked on the uncharted coral rocks, with the survivors eventually reaching Newfoundland some six months later. The wild hogs helped them survive this ordeal.

Still another group, this time English settlers bound for Virginia, were wrecked there in 1609. This band of settlers was led by Sir Thomas Gates and Sir George Somers. Their glowing reports of the lush vegetation and perfect climate led to the formation of a company to colonize the islands.

In April, 1612, the colonists left England for their new home, which they called Somers Island. The colony went well except that there was a shortage of coin, needed for the small commercial transactions of the islands. The deficiency was overcome through the minting of crude brass coins with a value of two pence, three pence, sixpence, and one shilling. One side showed a sailing vessel, while the other showed a wild hog and the words "SOMER ISLAND." The coins were undated.

This "hogge money" was believed to have been struck in 1616, since a document of that year describing the people said: "Besides meat, drink and clothes, they had for a time a certain kind of brass money with a hogge on one side in memory of the abundance of hogges that was found at their first landing."

✺ Were coins ever made of platinum?

It is strange to think of platinum as a metal used to strike coins, but then, fact is often stranger than fiction.

We know platinum to be a very hard, heavy, silvery metal that does not oxidize. The metal has been known since the beginning of recorded history, but it was not until about 1803 that William H. Wollaston, an English scientist, discovered how to make it malleable.

It was never found in any large quantity until about 1822 or 1823, when large veins were discovered in the Ural Mountains of Russia. It was found in the gold mines of Colombia, but for years had been discarded as a useless byproduct when mining gold. Smaller amounts were found also in California, Spain, and other parts of the world.

Nicholas I became Czar of All the Russias in 1825. He authorized that the three, six, and twelve rubles be struck from this metal. From 1828 to 1845 all of this series were platinum-struck. They fell into public disfavor, not being nearly as attractive as gold and silver, and in 1845 the government agreed to redeem all for gold or silver. It must be remembered that at that time the world market price of platinum was only about $1 an ounce.

Because the metal was slightly heavier than gold, counterfeit coins of platinum appeared from time to time. United States five-dollar gold pieces made of platinum and gold plated are known. In 1921 a counterfeit 1869 English sovereign was reported. In 1869 this rare metal still only sold for $4 an ounce.

The Russian platinum coins are rare today. Because of the rising price of the metal, more and more of them were continually being sold for their bullion content. What a shame! Today a three-ruble piece will bring over $100, while certain twelve-ruble pieces sell for in excess of $1,500.

✍ *What are Jackson Hard Time tokens?*

A large group of tokens, the size of the large United States one-cent pieces that circulated at the time, were struck from 1832 to 1844. They were called either Hard Time tokens or Jackson Hard Time tokens. The largest group encountered bear the date 1837.

Political views ran very strong in those days, especially concerning the continuation of the Bank of the United States. Henry Clay led the group in favor of renewing the Bank's charter, which would expire in 1836. Andrew Jackson, President from 1829 to 1837, vehemently opposed the Bank, especially on the grounds that it was privately controlled. Jackson won his fight and the Bank of the United States liquidated in 1836. But the following May all the banks in the country found themselves unable to meet their obligations, cause enough to call the tokens "Jackson Hard Time tokens," even though Andrew Jackson was no longer President.

The late Wayte Raymond (1887–1956), discussing these tokens in his *Standard Catalogue of United States Coins and Tokens,* suggested that there were two reasons for the large number of tokens issued during this period. First, a great deal of interest had been shown by the numismatists of the day, making them a popular selling item; and second, there was a need for the pieces as small change since "hard" money (gold, silver, and copper coins) was being hoarded because of the uncertainties of the times.

Lyman K. Low, well-known professional numismatist at the turn of the century, made a listing of one hundred and eighty-three varieties, his last revision being in 1900. The Low numbering system is still used to identify these pieces.

When did two countries issue almost identical coins?

The first permanent white settlement in what is now the State of Delaware was established by a group of Swedes in 1638. These settlers were transported to the New World on two ships, the *Kalmar Nyckel* and the *Fogel Grip*. The settlement, originally known as Fort Christina, is today the city of Wilmington.

To celebrate the three-hundredth anniversary of the establishment of this Swedish colony in America, Congress, on May 15, 1936, authorized the coining of 25,000 special commemorative half dollars. The face of the coin pictures the sailing vessel, the *Kalmar Nyckel*, in full sail, while the reverse shows Old Swedes Church of Wilmington, the first Protestant church erected in the New World. The coin is dated 1936, was struck in 1937, and bears the dates 1638 and 1938 in honor of the event that it commemorates.

When word reached Sweden that the coin was to be struck, a movement was begun to strike a four-kronor or silver-dollar-size coin to likewise honor the original Swedish settlers. But when Swedish numismatists saw that the United States coin was the size of their two-kronor coins they decided to make their piece that size. The Swedish Mint then ordered Erik Lindberg, the Royal Mint engraver, to prepare a design showing her king, Gustaf V, on the obverse, and with a reverse picturing the *Kalmar Nyckel* in full sail, similar to the United States coin's obverse.

A study of the two coins will attest to the great similarity of design on the half-dollar obverse and the two-kronor reverse. Pricewise, there is a great difference, with the U.S. piece selling for over ten times that of its Swedish counterpart. This is mainly because 508,815 two-kronor coins were struck, while the half dollars had a net coinage (some were returned to the melting pot) of only 20,993 pieces, making it scarce by present-day standards.

✒ *When did a coin series of one country attempt to copy that of another country?*

If you examine the coinage of Emperor Kuang Hsu (1875–1908) of China that was struck for use in Tibet you will discover that the design on the quarter-, half-, and one-rupee pieces of 1903 are quite similar to the comparable rupee pieces of India that were struck from 1862 to 1901. Since the British-Indian pieces were minted first, we know that these were copied by the Chinese.

Although the Chinese controlled Tibet, they recognized that the Indian coins were much better received than their own. And since they knew that most of the population was illiterate, they assumed that a "reasonable facsimile" would serve their purpose.

The Indian coins pictured the crowned bust of Victoria facing left and the words "VICTORIA QUEEN" or "VICTORIA EMPRESS." The Tibetan copies showed a mandarin's bust, facing left, with a mandarin cap on his head, even perched at the same angle as Victoria's crown. The garments of both were similar. The reverse is made up mainly of leaves and flowers in a circular wreath, and here, too, the similarity is even more striking.

A report in 1906 stated that the rupees of Edward VII were not nearly so well received, the design being strange to the Tibetans. This is all the more reason to believe that the appearance of the coin was of prime importance, similar to the Ethiopians' acceptance of the Maria Theresa taler of 1780.

⸨☞ *What is the origin of the phrase "Millions for Defense, But Not One Cent for Tribute"?*

In 1797 President Adams sent three envoys to France in an effort to iron out monetary differences. When it was whispered in Paris that a properly placed bribe would be needed before the envoys would be received by French officials, C. C. Pinckney, leader of the delegation and Minister to France, is said to have remarked, "War be it then, millions for defense, but not a cent for tribute."

This remark was recalled in 1836 when difficulties again arose between the United States and France, and the slogan appeared on copper tokens dated 1837.

✍️ *What is invasion currency?*

The World War II emergency currency has been called "invasion currency." This unique series of United States currency can be divided into two groups. The first was printed for use in the Hawaiian Islands. The second was issued to the troops invading North Africa.

The Treasury Department issued the following release on March 14, 1945, concerning the Hawaiian issue.

After the attack on Pearl Harbor, Hawaii became a danger spot in our defenses, and we could not be blind to the possibility that the Japanese might attempt to invade the Islands, as, indeed they evidently intended to do when we stopped them at Midway. As a defensive measure, we introduced the Hawaiian dollar, which is simply regular United States currency with the word "Hawaii" overprinted in large letters. We exchanged all regular dollar currency in Hawaii for Hawaiian dollars, and we were then ready for the Japanese from the point of view of money. Had the Japanese conquered Hawaii, the distinctive Hawaiian currency would have made it possible to take appropriate measures to prevent the enemy from using this currency to any advantage. In 1943 and early 1944, the Hawaiian dollar was put to further use in the occupation of certain Japanese-held islands in the Pacific, for the convenience of our naval personnel, since they operated out of Pearl Harbor. More recently, since our successes in the Pacific have removed all danger of an invasion of Hawaii, we

have discontinued issuing Hawaiian dollars and are gradually withdrawing these dollars from circulation by replacing them with regular currency as they are turned in to banks.

The Hawaiian series were one-dollar Silver Certificates and five-, ten-, and twenty-dollar Federal Reserve notes issued by the San Francisco Federal Reserve Bank. All used a brown Treasury Department seal in addition to the overprints of "HAWAII" on the front and back of each note.

The notes issued for the invasion of North Africa followed a different pattern. We again quote from the Treasury Department official news release:

In our first invasion operation, North Africa, we used yellow seal dollars. Yellow seal dollars, like Hawaiian dollars, are regular American currency, with a distinguishing mark to permit segregation if the situation so requires. We simply substituted yellow ink for blue in printing the seal on regular silver certificates of the

United States. We did not know whether we would be welcomed as allies or resisted as invaders; we could not be certain that we would not incur reverses. The yellow seal gave us the opportunity to segregate the currency if we should be driven from North Africa.

Since silver certificates were issued only in one-, five-, and ten-dollar denominations, this series of invasion currency included no twenty-dollar notes.

More than twenty years after their issuance, both types make their appearance from time to time at bank tellers' windows. Should one come your way, we suggest that you keep it as an interesting memento of World War II.

🎜 *What English coins did Wyon engrave?*

When mentioning Wyon, one must be more specific. There are Leonard Charles Wyon, Thomas Wyon, Jr., and William Wyon, all of whom engraved coins of England, and all of whom were closely related.

The family had migrated to England in 1727 from Cologne, Germany. No less than fifteen descendants of the German Wyon, Peter George, became recognized die sinkers or engravers. William and Thomas, Jr., were cousins and grandsons of Peter George, while Leonard Charles was the son of William.

William Wyon (1795–1851) was the eldest son of Peter Wyon, a well-known medalist. At the age of fourteen he was apprenticed to his father. He later served at the London Mint and was appointed Chief Engraver in 1828. Most of the heads of George IV and William IV, in the period from 1825 to 1837, that appeared on the face of their coins, were his workmanship. The earlier coinage of Victoria also used heads designed and engraved by W. W.

Cousin Thomas Wyon, Jr. (1792–1817), preceded William as Chief Engraver. He occupied this position from 1815 until his untimely death two years later. The coins of George III from 1812 through 1820 were his work.

The best known of the Wyons was Leonard Charles (1826–1891), the eldest son of William. Following family custom, he, too, was apprenticed to his father. Upon the death of his father in 1851, he succeeded as Chief Engraver. The British bronze coins of 1860 to 1895 were the work of this artist, as was much of the Canadian decimal coinage from 1858 to 1901.

My favorite, though, is Peter, William's father and Leonard Charles's grandfather. He designed a medal to James Sadler, the first English aeronaut, which proclaimed on its face: "Ascended from Birmingham, traversed upward of ½ miles in 1 hour & 20 minutes on October 7, 1811." And now we circle the globe in ninety minutes!

✍ *What caused the 1955 double-die variety one cent?*

This most unusual one cent, on which all letters and numbers on the obverse appear double, was the result of the very slight shifting of the hub when it was striking the working die.

The working die is used in the coining machine and after a limited number of strikes begins to break down. When this happens die breaks appear, and finally the die shatters. A new working die is then placed in the coining machine.

In preparing the working die for the one-cent piece, three blows of the hub are sufficient to give a true impression. The shift most probably occurred between the second and third strikes, since both sets of lettering appear equally strong.

This one-cent variety is not considered a freak, being recognized as a true variety in all catalogs. It first received public mention in the *Numismatic Scrapbook Magazine* of January, 1956. At that time the magazine stated: "The hurry-up call on the mints this fall to relieve an unforeseen cent shortage is probably the reason for putting into use an obverse cent die which is very much 'doubled.'" Two months later the editor, Lee F. Hewitt, wrote: "Doubled-die cents may turn out to be scarce . . . very few have been reported. Mint officials say they have no knowledge of the double-die being discovered during a press run, indicating that thousands of pieces were minted."

It is believed that the error was unintentional and occurred unnoticed at the Mint. The very slight mechanical failure that caused this variety to appear hurt no one and benefited the lucky finders, most of whom discovered their "prizes" on the eastern seaboard.

❦ Is the British sovereign minted in Canada considered part of English or Canadian coinage?

The Royal Canadian Mint, formerly known as the Ottawa branch of the Royal Mint, opened in 1908. British type sovereigns were struck there in most years from 1908 through 1919. They have always been considered part of the Canadian series since they not only were minted in Canada but circulated as legal tender in Canada. In their way they are similar to the sovereigns struck in Sydney, Melbourne, and Perth, which are always classified as Australian coins, not English coins. True, the design is identical to the English coins, distinguished only by the mintmark.

There is a further argument that can be presented. The Ottawa Mint was ready to strike coins early in 1908, but the gold sovereigns were not struck until late in the year. This was because the Master of the Mint wished to use locally mined gold, and the supply, from the Yukon Peace River and Larder Lake districts, did not arrive until December, 1908. As a result, only 636 sovereigns were struck, making the 1908 issue one of the rarer items. Reports in 1909 indicated that these pieces, with about $5 worth of gold, were already selling for $25 each. Today an uncirculated pieces sells for over thirty times that amount.

✍ Is it still possible to discover new die varieties of older coins?

Definitely yes! Because there is always the chance of discovering a new variety we find coin collecting infinitely more interesting. There can be the same thrill in discovering a new type of an old coin that there is in uncovering a buried treasure. And it can be just as profitable dollarwise.

This can be illustrated by telling the story of an 1849 Charlotte, North Carolina, Mint gold dollar. This coin has always been considered scarce because only a total of 11,634 pieces were struck the first year of issue. It comes with two different reverse designs, quite similar except that the wreath is of two different sizes. Where it is short, it is called the "open wreath" variety. Where it is longer and forms an almost complete circle, it is called the "closed wreath" variety. Until the early 1950's the Charlotte Mint dollar of 1849 had been known with only the "closed wreath" type of reverse.

It was the good fortune of Mr. Robert Schermerhorn of Dallas, Texas, to make the discovery that the 1849-C he had purchased at an earlier date had the hitherto unknown open-wreath reverse. This particular coin had previously been owned by two well-informed collectors, neither of whom had noticed the open wreath.

It was sold along with other coins of Mr. Schermerhorn at the auction sale held in conjunction with the annual convention of the American Numismatic Association, held in Chicago, Illinois, in August, 1956. At that time the coin was believed to be unique. (A second one has since turned up.) It realized $6,000.

Considering that it was purchased as an open-wreath variety, which sold for less than $100, it certainly paid to be observant.

And remembering that this coin had been owned for more than one hundred years by various collectors who had not recognized its rarity, we have every reason to believe that similar miracles are sure to happen as long as coins are studied by serious collectors.

〜 *What are Baron Gortz dalers?*

These were a series of copper tokens of Sweden issued between 1715 and 1719. They were the brainchild of a German, Georg Heinrich Gortz (or Goertz), Baron von Schlitz, better known merely as Baron Gortz.

Charles XII, King of Sweden (1697–1718), in 1700, at the age of eighteen, found himself pitted in a power struggle against Frederick IV, King of Denmark, Augustus, King of Poland, and Peter the Great, Czar of Russia. Against the first two he was victorious, but the power of the Russians caused his army's defeat and forced him to seek refuge in Turkey. Finally, in 1715, he returned to Europe to regain his throne. It was at this time that he met Baron Gortz.

The baron was a follower of John Law, the Scotsman who at that time controlled the finances of France. His philosophy for rejuvenating the Swedish Treasury was accepted by Charles XII, who made him his chief minister.

One of the methods for curing Sweden's financial problems was to strike copper dalers, and by law place them on a par with silver dalers. It is these pieces that are called "Baron Gortz dalers." Being of copper, and meant to represent a greater amount in silver, they would have to be classified as token money.

Gortz's monetary scheme failed (as did John Law's) and with the death of his protector, Charles XII, in 1718, he was arrested for treason and subsequently hanged.

Ten types of these copper pieces were struck, nine of which are easily recognizable since the reverse on all of these read

1
daler.
S.M.

As a set they are rare, but individual pieces seem to show up in junk boxes of tokens from time to time.

🖋 *Can you translate Latin legends that appear on American colonial coins?*

With the help of Scott & Co.'s *Coin Collector's Journal* the following is offered:

AMERICA INIMICA TYRANS.—America, hostile to tyrants.
AUCTORI CONNEC.—By authority of Connecticut.
AUCTORI PLEBIS.—By authority of the people.
BENEDICTE SIT NOMEN DOMINI.—Blessed be the name of the Lord.
CRESCITE ET MULTIPLICAMINI.—Increase and multiply.
DENARIUM TERRAE MARIAE.—Maryland penny.
EXCELSIOR.—Higher; more lofty.
E PLURIBUS UNUM.—One composed of many.
GEORGIUS TRIUMPHO.—I, George, triumph.
GEORGIUS, DEI GRATIA, MAGNAE BRITANNIAE, FRAN-CIAE ET HIBERNIAE REX.—George, by the grace of God, King of Great Britain, of France, and of Ireland.
IMMUNE COLUMBIA.—Free America.
IMMUNIS COLUMBIA.—Free America.
INDE. ET LIB.—Independence and Liberty.
IN UNITATE FORTITUDO.—In union there is strength.
LIBERTAS JUSTICIA.—Liberty through justice.
LIBER NATUS LIBERTATEM DEFENDO.—Being born free, I defend liberty.
NON DEPENDUS STATUS.—Independence of position.
NON VI VIRTUTE VICI.—I conquered by virtue, not by force.
NOVA CONSTELLATIO.—The new constellation. (The American Colonies united.)

NOVA CAESAREA.—New Jersey.
NEO EBORACENSIS.—New York.
NEO EBORACUS.—New York.
NOVA EBORAC.—New York.
QUARTA DECIMA STELLA.—The fourteenth star. (Vermont, fourteenth state.)
ROSA AMERICANA.—The American Rose.
SALVA MAGNA PARENS FRUGUM.—Hail, thou mighty mother of production.
UTILE DULCI.—The useful with the pleasant.
VERMONTS RES PUBLICA.—The Republic of Vermont.
VERMON AUCTORI.—By authority of Vermont.
VOCE POPULI.—By the voice of the people.
VIRT. ET LIB.—Virtue and Liberty.

✍ *Where is the gold medal presented by Congress in 1776 to George Washington?*

The medal referred to is the famous "Evacuation of Boston" medal, the first medal authorized by the Continental Congress. Through the courtesy of the Trustees of the Boston Public Library we quote from their *Bulletin* of October–December, 1919, which traced the history of this medal:

The gold medal commemorative of the Evacuation of Boston became the property of George Steptoe Washington, the son of Samuel Washington, who was the General's elder brother. The next owner of the medal was Dr. Samuel Walter Washington, eldest son of George Steptoe Washington. On the decease of the doctor at Hasewood, Virginia, in 1831, his widow became possessor of the relic. She gave it to her son, George Lafayette Washington, who married the daughter of her brother, the Rev. John B. Clemson, of Claymont, Delaware. On the decease of George Lafayette Washington, the medal became the property of his widow, Mrs. Ann Bull Washington, from whom with proper certificates and vouchers, by the generous cooperation of fifty

157

citizens of Boston, it has been secured to the permanent ownership of this city, with which it is so gratefully identified and has
been deposited in the Public Library.

Then it appears that the medal has been transmitted through
the descendants, in successive generations of General Washington's elder brother. They have fully appreciated its intrinsic and
symbolic value, and have anxiously taken care for its safety under
the risks and perils which have attended its preservation. It is,
itself, a most beautiful and perfect specimen of workmanship of
the die and mint, and is without a blemish or any perceptible
wear of its sharp outline. During the Civil War its then owner,
George Lafayette Washington, was residing eleven miles from
Harper's Ferry on the main route to Winchester, where the
belligerents held alternate possession. The medal, in its original
case of green seal-skin, lined with velvet, was enveloped in
cotton, and, deposited in a box, was buried in the dry cellar of a
venerable mansion where General Washington usually spent
many months of the genial portion of the year. The original case,
which fell into decay by this exposure, accompanies the medal in
its present repository.

The public announcement of the acquisition by the City of
Boston was in the form of a letter as follows:

Executive Department, March 20, 1876
To the Honorable the City Council:

Gentlemen—It affords me much pleasure to inform you
that the gold Medal presented to General George Washington by
the American Congress in 1776, commemorative of the evacua-

tion of Boston by the British troops, was recently purchased of the Washington family by a few of our citizens, to be given by them to the City of Boston and preserved in the Boston Public Library. This most valuable relic, so peculiarly interesting to Boston as commemorating the most important event in her history, has been placed in my hands, and by me transferred to the Trustees of the Public Library, in whose custody it is to remain, in accordance with the wishes of the donors. A copy of the subscription list, with the preamble stating the object of the subscription, is enclosed herewith.

Samuel C. Cobb, Mayor

You can obtain a bronze copy of this famous gold medal by sending $3.75 to the Superintendent of the Mint at Philadelphia, Pa. Ask for Medal No. 401.

What was the famous Bushnell Sale?

Charles I. Bushnell of New York City was an avid collector of early American coins and tokens. With his death on September 17, 1880, the collecting public in America knew that choice material would again be placed on the market.

The sale of the Bushnell collection in 1882 was handled by two young, energetic Philadelphia brothers, Samuel Hudson and Henry Chapman, operating under the name of S. H. & H. Chapman. The sale realized $13,900.47, an exceedingly high amount at that time.

Some of the individual pieces, many that today would sell for more than the amount realized in the entire sale, and their sales price are worthy of mention. The Lord Baltimore penny (possibly unique) sold for $550; the silver Virginia shilling in proof for $105; a Brasher doubloon for $505; a ring variety Chalmer's Annapolis shilling for $110; a Washington half dollar, 1792, with lettered edge for $126 and with plain edge for $365; a 1792 silver-center cent for $120; and 1856 proof set (9 pieces) for $64.

At the time that the catalog was issued, there was sharp

criticism of the Chapman brothers for the many inaccuracies that were noted in the sales catalog. Standish Barry was referred to as Barry Standish, Harvard was placed in New Haven, "smooth" edge was confused with "plain" edge; Salem, the home of witchcraft, was placed in New Jersey. Then there were certain coins that were judged genuine which were known to be forgeries. Some coins were misattributed, whether intentionally or unintentionally we do not know.

Regardless, the sale was a success and the Chapmans started their climb to become the foremost dealers of their day in the United States.

What is Maundy money?

The day before Jesus was crucified he washed the feet of his Disciples. This day became known as Maundy Thursday. Early English Christian kings, as part of the Easter week ceremonies, on Maundy Thursday washed the feet of a few selected "poor" subjects, then distributed food and clothing to them.

In 1572 Queen Elizabeth I took part, being accompanied by thirty-nine gentlemen and ladies-in-waiting, the number participating being the same as her years on earth.

As the ceremony developed over the years, it was found that the clothing did not always fit, or that the food spoiled. So instead money was given to these people, with which to buy for themselves the food and clothing. In time it became custom to give as many pennies to as many poor folks as the ruler was years old, plus additional amounts for food and clothing.

Since in earlier years these were silver one-, two- (half groat), three-, and four- (groat) pence pieces, even after these minor coins were made of other metals, specially struck silver pieces were used.

Today, when England strikes no silver coins at all for circulation, special one-, two-, three-, and four-penny pieces are still made of fine silver (.925 fine) for this Maundy Thursday ceremony. These pieces are now called Maundy money and, being quite rare, are highly prized.

❧ *What is the highest price paid for a United States commemorative coin?*

Back in 1892 the firm of Wyckoff, Seamans & Benedict, the manufacturers of the well-known Remington typewriter, knew the value of advertising. For the privilege of purchasing the very first Columbian half dollar struck, they paid the sum of ten thousand dollars. Considering the purchasing power of the dollar, this would be comparable to in excess of one hundred thousand dollars today. The check was drawn on the National Shoe & Leather Bank of New York City and dated September 29, 1892.

The coin itself is not a rarity, since 950,000 of them were struck dated 1892, followed the next year with an identical design (except for the date) of another 1,550,405 pieces. In 1892 the coin was an oddity because in all of the previous ninety-nine years of the existence of the Mint, this was the first commemorative coin struck.

This coin can be viewed today at the Field Museum in Chicago.

❧ *When was currency used as soap wrappers?*

After the defeat of Germany and Austria in 1918 by the Allied Powers, inflation ran rampant in both conquered nations. The printing presses continued to produce huge quantities of paper money. But the more produced the more worthless it became, until by 1922 it was not even worth the paper it was printed on.

An ingenious Swiss soap manufacturer bought up bales of Austrian paper kronen notes, noting that they were the proper size to use as soap wrappers. He imprinted his label on the blank reverse side of these notes and proceeded to wrap his soap with these colorful bills.

It is reported that sales increased because many folks purchased the soap, wishfully hoping that the currency would some day again attain its prewar worth.

✄ *Why is February 24, 1925, remembered by collectors of United States numisma?*

On February 24, 1925, one Congressional bill was signed that authorized three different half-dollar issues.

They are (1) the California Diamond Jubilee with a net mintage of 86,594, (2) the Fort Vancouver Centennial with a net coinage of 14,994 and (3) the Vermont Sesquicentennial with a net coinage of 28,162.

Of added interest is the fact that a grizzly bear is pictured on the California coin, a catamount on the Vermont coin, while a hunter (obviously looking for the bear or wildcat) is shown on the Fort Vancouver piece.

Congress authorized the striking of 300,000 pieces each of the California Diamond Jubilee and the Fort Vancouver Centennial half dollars and only 40,000 of the Vermont coins. Actually only 150,200 of the California pieces were struck (with 63,606 subsequently remelted), while 50,028 of the Fort Vancouver were struck (with 35,034 remelted). All of the Vermont issue was coined (with 11,838 remelted).

Certainly Congress was ill advised if the supply exceeded the demand to such an extent that after spending time and money to coin these commemorative pieces, more than 25 per cent of those coined were later returned and remelted into bullion.

🙞 *When were the star and crescent first used on coins?*

Coins of Juba II, King of Numidia and Mauretania (30 B.C.–A.D. 19?) are known that show the star within the crescent moon. This kingdom existed in North Africa and covered an area which is now Morocco and part of Algeria.

King Juba II was educated in Rome and was much favored by the Romans and their Emperor Augustus Caesar. For his loyalty  to Rome he was allowed to wed Cleopatra, the daughter of Mark Anthony and Cleopatra. Many of his coins have "King Juba" stamped on the obverse in Latin, and "Cleopatra," in Greek characters, on the reverse. Some coins even pictured Queen Cleopatra on them.

Whether or not it is coincidental that Turkey used the same device centuries later has not been explained. The heavenly bodies were held in awe until science later was able to explain their existence.

🙞 *Did you know that Hawaii was represented in American coinage long before she became a state?*

In March, 1928, Congress authorized the striking of 10,000 half dollars to commemorate the one-hundred-fiftieth anniversary of the discovery of the Hawaiian Islands by Captain James Cook of the British Royal Navy.

The face of the coin shows a bust of Captain Cook facing left, while the reverse pictures a Hawaiian warrior in full ceremonial dress with his hand extended in welcome. This is truly ironic since the adventurous captain was killed by Hawaiian natives on Hawaiian soil.

Captain Cook (1728–1779) discovered this group of twenty Pacific islands in 1778. He named them the Sandwich Islands after his sponsor, the Earl of Sandwich. After the discovery he sailed the Pacific Ocean in search of a northwest passage between the Pacific and Atlantic Oceans. It was on a return trip to Hawaii the following year that he was killed by unfriendly natives.

The Hawaiian half dollars were distributed equally between the mainland and the islands. Many of those sold on the islands became pocket pieces and thus became worn. Those sold on the mainland went into the hands of collectors. Since this series is collected only in uncirculated condition, it has become the scarcest coin in the U.S. half-dollar commemorative series.

🕭 *When did Germany make coins of porcelain?*

Germany was bankrupt after World War I. Inflation followed and the printing presses were kept busy manufacturing currency that became worth less by the day. It is at times like this that metal, any metal, is hoarded.

One of the first indications that porcelain was being used as a substitute for metal was a news dispatch from Meissen, Saxony, that was reported in *The Numismatist* of September, 1920. It read in part:

The first German porcelain money is being manufactured here and will consist of 300,000 twenty pfennig pieces for use on the Hamburg elevated railway. The city of Meissen, as well as several other towns, has ordered porcelain coins for local use, with a view to solving the small change scarcity, as well as obviating the present unclean and easily tearable paper currency. The German Republic is said to be about to introduce porcelain coins ranging from ten pfennigs to five marks.

Two months later photographs appeared of porcelain patterns of two-, three-, and five-mark coins, but with the notation that the project was being abandoned. But even though the federal government decided against porcelain coins, tokens issued for Saxony began to appear. These pieces were a chocolate brown with a reddish tinge. A later series appeared in 1921, of a different design and with a gilt edge. Before the year was over more than thirty varieties were known, being "fired" for different parts of Germany. Some were made for private firms and others for local governments.

By February, 1922, American collectors were warned in *The Numismatist* that because of the limited numbers made of each different issue and the high prices asked for them by German dealers, very possibly most were made, not as a money substitute, but to realize a profit for the issuer. The article even quoted a circular from Lippstadt that said in part: "The profit realized from the sale of the emergency money is to be devoted to the charitable enterprises of the Lippstadt district, especially for the care of babies and children."

Unlike metal, porcelain is prone to chip, crack, and break. This was soon realized. It is hard to conceive that the German Republic could seriously have considered its use. But then, we must remember that in this panicky period of German history, rational thinking was not always present. Possibly Germany was looking for a means of keeping her famous chinaware factories open, and to that end she succeeded for a limited time.

After 1921 no new issues were reported, so we can well assume that Germany's porcelain coinage was limited to 1920 and 1921.

✍ Has anyone assembled a complete collection of United States coins?

In 1951 the numismatic world was astonished to hear that such a collection had been completed. The possessor of this fabulous collection is a Baltimare financier named Louis Eliasberg. Except for minor die varieties, it is considered complete.

According to the announcement of the Baltimore National Bank, when it invited the public to inspect the coins, "Sixty years went into making this United States collection." Among the rarities are the finest known "Without Pole to Liberty Cap" 1796 half cent; the finest known Liberty Cap 1793 one cent; the finest proof of the five known 1913 Liberty Head five cent; the unique 1873-CC dime; an 1894-S dime (24 struck, but few known); one of a dozen known 1876-CC twenty-cent pieces; one of five known 1827 quarter dollars; one of seven known 1838-O halves; one of three known 1853-O halves, without arrows and rays; the Stickney Specimen 1804 silver dollar; one of five known 1885 trade dollars; an 1861-D gold dollar, the rarest date; one of no more than half a dozen 1841 quarter eagles; an almost unique 1870-S three-dollar gold piece, a second specimen of which is in the cornerstone of the San Francisco Mint; one of three known 1822 half eagles; one of six (or less) 1858 eagles; one of sixteen extra-high-relief 1907 Roman Numerals double eagles, struck piedfort (double thickness).

The list goes on and on. And each coin was the finest obtainable. This is one collection we hope remains intact and properly housed for all to view.

166

✒ Why is the 1933 ten-dollar gold piece so expensive?

When Franklin Delano Roosevelt became President in 1933, the economy of the country was at a low ebb. One of the first steps taken by the newly elected F.D.R. was to propose legislation to help bring the nation out of the depression. Within a week of his inauguration the Act of March 9, 1933, "An Act to Provide Relief in the Existing National Emergency in Banking and for Other Purposes," became law. Among other things this law prohibited the hoarding of gold coin, gold bullion, and gold certificates. It required that all three be delivered to a Federal Reserve Bank, agency, branch, or member bank by May 1, 1933. It did allow for a maximum of $100 worth of gold of numismatic value to be held by collectors or others. Of course the bill provided for reimbursement in any other lawful money. This redeemed gold, together with that on hand, was remelted into bullion.

We can assume, in spite of a recorded mintage of 312,500 pieces, that most of the 1933 gold eagles had not gone into circulation before March 9, 1933. Minting could have started only after January 1, 1933. The minted coins then had to be released by the Treasury Department to the Federal Reserve Banks. These banks then only passed them on to member banks upon request. And certainly not many could have been requested in the depth of the depression.

And so, the ten dollar gold piece of most recent date is one of the five rarest in the whole series that has been coined almost every year from 1795 to 1804 and from 1838 to 1933.

✒ What is Bryan money?

A series of tokens was issued concurrent with the Bryan–McKinley presidential campaigns of 1896 and 1900. One of the major issues concerned the subject of free silver. In 1873 silver was demonitized and the United States was placed on a gold standard. William Jennings Bryan, the Democratic candidate, opposing William McKinley, advocated the restoration of silver at a ratio of 16 to 1 with gold. As a result, silversmiths such as Tiffany & Co. and Gorham Manufacturing Co. issued large silver tokens showing a dollar's worth of silver. One type was more than twice as large as a silver dollar and had wording similar to "A government dollar contains 412½ grains coin silver 900/1000 fine.

This piece contains 870 grains of coin silver, in value the equivalent of one gold dollar." At another date the grains were stated as 776⅛ instead of 870, showing the changing market price of silver. Similarly, a small silver token was struck, about fifty-cent size, which preached its sermon with "A government dollar contains 412½ grains of silver 900/1000 fine. This piece of silver is the size and weight of a government dollar . . . and its value July 5th, 1900 was 48 cents." A second type was also minted. These pieces were satirical in character and usually were made of base metal. They used such phrases as "Free Coinage," "16 to 1," "In Bryan We Trust-Nit," "Vote for 100¢ Dollar and McKinley," etc. These satirical pieces in many cases looked quite similar to United States coins. As a result, in certain areas they were outlawed as counterfeits, while in other communities the law-enforcement agents saw them for what they were, merely laughed, and allowed them to be distributed without interference. In 1926 the well-known numismatist, Farran Zerbe, cataloged and described over 140 types. His numbering system is still used when referring to these "Bryan" pieces.

Was Henry Ford a numismatist?

In all my research into coin collecting I have never come across the name of Henry Ford except on one occasion. In 1922 the auto magnate received a gentle ribbing from the gentlemen of the press because he purchased a "bunch of Confederate Money" for $10. Little did the reporters realize that the astute Mr. Ford was, as usual, making a wise investment, since it can be assumed that his ten-dollar purchase could today be sold for more than fifty times its purchase price. At that time individual Confederate notes sold for only pennies, where today they sell for $1 or up. It is also possible that the currency was being purchased as a gift for Mrs. Ford, since she definitely was a numismatist. This fact was established when, after her death, Stack's, the well-known New York coin dealers, sold at auction rarities from her collection.

Mrs. Ford's collection included about forty U.S. pattern coins, some three hundred large cents and proof sets of 1859, 1865, 1867, and all the dates from 1869 through 1914. The proof sets alone probably did not represent an investment of more than $400. At the time of the sale, December, 1951, the set of 1877 alone was worth $400!

Why was a Canadian 1947 maple leaf variety minted?

Canadian coins of King George VI bore the legend "GEORGIUS VI D. G. REX ET IND. IMP." (George VI, by the Grace of God, King and Emperor of India). With India gaining her independence in 1947, it became necessary to change the wording on the coins. A delay in executing the dies and an urgent need for coins in early 1948 made the Mint officials decide to use the 1947 dies.

In order to identify the coins actually minted in 1948 from those struck in 1947, it was decided to punch a small maple leaf to the right of the date 1947. When the 1948 coins finally appeared the new legend "GEORGIUS VI DEI GRATIA REX" replaced the one previously used on Canadian coinage.

Mint records indicate that in each coin denomination, more coins with the 1947 maple leaf were struck than those bearing the date 1948. Following are the mintage figures:

Denomination	1947 M. L.	1948
one cent	43,855,448	25,767,779
five cents	9,595,124	1,810,789
ten cents	9,638,793	422,741
twenty-five cents	4,393,938	2,564,424
fifty cents	38,433	37,784
dollar	21,135	18,780

Did you know that U.S. Secret Service agents confiscated a painting because it showed some currency?

In 1892, Charles A. Meurer of Cincinnati executed a beautiful still-life in his studio in Paris. He called it "My Passport." This painting, with a patriotic flavor, showed a table upon which lay an open passport, several letters, some loose change, and three pieces of United States currency. These bills were a one-dollar silver certificate, series 1886, a five-dollar legal-tender note of series 1880, and a twenty-dollar legal-tender note of the same series.

This painting was exhibited at the World's Columbian Exposition in Chicago in 1893. Because it was too realistically executed, and because the counterfeiting laws were then so stringent, the picture was seized by federal agents.

Only after red lines were painted through each bill was the painting returned to its owner. The many copies that exist today all prominently show these red lines.

 Can you describe the Washington Funeral Medal?

This famous medal is oval, measuring one inch by one and a quarter inches, with the bust of Washington facing left. Under the bust are the initials G. W., and as a border appears the legend "HE IN GLORY, THE WORLD IN TEARS, OB D. 14, 99." This last part translates to "died December 14, 1799."

The Funeral Medal was issued following a proclamation of President John Adams, setting the anniversary of George Washington's birthday, February 22, 1800, as the official day of mourning when the public should show its "grief by suitable eulogies, orations, or by public prayer."

The medal was designed by Joseph Perkins of Boston, who used as a model a profile of the President drawn by Joseph Wright in 1790. For the men, the medal was worn as a badge, as was customary at that time. For the ladies, the custom was to place it in a locket to hang around the neck. A copy in gold is owned by the Smithsonian Institution, enclosed in a glass case with a loop at the top, undoubtedly made to be worn by a lady.

✿ Why were the Lord Baltimore coins struck?

The colony of Maryland was first settled in 1634. Two years earlier a charter had been offered to George Calvert, the first Baron Baltimore, to establish a sanctuary in North America for religiously persecuted Catholics. He died before the charter was signed and it was issued to his son, Cecilius. The first settlers, both Catholic and Protestant, established the colony under the command of Lord Baltimore's younger brother, Leonard Calvert. Another brother, Philip, became Secretary of State.

Just as the other settlements in North America had their problems finding a medium of exchange, so also did Maryland. In 1650 taxes were collected in the form of corn. Powder and shot also served in lieu of currency.

As the situation progressively worsened, Lord Baltimore attempted to remedy it in England by privately having coins struck. Dies were prepared and trial pieces sent from England with the following letter:

> To my most affectionat loving brother, Philip Calvert, Esq'r at St. Mary's, in Maryland.
>
> I sent a sample of the Maryland money, with direction for the procuring it to pass, because I understood by letters this yeare from the Governor and you and others that there was no doubt but that the people there would accept of it, but which if we find they do, there wilbe meanes found to supply you all

there with money enough; but though it would be a very great advantage to the Colony that it should pass current there, and an utter discouradgment for the future supply of any more, if there be not a certain establishment this yeare and assurance of its being vented and currant there, yet it must not be imposed upon the people but by a Lawe there made by their consents in a Generall Assembly, which I pray faile not to signify to the Governor and Councell there to gether from me, by shewing them this Letter from

Your most affectionat Brother
C. Baltemore

London, 12th October, 1659

After lengthy discussions the council passed a resolution in April, 1661, authorizing the establishment of a mint within the colony, and effecting laws to prevent clipping, counterfeiting, and debasing the new coinage. But in fact the mint was never built and newly minted coins were delivered from England.

These coins were undated, showed a head of Cecil, Lord Baltimore, on the obverse, while the reverse pictured the family coat of arms. They were struck in silver in denominations of shillings, sixpence, and groats (four pence). A penny of copper, with a different reverse, was also minted. It is so rare as to suggest that it was never struck for circulation but only as a pattern.

The council made certain that the coins would circulate by passing a law in April, 1662, requiring every householder and freeman "to take up ten shillings per poll of the newly issued coins, for every taxable under their charge and custody, and pay for the same in good casked tobacco, at two pence per pound, to be paid upon tender of the said sums of money, proportionately for each respective family."

What is a double-denomination bill?

This is a piece of currency that has one value on its face and another on its reverse.

With the introduction of the small-size bill in 1929, notes were first printed twelve at a time, later eighteen, and currently thirty-two. The chance of any error of this type escaping the eyes of the various inspectors is very slim. As a result, the few known bring extremely high prices.

Back in 1891 a twenty-dollar national bank note with a ten-dollar reverse was reported being received by a bank in Washington, New Jersey. The bank's cashier returned the freak note to the Treasury Department with a caustic letter saying that he was not in the business of collecting freaks.

At that time the large-size national bank notes were printed four to a sheet. The tens and twenties were printed together with three tens and one twenty, one above the other. The error occurred because the sheet was reversed at the time of the second printing. This meant that a second error also had to be in existence, with a ten-dollar face and a twenty-dollar reverse.

Some months later, in nearby Newark, New Jersey, the mate made its appearance. But in this case the proud possessor refused to part with the piece, even though offered a handsome profit.

Why is P. T. Barnum pictured on a United States coin?

To commemorate the one-hundredth anniversary in 1936 of the incorporation of the city of Bridgeport, Connecticut, and at the same time honor her most distinguished citizen and one-time mayor, Congress authorized the striking of 25,000 fifty-cent pieces. All were issued at $2 apiece and the $1.50 profit per coin helped defray the expense of the centennial celebration.

Phineas Taylor Barnum, whose profile covers the obverse of

this coin, gained his fame as the impresario who introduced Jenny Lind and "General" Tom Thumb, and founded the circus which became world-famous as "Barnum & Bailey." The wealth that he acquired as a showman was largely spent to improve his home town of Bridgeport.

Barnum was considered by many to have been the greatest showman that the United States has produced. His first endeavor in this field took place in 1834, when he purchased a Negro woman who was reputed to have been George Washington's nurse. Since Washington had been born 102 years earlier, this woman had to have been well over 120 years of age. Barnum claimed that she was 161 years old. He "showed" her for a short while before she died.

Finding show business lucrative, he started the American Museum in New York City, filling it with freaks and oddities of every description. From his home town of Bridgeport, he introduced Charles Stratton as "General" Tom Thumb. The "General," Barnum's best-known attraction, won him fame and fortune.

The success of the coin (P. T. was not around to plug it) was far slower than his freaks. In 1940 it still catalogued for only $2; by 1949 it had advanced to $3; by 1958 it reached $8.50; but by 1966 it had really taken off, selling for more than $40.

✐ What is the history of the Canadian dot coins?

The death of King George V in January, 1936, made it necessary to start preparing new dies for 1937 with the likeness of King Edward VIII. His abdication in December, 1936, came at a very inopportune time as far as the Royal Canadian Mint was concerned. Very little time remained to prepare new dies for King George VI.

With a need for one-cent, ten-cent, and twenty-five-cent pieces in early 1937, it was decided to use the 1936 dies but identify the coins struck in 1937 by punching a small hole in each reverse die under the date.

Although 678,823 one-cent pieces were struck, only four are known, and while 192,194 ten-cent pieces were struck, only four of the "dot" variety are known. A large number of the 153,655 dot quarter dollars have been found, making them scarce but not rare.

It is believed that the punch mark was quite shallow and that dirt or dust clogged the punched hole after a short time, causing few one-cent and ten-cent pieces to be found with the dot visible. Possibly others may turn up, but after more than thirty years it is unlikely that more than a dozen of each could ever become known.

✈️ *What is the Astor Peace Medal?*

The success story of John Jacob Astor (1763–1848) must have given every emigrant from Europe the faith needed to enter new surroundings, learn a new language, and know that he could better his lot financially.

Starting as a twenty-one-year-old penniless emigrant from Germany, Astor started his own business in New York City a few years after his arrival, trading in musical instruments and furs. This led to his entering the China trade which, although hazardous, offered large profits if the vessels made a safe return. Withal, John Jacob Astor became the wealthiest citizen of the young United States.

In 1808 he organized the American Fur Company, obtaining a charter from the New York State legislature. Trading posts of the company were established along the Missouri and Columbia rivers and their tributaries. This allowed for the use of inexpensive river transportation. Astor arranged that each trading post be a self-contained fort that could be easily defended against Indian attack. Each was well supplied with all the needs for the fur trappers and the local Indians.

To help maintain a friendly relationship with the Indians he had medals struck that were quite similar to the peace medals given out by the United States government. But in place of the bust of the President, his bust appeared, with the words "PRESI-DENT OF THE AMERICAN FUR COMPANY." The reverse showed clasped hands, crossed peace pipes and tomahawks, and the words "PEACE AND FRIENDSHIP," almost identical in design to the government medals. In addition the name of the trading post appeared.

Mr. Astor's imitation of government peace medals may have

been presumptuous, but it was a useful means to placate the Indians who were resentful of the foreign trespassers.

On what U.S. coin is the Capitol pictured?

The double eagle or twenty-dollar gold piece minted from 1907 to 1933 shows the Capitol in minute size in the lower left-hand corner on the obverse side of the coin. Its position helps create the illusion that Miss Liberty, with torch in hand, is floating above the nation's Capitol as a guardian angel.

This is the coin considered by many to be the most artistic ever designed in the United States series. This position is well taken, since it is the work of a famous American sculptor, Augustus Saint-Gaudens, who was commissioned by President Theodore Roosevelt to redesign the U.S. eagle and double eagle. The artist, born in Dublin, Ireland, in 1848, did not live long enough to see his coins widely circulated, since he died in 1907, the first year of issue of both pieces.

What is the best-known Roman coin?

Since the publishing in 1965 of James A. Michener's best-selling novel, *The Source,* I believe that the sesterce of the Emperor Vespasian commemorating the conquest of Judea is the best-known Roman coin. This brass piece is pictured twice and discussed in detail in the book.

Upon the death of Otho on April 19, A.D. 69, the Roman Senate proclaimed Aulus Vitellius emperor. But the soldiers of General Titus Flavius Vespasianus disapproved of the choice and proclaimed him their emperor on July 1. Even though Vespasian

was in Alexandria and not in Rome, public support caused rioting in Rome and Vespasian's followers overcame the soldiers of the new emperor and Vitellius was murdered. The Senate then confirmed the election of the Emperor Vespasian.

One of the new ruler's first acts was to seek revenge for the annihilation of the Roman garrison at Jerusalem in A.D. 66. A strong army led by Vespasian and his son, Titus, accomplished this task in 70. The occasion was celebrated with a triumphal parade into Rome, with captives and the spoils of war.

To commemorate the event itself, coins were struck that showed a weeping woman seated, representing Judea, and a standing Roman soldier, with his shield and helmet on the ground nearby. The wording on the coin read "IVDEA CAPTA" (Judea captured).

ஜ்ஐ *Who is J. O. P.?*

Canadian dollars dated 1935 to 1949 have been seen with the initials J. O. P. punched into them. For many years the meaning of these initials was not generally known to numismatists. But in October, 1959, Larry Gingras, a member of the Canadian Numismatic Association, wrote in its monthly magazine, *The Canadian Numismatic Journal*, a fascinating tale. On a visit to the city of Nelson in British Columbia, Mr. Gingras found the answer and reported it to his fellow collectors.

The initials were those of Joseph Oliva Patenaude, a jeweler of Nelson. He lost his jewelry business in 1930 in a legal fight for a less expensive means of refining silver ore. Along with other citizens of Nelson, he financially backed a Mr. French, who had developed new mining techniques. But the opposing mining interests brought charges of patent infringements, which the courts upheld. After losing his jewelry business he became an optometrist and continued this business until he retired in 1950. He was a strong advocate of the introduction of a silver dollar into Canada's monetary system. When Canada issued her first silver dollar in 1935 he was so pleased that he purchased one thousand of them, counterstamped them with his initials, and used them when paying bills or when making change. He believed that he could show how widely silver coins circulated by tracing those that bore his initials. As Mr. Gingras put it: ". . . each coin bore a counterstamp for the same reason that one tags wildfowl—to assist in following their circulation." He followed the same procedure to a lesser degree in the years through 1949. After his retirement he discontinued the habit.

Just as in the United States, counterstamping of Canadian coins is considered an illegal act. Nevertheless, all who knew Mr. Patenaude agreed that his motives were good and that he did not deliberately violate the laws of Canada.

J. O. P. died at the age of eighty-five in 1956.

Are there any 1933 twenty-dollar gold pieces in private collections now?

Under the terms of the act of March 9, 1933, "An Act to Provide Relief in the Existing National Emergency in Banking, etc.," gold was recalled and all gold coins on hand at the Treasury Department or in Federal Reserve Banks were returned to the mint and remelted into bullion.

As of that date no double eagles dated 1933 had been officially released by the Treasury Department. Nevertheless a few had gotten into private hands. By 1954 all were believed returned except for one piece that was in the King Farouk collection.

After Farouk was deposed the Egyptian government decided to sell his collection at public auction. The sale was to take place in Cairo on February 24 through 28 and March 3 through 7, 1954. A catalog of 2,798 lots was prepared by Sotheby & Co. of London. Lot No. 185 listed all double eagles from 1924 to 1933, lacking only the 1926-S and 1927-D.

When the catalog appeared, the United States government requested that the Egyptian government return the 1933 coin, claiming that the coin must have been obtained illegally. It was withdrawn from the sale and returned by the Egyptian government.

Since early 1954 none have appeared, or even been hinted about, leading us to assume that none today are in private collections.

🌺 What is a "shooting coin"?

At Breslau, in Silesia, in 1561, the aldermen of the city presented a double ducat to the champion of a shooting match. Other cities, not to be outdone, held shooting matches and presented a special coin or medal to the winner.

In numismatics, we generally think of the Swiss series of shooting festival coins as "shooting coins." This series started in 1842 at Chur in the Canton of Graubunden. Festivals were held with a fair degree of regularity until 1885 in fourteen of the twenty-two Swiss cantons. These pieces were minted of silver and, having a limited mintage, were highly prized. The following is a list of this series, showing the number minted and the location of the event:

Year	Coin	Number Minted	Minted for
1842	4 Francken	6,000	Chur in Graubunden
1847	40 Batzen	3,200	Glarus
1857	5 Franken	5,195	Bern
1859	5 Franken	6,000	Zurich

1861	5 Francs	6,000	Stanz in Nidwalden
1863	5 Francs	6,000	La Chaux-de-Fonds in Neuchatel
1865	5 Francs	10,000	Schaffhausen
1867	5 Francs	6,000	Schwyz
1869	5 Francs	6,000	Zug
1872	5 Francs	10,000	Zurich
1874	5 Francs	15,000	St. Gallen
1876	5 Francs	20,000	Lausanne in Vaud
1879	5 Francs	30,000	Basel
1881	5 Francs	30,000	Fribourg
1883	5 Francs	30,000	Lugano in Ticino
1885	5 Francs	25,000	Bern

Sometimes the amount was shown on the coin, other times not shown but implied by the weight and size of the coin.

An attempt to continue the series was tried with five-franc pieces struck for shooting festivals in Fribourg in 1934 and again in Lucerne in 1939.

These beautiful coins remind us of the skill of the Swiss men, where every male citizen is a soldier and is taught from youth to be proficient in the use of firearms and where in the past this proficiency was rewarded with the presentation of a beautiful coin.

✎ When was there a United State of America?

Sometime between July 1, 1905, and June 11, 1906, when Charles H. Treat was Treasurer of the United States and Judson W. Lyons was registrar of the Treasury, an error was made on one plate that printed the one-dollar silver certificates. Instead of reading "Treasurer of the United States," the engraver had a lapse of memory and left off the final "s." Only one bill is known to exist today that acknowledges Chas. H. Treat as Treasurer of the United State.

The variety with the "s" is quite common and since this error is not widely known, it is very possible that other specimens may show up. This is not a glaring error because the engraving of the title under the name is quite small and could be easily overlooked.

🏵 What are Canada's "Graceless" coins?

Upon the death of Edward VII in 1910, George V became king of the Dominion of Canada as well as the king-emperor of the British Empire.

The Canadian decimal coinage has always pictured the British monarch on its face, and with both Edward VII and Victoria the legend had read "EDWARDUS VI DEI GRATIA REX IMPERATOR" or "VICTORIA DEI GRATIA REGINA." Now, with the introduction of the new coinage in 1911 for George V, the new dies were engraved "GEORGIUS V REX ET IND. IMP." Inadvertently the words "DEI GRATIA" (by the Grace of God), had been omitted.

Public disapproval was immediately evidenced and new obverses were engraved for the following year's coinage. Naturally, since the "Graceless" coins appeared only in 1911, this one year's coins make up a separate type of coinage. As a result the one-, five-, ten-, twenty-five-, and fifty-cent pieces of 1911 have a higher premium value than either the preceding or following year.

A true bargain, unnoticed by most, announced to the American collector that a specimen set was being issued. The January, 1912, issue of *The Numismatist* had an article headed "New Canadian Coins," which read as follows:

We are informed by R. W. McLachlan, of Montreal, that the new Canadian half dollar has been issued. Mr. McLachlan has forwarded a specimen, which will be reproduced in *The Numismatist*. He also has received the following communication from the Deputy Master of the Ottawa Mint, which would indicate that the silver dollar is not to be issued this year:

13 December, 1911

Specimen coins of the new issue of the New Reign in silver and bronze are now ready.

The price of case and contents will be two instead of three dollars. A place has been provided in the case for the silver dollar, which has not been coined this year.

Cases without this blank will be ready in January for those who prefer them.

Applicants are requested to state their preference.

James Bonar, Deputy Master

Records indicate one thousand sets were sold, but this figure is believed to be incorrect, for the cased set today sells for in excess of *four thousand dollars*. What a buy our grandparents missed!

What is the history of the Rosa Americana coins?

Recognizing the need for coins for use in the young American colonies, George I of England granted a letter of patent in 1722 to one William Wood. By the terms of this patent, Wood was to mint two-pence, pence, and half-pence pieces of a mixture of silver, brass, and pewter. The patent spelled out in detail the number of pounds of metal that could be used each year. It did not specify the design except to state that the king's portrait, name, and titles must appear on one side and that the word "America" appear on the other side.

We can assume that the idea of the rose, which is pictured prominently on the reverse, was Wood's idea, since it was not

mentioned in the patent. Around the rose were the words "ROSA AMERICANA UTILE DULCI" (the American Rose, the useful with the pleasant). The face of the coin shows the king's bust and the words "GEORGIUS D. G. MAG. BRI. FRA. ET HIB. REX" (George, by the Grace of God, King of Great Britain, France, and Ireland), or merely "GEORGIUS DEI GRATIA REX" (George, by the Grace of God, King). As with most coins of that time, the value was not stated, and the denomination recognized only by the size of the piece.

The right of coinage can be most profitable, but it is doubtful that William Wood made his fortune by being granted this right of coinage. Under the terms of the document he was required to hire a "clerk" who was to receive £200 per annum, a large salary at that time. He further was required to pay an annual "rental" of £100 to the Clerk of the Treasury. Then, we are told that the Rosa Americana coins were not popular with the American colonists, probably because they were made in England and not in the colonies.

Coins of all three denominations dated 1722 and 1723 circulated quite widely, and can be purchased in the range of $20 to $150. The two pence and pence of 1724 are known, but are considered uncollectable, as none have come on the market in many years.

What is an Indian Peace Medal?

Medals were presented to the North American Indians as a gesture of friendship (after their lands had been seized) by the white settlers.

Both in British North America and in French North America (Canada) medals were presented in the name of the European monarchs who claimed the land. The early medals were generally oval in shape and made of silver. They had a loop on the top so that the Indian chief could hang it about his neck.

In the United States, the custom of presenting medals to Indian chiefs continued even after the Civil War. The U.S. medals pictured the President on one side, while the reverse usually had a fitting description such as "Peace and Friendship."

Many counterfeits exist of the early medals and the medal collector can never be absolutely sure if a medal is authentic unless he actually digs it up at an Indian burial site.

Did Benjamin Franklin truly prefer the turkey to the eagle?

It is an oft-told story that the elder statesman of the American Revolution would have preferred the picture of the turkey to that of the eagle on the national emblem. I consider that his remarks on the subject were said in jest.

Every story written on the subject stems from a letter the aged Franklin wrote to his daughter, Mrs. Benjamin Bache. The letter was mainly concerned with the formation of the Society of the Cincinnati in 1783 by the officers of the Continental Army. His concern was that this fraternal organization might become a strong political group. The letter read in part:

For my own part I wish the bald eagle had not been selected as the representative of our country. He is a bird of bad moral character; he does not get his living honestly; you may find him perched upon some dead tree, where, too lazy to fish for himself, he watches the labor of the fishing hawk, and when that diligent bird has taken a fish and is bearing it to his nest for the support of his mate and young ones, the bald eagle pursues him and takes it from him. With all this injustice he is never in good care, but, like those among men who live by sharping and robbing, he is generally poor and often very lousy. I am, on this account, not displeased that the figure [on the badge of the Cincinnati], is not known as a bald eagle and looks more like a turkey. For in truth the turkey is a much more respectable bird, and withal a true, original native of America. Eagles have been found in all countries, but the turkey was peculiar to ours. He is besides (though a little vain and silly, 'tis true, but not the worse emblem for that), a bird of courage and would not hesitate to attack a grenadier of the British guards, who would presume to invade his farmyard with a red coat on.

No, I believe that the eminent Dr. Franklin was quietly chuckling at his own remarks, and never meant them to be taken seriously.

✇ *What is the Dix token?*

Of all the tokens issued during the War Between the States as a substitute for the elusive one-cent piece that was hoarded by a jittery public, the Dix token was probably the most used of the "patriotic" type coppers.

One side pictures the United States flag encircled with the words: "THE FLAG OF OUR COUNTRY," while the reverse shows the word "DIX" circumscribed with "IF ANYONE ATTEMPTS TO TEAR IT DOWN, SHOOT HIM ON THE SPOT."

Dix refers to John Adams Dix (1798–1879), the New Hampshire–born statesman and railroad builder, who served as a United States Senator and later, for only two months in 1861, as Secretary of the Treasury under President Buchanan. During the Civil War he served the Union as a major general.

During the period of tension preceding the war, when the federal government was attempting to prevent southern states from seizing government property, Dix was informed that a Captain Breshwood refused to obey a general order to secure American property. This resulted in the following telegram being sent:

Treasury Department, January 29, 1861.—Tell Lieutenant Caldwell to arrest Captain Breshwood, assuming command of the Cutter, and obey the order I gave through you. If Captain Breshwood, after arrest, undertakes to interfere with the command of the Cutter, tell Lt. Caldwell to consider him as a mutineer and treat him accordingly. If anyone attempts to haul down the American Flag, shoot him on the spot.

John A. Dix
Secretary of the Treasury

The contents of the telegram somehow became widely known. When the flood of patriotic Civil War tokens was issued in 1863, the Dix token was designed and widely distributed. Many varieties exist, including a humorous one with an error by the die sinker. This resulted in the slogan reading, "If anyone attempts to tear it down, shoot him on the spoot."

🕊️ *Who is Pistrucci?*

The name is most familiar to numismatists as that of the man who designed the reverse of the English coins that show St. George slaying the dragon. This design appeared on crowns of George III, George IV, Victoria, Edward VII, and George VI. It also appeared on gold coins of all the aforementioned and also George V.

Benedetto Pistrucci was born in Rome in 1784 of a well-to-do family. His father was a judge and hoped that young Benedetto, too, would follow the legal profession. But Pistrucci showed no talent in this direction. His artistic ability was noted in his early years and at fifteen he was apprenticed to a gem engraver.

By 1814 his skill for producing portrait cameos was well known, and with the defeat of Napoleon and Europe in a state of turmoil, he felt that London offered the best opportunities.

A cameo of George III, commissioned by Sir Joseph Banks, brought him to the attention of the Royal Mint in 1816. His first commission from the Mint was to produce a cameo of St. George slaying the dragon. His original design was first used by the Mint on the gold sovereign of 1817. The following year the Chief Engraver, Thomas Wyon, Jr., died, and Pistrucci was offered the position. He accepted, and held the post until 1825.

His masterpiece was the Waterloo Medallion which he began in 1817 and partially completed some thirty-three years later. This medal had a diameter of 4¼ inches. Because of its great size there was fear that the dies would crack if hardened. Therefore only trial pieces were struck, in soft metal.

Pistrucci was subjected to much criticism because he was paid £2000 for a medal that was never quite finished. When he died in 1885 *The Illustrated London News* said about the medal:

The Master and Moneyers of the Mint were plagued with early applications for proof impressions of the glorious medal. Collectors reserved central circles in their cabinets for examples of the coming wonder. Years passed by, and nothing was heard about it. George the Fourth died, and collectors were still impatient. William the Fourth died, and Mr. Hamilton assured us that it was in hand—would be a glorious work, and one well worth waiting for. Then came the Mint Commission of 1848, and it was not forthcoming. . . . The Great Captain whose Victory it was designed to commemorate died, and yet no medal; and now forty years after the event Pistrucci himself dies, and the medal is unpublished and unknown to the Master of the Mint.

Had the medal been finished in a reasonable time, Pistrucci

would never have received the newspaper publicity that naturally was aimed at an artist who was paid approximately $10,000 (quite a fortune in the early nineteenth century) for a work that was never completed. Possibly Pistrucci has gained more fame because his medal remained unfinished.

✦ What is the origin of the motto "In God We Trust"?

The archives of the Treasury Department reveal two letters that possibly led to the adoption of the motto. The first letter, addressed to the Secretary of the Treasury, was from a man of God who desired that the citizens of the United States be made more aware of God's guiding hand in our day-to-day affairs. The second was a letter of instructions from the Secretary of the Treasury to the Director of the Mint to suggest how this idea could be realized. That the first letter was saved suggests that its recipient felt that it had merit and that it was this first letter that led to his writing the second letter.

The first letter was addressed to Salmon P. Chase, Secretary of the Treasury, and read:

Ridleyville, Pa., Nov. 13, 1861
Dear Sir: — You are about to submit your annual report to Congress respecting the affairs of the national finances.

One fact touching our currency has hitherto been seriously overlooked. I mean the recognition of the Almighty God in some form in our coins.

You are probably a Christian. What if our Republic were now shattered beyond reconstruction. Would not the antiquaries of succeeding centuries rightly reason from our past that we were a heathen nation. What I propose is that instead of the goddess of liberty we shall have next inside the 13 stars a ring inscribed with the words "perpetual union"; within this ring the allseeing eye, crowned with a halo; beneath this eye the American flag, bearing in its field stars equal to the number of the States united; in the folds of the bars the words "God, liberty, law."

This would make a beautiful coin, to which no possible citizen could object. This would relieve us from the ignominy of heathenism. This would place us openly under the Divine protection that we have personally claimed. From my heart I have felt our national shame in disowning God as not the least of our present national disasters.

To you first I address a subject that must be agitated.

(signed) N. R. Watkinson
Minister of the Gospel

Exactly one week later the Secretary of the Treasury wrote the following memo to the Mint Director:

Treasury Department, Nov. 20, 1861

Dear Sir: No nation can be strong except in the strength of God, or safe except in His defense. The trust of our people in God should be declared on our national coins.

You will cause a device to be prepared without unnecessary delay with a motto expressing in the fewest and tersest words possible this national recognition.

Yours truly,
(signed)   S. P. Chase

James Pollack, Esq., Director of the Mint, Philadelphia, Pa.

Trial pieces and pattern coins were struck, bearing such mottos as "Our country, our God," "God, our Trust," "Our God and our country." Further correspondence in the archives revealed a letter from the Secretary to the Mint Director suggesting a change in a pattern piece to "In God We Trust."

This motto first appeared on the bronze two-cent piece of 1864. In 1866 it was first used on all quarters, halves, silver dollars, and all gold coins. It first appeared on the one cent in 1909, the dime in 1916, and the nickel in 1938. Even though the motto was used by all the coin denominations it was not made mandatory on all coins until an Act of Congress was signed into law by President Eisenhower on July 11, 1955. (It had been made mandatory on gold and silver coins in 1908.)

What is the difference between a Federal Reserve note and a Federal Reserve Bank note?

Space would not permit an answer on the economic distinctions. Generally, the Federal Reserve Bank notes, rarely seen today, can be considered in the same class with the National Bank notes. Both state on their face "National Currency." The last issue of either National Bank notes or Federal Reserve Bank notes was the Series of 1929, which was discontinued in 1933. Both carried a brown Treasury Department seal.

Federal Reserve notes, the most prevalent series used today, are authorized in denominations of one, two, five, ten, twenty, fifty, one hundred, five hundred, one thousand, five thousand, and ten thousand dollars. (Actually none above $100 have been printed since 1945.) To date no two-dollar notes have been printed, the supply of two-dollar United States notes (red seal) filling present needs. These notes all bear a green Treasury Department seal.

There are other noticeable differences between the two currencies, although the basic design is similar and the reverses are identical. The Federal Reserve notes have the signatures of only the Treasurer of the United States and the Secreatry of the Treasury. The Federal Reserve Bank notes show the alphabetical letter for the Federal Reserve district (A for Boston, B for New York, C for Philadelphia, D for Cleveland, etc.) in four positions on the face, as well as the additional signatures of the Governor and Cashier, Governor and Deputy Governor, Governor and Assistant Deputy Governor, or Governor and Controller.

Should you find a brown seal note, save it. It might have a nice premium value.

What is Heath's Counterfeit Detector?

In 1864, an ingenious gentleman named Laban Heath obtained permission to use plates of The American Bank Note Company, which company printed much of the paper money in circulation at that time.

Heath prepared illustrations from these plates that could be helpful in instructing anyone who had to handle money how to distinguish a counterfeit bill. By comparing notes offered with his illustrations and having an understanding of engraving techniques, counterfeits could be readily detected.

Heath's volume was widely used and endorsed by banks, since counterfeiting was far more prevalent then than it is today. Further, in 1864 notes of private banks circulated freely alongside the new "greenbacks" and national bank notes that had only recently come into being. Most of these notes had parts mechanically made by intricate ruling machines. Mr. Heath's explanations of the techniques of manufacture, along with the engravings, pointed up the obvious places where counterfeiting would be difficult.

The success of the first volume led to a second volume in 1867. By now, most state bank notes had been withdrawn. Heath obtained from the United States Treasury Department, and the American, National, and Continental Bank Note companies, all of whom engraved currency for the government, genuine designs from the original government plates used on United States paper money, both large-size bills and fractional currency. This new volume bore the impressive title of *Heath's Greatly Improved and Enlarged Infallible Government Counterfeit Detector, At Sight.*

For this second volume, Laban Heath received a commendation from the Sergeant at Arms of the U.S. House of Representatives, duly endorsed by fifty-three members of the House. Heath never updated his book after 1867. With changes in designs, his book soon became outmoded, and later a collector's item.

What is the history of the
British Columbia gold coins?

In 1818 gold was discovered in the mountains of British Columbia. The strikes were quite sizable and "gold fever" ran high.

This remote province had no facilities for assaying the metal and for exchanging the gold dust for usable currency. The closest place where this could be done was in San Francisco. Naturally the government disliked the idea of gold being exported to another country, although there were actually no legal restrictions.

Captain W. D. Gosset, treasurer of the colony, petitioned for the establishment of an assay office and mint for New Westminster, the colony's capital. This was in 1859. By the next year an assay office was in operation. In 1861, the governor of this Crown Colony (later to become a province), urgently requested permission of London to establish a mint. His argument was that coins were so scarce that they commanded a 5 per cent premium, while the cost of production would not exceed one half of one per cent. He suggested that coins comparable to the United States ten-dollar and twenty-dollar gold pieces be struck.

London approval was received in 1862 and mint machinery was purchased for about $2,500 in San Francisco. The Tower Mint in London prepared dies for both the ten-dollar and the twenty-dollar gold coins and shipped them to New Westminster.

Now comes the irony. The gold mines, after four years of being worked, became depleted. The amount mined was negligible. The governor, Sir James Douglas, ordered the machinery dismantled and stored away. Captain Gosset, the sponsor of the project, ordered a limited number of each denomination struck off, both in gold and in silver before the machinery was dismantled. These were presented as souvenirs to certain officials and friends.

Reports vary as to the number of each struck. Probably not more than ten of each denomination in gold and silver were made. They are listed as "very rare."

*What U.S. President was pictured
on a U.S. coin while he was in office?*

Only Calvin Coolidge had this distinction. This un-
assuming Vermont lawyer, who was Warren Harding's Vice
President, would probably never have become President except
for the untimely death of President Harding on August 3, 1923.
After serving a full four-year term from 1925 to 1929, he wisely
chose not to run for re-election. We say "wisely" because his
successor, Herbert Hoover, started his term in an era of "prosperity" and ended it in a gloomy sea of "depression."

Possibly because of the prosperous times, Coolidge, along with
Washington, was chosen to have his bust placed on the new
commemorative half dollar that was authorized for issuance in
conjunction with the celebration of the Sesquicentennial of American Independence, July 4, 1926. The event was highlighted with
a government-sponsored fair, held in Philadelphia from June to
December, 1926.

Because of the good times it was anticipated that the demand
for such a half dollar by visitors to the fair would be great. As a
result, Congress authorized the striking of one million pieces.
With an issue price of $1 per coin, the demand was sadly lacking
and when the fair ended, 858,880 pieces were returned unsold to
be melted down into bullion, resulting in a net coinage of 141,120
pieces. The coin was executed in extremely low relief, which may
have contributed to its lack of popularity.

Fifteen years after mintage it still sold for only $1.50. By 1953
it had advanced to $4, doubling to $8 by 1958, and by 1966 it was
triple the 1958 price.

✏️ How can you identify coins of the Holy Roman Empire?

The Holy Roman Empire was reputed to have its beginnings with the crowning of Charlemagne in A.D. 800. However, its true beginning was with the coronation of the German king, Otto I (936–973). But not until 1438, when the Hapsburg dynasty came into power with Albert II, did the word *Empire* truly apply. This great empire played an important role in European history from 1438 until 1806, when Francis II relinquished the title and was crowned solely as King of Austria. As emperors the Hapsburgs were the rulers of a large territory that was made up of Germany, Austria, Hungary, and Bohemia.

The coins struck in the name of the Empire read "DEI GRATIA ROMANORUM IMPERATOR SEMPER AUGUSTUS GERMANIAE HUNGARIAE BOHEMIAE REX" (By the Grace of God, Holy Roman Emperor, ever august, King of Germany, Hungary and Bohemia) or the initials "D.G.R.I.S.A. G.H.B.R.," or with some or all of the Latin words partially spelled out.

Just to confuse you more, for a short time Charles VI (1711–1740) also claimed Spain and during that period "HISP.," "HIS.," "HI," or merely "H" appeared between the "G" and the "H"!

✏️ What is the history of the English copper two-penny coin?

If you have studied the coinage of England you know that the only two-penny coin of copper was dated 1797. This coin is better known as the "cartwheel" because of its size and wide border.

The story of this coin is the story of Matthew Boulton, English engineer, draftsman, and manufacturer. Born in 1728 in Birmingham, Boulton learned manufacturing, business, and commerce from his father. By 1762 he was a successful businessman employing close to 1,000 people. In 1777 he formed a partnership with James Watt, inventor of a much-improved steam engine. Their union resulted in a large plant to manufacture steam engines in the Soho district of London.

At about this time Boulton became concerned with the token money that was used in lieu of farthings, half pennies, and pennies. Many were badly made forgeries of short weight. Since the government took a do-nothing attitude, the workman, the tradesman, and the public generally suffered financial loss from these fraudulent pieces.

Because of this situation, Watt decided to design a coining press, run by a steam engine, to produce better coins that could not easily be counterfeited. He started this project because the government had promised him a contract to produce copper coins after the machinery had been perfected. Although the government reneged in 1787, when the new machinery was ready to produce, he did obtain contracts for certain colonial coins.

Finally, in 1797, he received his first order from the British government. This was to strike five hundred tons of copper farthings, half pennies, pennies, and two pennies from the designs that he had developed in his effort to reduce the possibilities of counterfeiting. The essence of the design was that all lettering was incused, while the figures on the coins, a bust of George III on the face and a seated Britannia on the back, were raised.

The farthings and half pennies were never struck, except as trial pieces. Four hundred and eighty tons of copper were used for the penny and only twenty tons for the two penny. The penny weighed exactly one ounce and the two penny exactly two ounces. The tolerances were so fine that the coins were used for many years as weights by scalemakers.

Britishers admired the coins, but objected to the weight and size of the two-penny pieces. They were too cumbersome to carry around. As a result, after 722,160 were struck in 1797 and 1798 (all dated 1797), this denomination was never struck again in copper.

Its popularity as a keepsake is attested to by the fact that almost every accumulation of English coins examined by this writer (in the United States) include at least one example of this English cartwheel.

🕸 Did the United States strike fifty-dollar gold pieces?

In 1854 a group of California citizens petitioned Washington through Senator William Gwin for the striking of fifty-dollar gold coins. The Senator prepared a bill to coin a "Union" of $100, a "Half Union" of $50, and a "Quarter Union" of $25. Congress quickly killed the bill. Not only were the majority satisfied with the double eagle ($20), eagle ($10), half eagle ($5), and quarter eagle ($2.50) of gold, but any coin larger than a double eagle was too cumbersome to carry.

Although the issue of gold coins with a value above $20 was quite dead by 1877, two patterns for a fifty-dollar gold piece or quintuple eagle were prepared in 1877. While copper copies were known, the existence of gold copies was not known until 1909. The designs of both were quite similar to the double eagle and they differed only slightly from each other.

The June 6, 1909, issue of the New York *Sun* had the first public announcement of the new find:

PAID $10,000 for $50.—*Highest Price ever given for an American Coin.*—Two $50 gold pieces struck in the United States Mint at Philadelphia in 1877, were sold yesterday· at the Numismatic

Club to William Woodin, a wealthy collector, of New York, for $10,000 each, the highest price ever paid for an American coin. Both were perfect specimens. Fifty-dollar gold pieces were struck from octagonal private dies during the early mining days of California, but so far as is known to numismatists, the two pieces sold this afternoon are the only ones of this denomination ever minted by the Government.

The following year Mr. Woodin returned the pieces to the government and they repose in the Mint Collection at the Smithsonian Institution in Washington today.

ᔰ *Do the coins of Canada offer die varieties such as are found on United States coins?*

Yes, but probably not as many varieties, possibly because the United States coinage began in 1793 while the Canadian decimal coinage started only in 1858.

In the large cents (1858–1920) alone, an interesting collection can be made of coins with re-engraved dates, small and large dates, small and large leaves, and recut letters and numbers.

In the five-cent silver series, the 1874-H comes with a plain and crosslet "4," just as is found on the U.S. half cents of 1804 and other denominations. The five-cent nickel has an interesting variety in 1926, with the "6" in the date close to or far from a maple leaf in the design.

The ten-cent series has many interesting varieties beginning with the wide and narrow "D" of 1870. Most are variations in size or style of numbers in the date, but some relate to the design of the leaves on the reverse.

Besides the waterline varieties on the silver dollars, this series is especially strong in varieties. Well known are the 1947 dollars with either blunt or pointed "7." In 1965 four major varieties of dollars were discovered. These are concerned with large or small beading on the obverse and pointed or blunt "5" in the date on the reverse. Both types of obverses have been found with both types of reverses, making for four die variations.

All of the 1953 issue come with or without shoulder straps showing on the bust of Elizabeth II. This and other types of detail or lack of detail on coins may seem very minor to the non-collector. But to the majority of numismatists, if a new variety is discovered and is believed worthy of inclusion in the next standard catalog, then it is a type to be collected.

Just as the astronomer hopes to discover a new star, part of the fun of collecting is knowing that it is possible that you might be the one to discover a new coin variety.

What are "Roosevelt's Godless Coins"?

President Theodore Roosevelt commissioned the great Irish-American sculptor, Augustus Saint-Gaudens, to execute new designs, beginning in 1907, for the eagle ($10 gold) and double eagle ($20 gold), since the current designs had been in use since 1838 on the eagle and since 1854, the first year of issue, on the double eagle.

Except for the minor coins, all United States coins at this time had on their face "In God We Trust." The new designs of Saint-Gaudens, approved by T.R., left off the motto. Immediately a cry of protest was heard and "Roosevelt's Godless Coins" were subjected to the severest criticism.

Ridicule ran rampant. The Fort Worth *Telegram* reported:

"Two of the Roosevelt 'anti-In God We Trust' coins are in Fort Worth. A Main Street saloon keeper might have had a third, but he declined the medal style coin which is now quoted at $28 market value, because he didn't think it was real money."

President Roosevelt resisted this criticism, publicly stating "We looked into the law and found there was no warrant therein for putting 'In God We Trust' on the coin."

By the following March, the House committee on coinage, weights, and measures reported favorably on a bill requiring all gold and silver coins of the United States to bear the motto "In God We Trust." The reverse dies of both denominations were immediately re-engraved to add the motto. As a result, part of the 1908 coins of each denomination have no motto and part have the motto.

Therefore all the 1907 and some of the 1908 eagles and double eagles are T.R.'s godless coins.

✍ What is the history of the Bahama penny?

Before we proceed with the history, one correction. The coin has a value of a half penny, not one penny.

The group of tiny islands north of Cuba and east of Florida are known as the Bahama Islands. This tropical paradise had a bloody history of warfare between Spaniards, Frenchmen, and Englishmen for some thirty-five years, until 1708, when it was abandoned by all and became a pirate's refuge. Between 1708 and 1717 the pirates had full reign, using the island of New Providence as their central meeting place.

In 1717 British forces again occupied the islands and issued a general pardon to all the outlaws who dwelled there. Then as now, almost the entire population of these many islands was centered on New Providence Island where the capital city of Nassau is located.

In 1806 the British government contracted for the minting of coins by Matthew Boulton, who had set up a modern mint in the Soho district of London. Five hundred pounds of copper were ordered stamped into coins. The design selected had the normal obverse with the bust of George III and the date 1806 or 1807, while the reverse pictured the Great Seal of the royal colony. The seal shows a ship under full sail, with a mountain peak in the background. Two other sailing vessels appear in the distance. Above the ship in bold letters is "BAHAMA," while below is the legend "EXPULSIS PIRATIS RESTITUTA COMMERCIA" (pirates being driven away, commerce is restored).

✒ *What is a Fractional Currency Shield?*

United States fractional currency came into existence in 1862. The Civil War caused people to hoard their hard money (coins) and a shortage of small change developed. To ease the situation paper money with a value of three cents, five cents, ten cents, fifteen cents, twenty-five cents, and fifty cents was issued by the federal government. Almost immediately, counterfeit notes made their appearance.

To help banks determine a genuine from a counterfeit bill the Treasury Department designed a large frame upon which was imprinted a shield with the American eagle on top. Within the shield thirty-nine specimen notes were pasted.

These so-called "shields" were sold to banks as counterfeit detectors, whereby a dubious note could be placed next to a known genuine note on the shield and compared.

After the War Between the States, these unpopular "shinplasters" were redeemed and coin once again flowed freely.

Banks removed these shields from their walls and most ended up being stored in basement space. Some were purchased by collectors and remained intact. Most either deteriorated in damp basements or were sold to collectors who soaked off the notes in order to obtain copies of the rare Grant and Sherman Specimen fifteen-cent notes. These were placed on the shield in anticipation of their being issued, but they never were printed except as proofs or essays, and in very limited numbers.

A Fractional Currency Shield in fine condition is truly a rarity as well as a beauty to behold.

✌ When was "O.K." first used?

This hardly seems like a proper question for a book on numismatics. According to one dictionary, O. K. was "first used in name of Democratic O. K. Club (earliest recorded meeting March 24, 1840, in which O. K. is abbreviation of *Old Kinderhook,* name of the native village of Martin Van Buren, whom the club supported for a 2nd term."

Lyman H. Low, a New York professional numismatist of the late nineteenth and early twentieth century, made a listing of Jackson Hard Time tokens. His No. 56, dated 1840, pictures Van Buren encircled with the words "THE SOBER SECOND THOUGHTS ABOVE°OF THE PEOPLE ARE O. K.°."

Mr. Low had his own version of the origin of the term. Low wrote that Andrew Jackson lacked formal education and that even his biographer, Parton, said that "he was not a well-informed man." He also wrote that Jackson was "associated with the mystical initials OK, popularly believed to have been used by him upon his files of legal documents to show the papers were Orl Korrect (All correct)."

I believe that Mr. Low was just guessing and that in 1840 "O. K." referred to a Van Buren Democrat. In other words, "the people are O. K." meant that the people are good Democrats.

🙠 *What unusual money did Marco Polo mention?*

That adventurous explorer and merchant of the thirteenth century, Marco Polo, told of his travels into Cathay.

He described how the Chinese worked wells of salt brine. They boiled off the water until only the precious salt remained. This salt was then molded into cakes weighing about one half pound each. Each cake was then stamped with a government seal and could be used as currency by a salt-starved people. Polo valued eighty cakes as having the value of one gold saggio.

Undoubtedly the need for salt continued for the next five centuries, because an article in 1879 tells of Chinese hill tribes raiding villages in the valley in order to steal salt. The villagers, in turn, discovering the great need of the hill tribesmen for salt, acquired quantities which they in turn used to bargain for precious metals owned by the hill dwellers.

🙠 *When did the United States mint a fifty-dollar gold piece?*

The only regularly authorized fifty-dollar gold piece (patterns had been made earlier) was struck as one of the coins to honor the opening of the Panama Canal. To commemorate the occasion, the Panama-Pacific International Exposition was held in San Francisco in 1915.

In January, 1915, Congress had approved the minting of 3,000 pieces, half to be round and half to be octagonal. It had been decided to use two shapes because the fifty-dollar pieces privately minted at the time of the California gold rush were known both ways.

Since San Francisco had a branch mint, it was decided that these commemorative pieces, which included a half dollar in silver and a gold dollar and quarter eagle, should be struck there. At the time, this was most unusual, since no branch mint had ever produced a commemorative issue. This presented one problem. No equipment in San Francisco was capable of striking the fifty-dollar coins. This called for the Philadelphia Mint shipping a hydraulic press to the West Coast. This giant press was not generally used to strike coins, but was reserved for the striking of medals, which because of their high relief need great pressure in order to bring out all the details of the design.

It was decided to strike the octagonal pieces first, with full-dress ceremonies. The day chosen for the event was June 15, 1915, and a schedule of dignitaries were lined up to have the honor of striking the first few coins. The superintendent of the San Francisco Mint, T. W. H. Shanahan, clothed in a cutaway jacket, struck the first piece. The Honorable Julius Kahn, the California congressman who introduced the bill authorizing the coinage, pulled the lever that struck the fourth piece. Pieces number 24 and 29 were struck for General George Washington Goethals, the Army engineer who completed the construction of the Canal. He had requested a coin for each of his two sons, and specifically asked for the twenty-fourth and twenty-ninth strikings since those strikings corresponded to each son's age. Coins one through twenty-nine went to dignitaries and thirty through one hundred to various Mint officials and employees.

In spite of the limited number struck, 1,500 of each type, the supply far exceeded the demand. Eight hundred fifty-five of the octagonal and 1,017 of the round pieces were returned to the Mint and remelted. So, with a net coinage of 645 octagonal and 483 round coins, these two gold "slugs" rank among the rarest in the United States series of coins.

At the time of issue either gold piece could be purchased at double face or the whole set, including half, dollar, and two and a half, for $200. Ask a coin dealer today what this set sells for!

Why is the Mexican two-peso silver coin undated?

If you are not familiar with Roman numerals, this coin could be just as difficult to read as one with the date in Chinese or Sanskrit.

The coin was struck in 1921 to honor the hundred years of freedom from Spanish rule. The dates MDCCCXXI (1821) and MCMXXI (1921) are both shown on the coin on the obverse along with the Mexican eagle with the snake in his beak. The reverse pictures a magnificent classic reproduction of the Winged Victory that stands on the top of the Monument of Independence in Mexico City. The Greeks called this winged goddess Nike, while the Romans gave her the name of Victoria. From the latter comes our word "victory."

With the classic Greek or Roman statue as the central design, it was only fitting that the date follow the classic trend. Since many folks today understand Roman numerals, it seemed fitting to use them on the coin. Possibly the idea was suggested by the first United States twenty-dollar gold pieces of 1907, designed by Saint-Gaudens, on which the date was written MCMVII.

This large silver piece is truly beautiful. This is evidenced by the fact that although over one and a quarter million pieces were struck, it is truly scarce and commands a high premium.

Has Lincoln been pictured on any coins other than the one-cent piece?

Abraham Lincoln has been memorialized by thousands of medals struck in his honor. His face has appeared on postage stamps of nations around the world. But aside from the one-cent piece only one other United States coin has shown his strong, granitelike features. This is the commemorative half dollar of 1918 issued to honor the one-hundredth anniversary of the admittance of Illinois into the Union.

As we have seen, the first United States commemorative coins were the Columbian half dollars of 1892 (and 1893), followed by the Isabella quarter dollar of 1893 and seven years later by the Lafayette dollar. All of these coins were silver, but the pattern had not been established as to which denomination was best suited for future commemorative issues.

In 1903 a gold dollar was selected as the appropriate coin for a commemorative piece when the Louisiana Purchase Centennial was to be celebrated. Likewise in 1904 and 1905 the gold dollar was used to honor the Lewis and Clark Centennial Exposition in Portland, Oregon.

For the Panama Pacific Exposition of 1915 a new concept was initiated, with the coining of a set made up of a silver half dollar, a gold dollar, a quarter eagle, and two fifty-dollar gold "slugs."

With the 1918 Illinois Centennial the pattern was re-established to use the half dollar when authorizing a new commemorative coin. This concept has been followed with only two exceptions. These were the Grant Memorial gold dollar of 1922 and the Sesquicentennial quarter eagle of 1926, both of which also had half dollars simultaneously struck.

This Illinois Centennial piece shows the bust of a beardless Lincoln. One hundred thousand coins were authorized and struck, and none were remelted. The majority were sold through the "County Centennial Committees of the State," at a price of $1 each. The fifty-cent profit was retained by the local committee to defray costs of the local celebration of the event. If not needed for this purpose, the committee used the funds for some war relief, since World War I was still in progress.

The monetary appreciation of this coin has not been spectacular, but it has been steady. In 1940 it still catalogued for $1, in 1947 for $4, in 1957 for $10, and by 1966 it had risen to $27.50, Considering that the original distribution was to local citizens, many of whom probably used the coin as a pocket piece, the coin can still be said to be reasonably priced at $27.50.

♨ *Is it true that the word "Dixie" had a numismatic beginning?*

Yes, and the beginning was in New Orleans in the 1830's. At a time when all the currency in the United States were state bank notes, some good, some not so good, and most of them worthless, the notes of the Citizens' Bank of Louisiana, located in New Orleans, were always accepted at par.

Because New Orleans was a bilingual city, with as much French spoken as English, the notes stated their value in both languages. The note that circulated the most was the ten-dollar denomination. On its face appeared not only "TEN," but the French "DIX." The notes came to be called "dixes" and New Orleans became known as the home of the dixes.

According to W. A. Philpott, Jr., writing in *The Numismatist* in 1952, southerners became enamored with the name in 1860. It seems that in the previous year a composer by the name of Dan D. Emmett wrote a song for a minstrel troupe known as Bryant's Minstrels. This group sang a new song by Mr. Emmett in New York City, which began, "I wish I wuz in de land of the dixes." Of course this last word soon became corrupted to "dixie." When the song reached New Orleans the following year, it was an immediate success and the Southland had a new nickname.

So when you think of Dixie Land, think not only of New Orleans, and pralines, and corn pone, and southern fried chicken, but also think of a colorful bank note of the Citizen's Bank of Louisiana.

✒   *What are the Althing coins?*

Iceland was first established as an independent nation in A.D. 874. By 930, a governing body known as the Althing (The Assembly of All) was functioning. This lawmaking body is considered to have the longest uninterrupted history of any legislative group in recorded history.

SILVER 10 KRONUR

To celebrate its one-thousandth anniversary, Iceland issued three beautiful medal-like coins, a ten-Kronur piece in silver, a five-Kronur piece in nickel, and a two-Kronur piece in bronze. This three-piece set was a limited issue and is quite rare.

There is an unresolved argument among numismatists as to whether these "Althing coins" are truly coins or are merely commemorative medals. Richard S. Yeoman's *A Catalog of Modern World Coins* does not include this set of coins (or medals).

John S. Davenport's *European Crowns and Talers Since 1800* lists both the ten-Kronur and five-Kronur pieces.

Since each piece has the denomination indicated on the edge, it is this writer's contention that they truly are coins, even though, like many rare commemorative issues, they were never circulated as such.

🎔 What is a Levant taler?

The taler of Maria Theresa, date 1780, is known as the Levant taler. It is still being struck and circulated today. It can truly be said to be the only "trade dollar" still in use in a world where paper money and bank credit are generally accepted.

The coin shows a bust of Maria Theresa (1717–1780) on the obverse and a crowned imperial eagle on the reverse. The wording on the coin translates to: "Maria Theresa, By the Grace of God, Empress of the Holy Roman Empire, Queen of Hungary and Bohemia, Archduchess of Austria, Duchess of Burgundy and Countess of Tyrol."

Although the coin was dated 1780, historians state that it was not struck until 1783, at the Vienna Mint. For some unexplainable reason it came to be accepted as a trade coin in Ethiopia, Aden, Arabia, Bahrein, Borneo, Eritrea, Syria, and other parts of the Middle East. Because of its acceptance along the eastern shores of the Mediterranean Sea, known as the Levant, it became known as the Levant taler.

Its acceptance in so many countries that traded with Europe, while other European coins were refused, led the London, Rome, and Brussels mints to strike identical coins. Attempts to introduce other coins, even similar in appearance, met with failure. Italy struck a tallero for Eritrea in 1918, even picturing a woman looking like Maria Theresa, but it was not accepted. Menelik II, in his own country, Ethiopia, struck a silver tallero, which his own subjects refused to accept while willingly accepting the Levant taler.

It seems that the illiterate natives, in whatever country, recognized the design and details of the Maria Theresa coin, and always finding that it bought what they wanted in trade, would not take a chance on a substitute.

Is the use of the eagle as a device on a coin of recent origin?

On the contrary, early Roman coins used the eagle as a symbol of courage.

The eagle is a member of the falcon family and falconry was a sport of the ancient Persians, Egyptians, and Chinese. It was believed to have spread from Asia to Europe. Being a sport of kings, the falcon or eagle became identified with royalty as well as with courage.

The Romans invaded and conquered England, introducing the eagle to the Britons. Henry II, King of England (1154–1189), used it for his emblem and thereafter it became a part of British heraldry. Since most of the early colonists who settled in America came from England, this symbol crossed the Atlantic with them. Their descendants chose the eagle as the national bird of the new nation.

Certain stylized designs of the eagle on modern Mexican coins are quite similar to the eagle that appeared about A.D. 250 on Syrian tetradrachms struck at Antioch. The badge of Ptolemy I (323–285 B.C.) was an eagle on a thunderbolt (bolt of lightning).

The U.S. ten-dollar gold pieces of 1907–1933 picture an eagle in an almost identical position, suggesting that the designer, Augustus Saint-Gaudens, was inspired by this beautiful coin of ancient Egypt.

We consider the Teutonic Knights as the most warlike of the Europeans. Their descendants in Germany and Austria (Holy Roman Empire) used the eagle freely on their heraldric devices and upon their coinage.

✒ *Did you know that in 1823 a medal for literary achievement was presented to an American Indian?*

At a time when Indians were being presented Peace Medals in an attempt to win their friendship, a medal for literary merit was probably unique.

The Indian was a Cherokee chief by the name of Sequoyah. His English name was George Gist (or Guess). For his contribution in developing an eighty-five-character alphabet and preparing a grammar of the Cherokee language, the United States presented him with a medal in the name of his people.

For the ceremony Chief Sequoyah and the important members of the Cherokee Nation came to Washington. Copies of the medal were also presented to the dignitaries, Indian and American, who attended this ceremony. The medal was similar on both sides, showing crossed Indian tobacco pipes, symbolizing Indian-American friendship, and the words "Presented to George Gist, by the General Council of the Cherokee Nation, for his ingenuity in the invention of the Cherokee alphabet." On one side the words were in English, while on the other side they were written out in the new Cherokee characters that Sequoyah had invented.

This Cherokee chief might possibly be forgotten today except for the fact that when the giant redwood trees of California were given a botanical name, the name chosen was *Sequoia gigantea*, in honor of a great American Indian.

How many Confederate half dollars were struck?

The first indication that the collecting public had that the Confederate States of America struck a half dollar was in an article in the *American Journal of Numismatics* of April, 1879. The story referred to a letter from a B. F. Taylor, M.D., of New Orleans, who claimed to own one. He stated that four had been struck. When a Philadelphia numismatist by the name of Mason asked to see Dr. Taylor's coin, he was sent a rubbing. From this rubbing the world was first apprised of its design.

The obverse was the "Seated Liberty" design common to all United States silver coins of the period and was dated 1861. The reverse was described as "a Liberty cap above the American shield, the Union of the latter containing seven stars, representing the seven seceding States, the whole being surrounded with a wreath of sugar cane and cotton in bloom and the legal 'Confederate States of America' above and 'Half Dol.' below."

In July, 1879, the *American Journal of Numismatics* reported that Dr. Taylor informed them that one was presented to Professor Riddell of the University of Louisiana, one to Dr. Ames of New Orleans, one was sent to the government, and the last kept by himself.

Three years later, an interesting letter was written to the *New Orleans Picayune:*

No. 26 St. Charles Street
New Orleans, April 24, 1882

Editor Picayune:
The story copied in your paper from the Augusta *News* of the 14th, purporting to be made by A. H. Peterson, of Denver,

to the effect that "one Dr. B. F. Taylor, Chief Coiner of the Mint in 1861, tried to strike off a large number of coins after the war solely to sell to numismatists at high prices" is wholly untrue. Three years since, the facts and history, with the proof thereof, were published in the "Picayune" of the four Confederate coins made in 1861. About the time above mentioned I sold the coin then in my possession through Messrs. Mason & Co., numismatists, of Philadelphia, to Mr. Scott, of New York, with the die. That gentleman recently sold, as reported in THE NEW YORK TIMES, the same coin at public auction for the sum of $870. It is true that Mr. Peterson did, in 1861, make the die, but neither he nor any one person ever had it in their possession, nor were there any coins "attempted" to be made subsequently, but the coin and die were delivered to the Messrs. Mason & Co., as they will testify. After diligent inquiry during the past three years, I have been unable to locate but one of the other four pieces, and that one is now in this city. The foregoing facts are given in justice to the public and to all parties concerned, but more particularly to the numismatist who paid his $870 for the coin.

Very respectfully,
B. F. TAYLOR, M.D.

The Mr. Scott referred to was J. W. Scott of Scott & Company, later Scott Stamp & Coin Company, who purchased some five hundred U.S. half dollars of 1861, shaved the backs smooth and restruck them with the Confederate reverse. Today even these restrikes are considered rare coins.

 Why do some Canadian coins have a mintmark?

Mintmarks are used only on the coins of a country that operates more than one mint. While the United States has at various times had mints at Philadelphia, Denver, San Francisco, New Orleans, Carson City, Charlotte, and Dahlonega, Canada has only one mint, located at Ottawa. She, therefore, has no need of a mintmark on her coins and uses none.

But prior to the establishing of the Royal Canadian Mint at Ottawa in 1908, all her coins were struck in England. Most were made at the Tower Mint in London. These have no mintmark. But at certain times the mint in London found it necessary to contract out the manufacturing of coins. When this happened, Heaton's Mint in Birmingham took the overflow. Those coins struck in Birmingham were identified with the mintmark "H."

No Canadian coins dated after 1907 have a mintmark, since from 1908 all were made in Canada. But prior to 1908, in certain years, coins were struck both at the Tower Mint and at Heaton's Mint. This gives the collector two varieties of certain Canadian coins. The following is a listing of coins that appear identical except that one will have no mintmark and the other will have an "H" on the reverse in the six o'clock position: One cents of 1900 and 1907; five cents of 1902 and 1903; ten cents of 1902 and 1903; twenty-five cents of 1902; fifty cents of 1871.

☙ How is it possible to tell a small California gold coin from a token?

Private California gold coins with a value of twenty-five cents, fifty cents, and one dollar were minted from 1852 to 1882. They were struck to fill a need for small change. In 1850 the California legislature passed a law providing for severe penalties against any being produced by "unauthorized persons." This would imply that there were persons authorized and that most of the known pieces had at least state sanction.

The genuine pieces can be recognized because the amount was stated on the reverse, either by "C," "Cents," "Dol," or "Dollar." They were either round or octagonal. Genuine pieces come both dated from 1852 to 1881 and also undated.

The tokens may be similar in appearance to the coins, even bear an early date, but will not state the amount in dollars or

215

cents. Most are of fairly recent origin, with a great many struck for sale at the Panama-Pacific Exposition, held in 1915 at San Francisco. In 1932, B. Max Mehl, largest retail coin dealer in the country at that time, was offering a set of round and octagonal quarter-dollar size and half-dollar size for $3. Although he referred to them as "California Gold Pieces," he did not call them coins, merely "keepsakes."

The tokens as well as the coins are usually of full weight. For this reason, many of the genuine pieces were remelted years ago because in their desire to give value received, these early coiners often had as much as 10 per cent excess gold in a coin, making it profitable to remelt into bullion. Therefore, even though made in large quantities, they are extremely scarce today.

 Does England have an organization comparable to The American Numismatic Association?

Yes, but it is not as old as its American counterpart. It was founded in 1903, whereas The American Numismatic Association was founded in 1891. The announcement of its formation appeared in *Spink's Numismatic Circular* of September, 1903, and ran as follows:

A thousand years ago the British Coinage was, as it is today, the popular standard of currency for the civilized world, yet it has often been remarked that British numismatists encourage the study and elucidation of the money of any other country in preference to that of their own. That there is much truth in the charge cannot be denied, for there is no Society, Journal, Magazine or Publication which has as its primary object the advancement of the study of the Coinage of the English-speaking race. Even the Numismatic Society of London devotes but a small proportion of its work and influence to this objective, and for the last twenty-years not one third of the pages of its Journal—The

Numismatic Chronicle—has been devoted to anything directly or indirectly connected with the monetary system of our coinage, it is scarcely to be expected that any other nation will do it for her, and yet that is what she is doing for all others but herself.

The British Numismatic Society has been formed to meet this requirement, and its object is the encouragement of the historical study of the coins, medals and tokens of the English-speaking race throughout the globe. Included in the subjects to be considered are the various series of ancient Britons, Romano-Britons, Anglo-Saxons, Normans, English, Welsh, Scots, Irish and Angelo-Gauls, also those of the Colonies and Dominions comprised in the British Empire, and the United States of America—so closely connected with our history in the past, and still allied to us by ties of language and descent.

The article then mentioned London as the meeting place and the publication of an annual to be called *The British Numismatic Journal*. There followed a list of some forty gentlemen who indicated their intention of joining. This impressive list was headed by His Grace The Duke of Bedford and The Right Honorable The Earl of Powis. By December, 1903, they reported that "upwards of 270" distinguished citizens had already joined. In 1905 they proudly reported that honorary memberships had been accepted by Queen Alexandra (wife of Edward VII), the Princess of Wales, the King of Spain, the Queen of Italy, the King of Greece, the King of Denmark, and many of lesser rank.

There is an older and more sedate organization known as The Royal Numismatic Society, which would compare to the American Numismatic Society, which was founded in New York City in 1858. Both organizations are more concerned with numismatics on a worldwide basis than on a national basis.

✍ Why are there different color seals on U.S. currency?

In all the years of the large-size bills, from 1863 to 1929, there was no planned and accepted use of color in the Treasury Department seal that appears on each piece of United States paper money. United States Notes were printed with red or brown seals, Silver Certificates with red, brown, or blue seals, National Bank Notes with red, brown, or blue seals, and Federal Reserve Notes with either blue or red seals.

With the introduction, in 1929, of the small-size notes, uniformity was prescribed, not only to the design on notes but as to the color of the seal. Today we can glance at a note and recognize the type merely by noting the color of the seal. All United States Notes bear a red seal, Silver Certificates a blue seal, Federal Reserve Notes a green seal, and the very seldom seen National Currency (National Bank or Federal Reserve Bank) Notes a brown seal.

But do not be disturbed as to which type of currency you have in your pocketbook. The purchasing power of one is identical to that with another color seal.

✍ Did you know that only a century ago Indian Peace Medals were still being presented?

The October, 1866, issue of the *American Journal of Numismatics and Bulletin of the American Numismatic and Archaeological Society* (quite a title!) carried the story of the presentation of a silver medal and a certificate of merit to a Blackfeet Indian Chief. The contents of the certificate tell the story:

To HOO-KE-OP, THE CHIEF:

I am informed by the two commissioners sent by me last spring to treat with the Indians on the Upper Missouri River country, of the friendly act of Hoo-Ke-Op, the chief, a member of the Blackfeet tribe of Indians, in rescuing from captivity a white woman named Fanny Kelly in 1864. I thank Hoo-Ke-Op, the chief, for his noble conduct in this matter, and as a memento of my friendship for him so long as he remains friendly with the white man I direct that a silver medal be given to him, that all my red children and all my white children when they look upon it may know that the Great Father at Washington is very much pleased with him. I also direct that one hundred silver dollars be given to Hoo-Ke-Op, the chief, and I write my name on this paper to be given to him that he may know that the silver medal and the silver dollars are sent to him from Washington.

ANDREW JOHNSON
President of the United States

O. A. Browning, Secretary of the Interior
D. N. Cooley, Commissioner of Indian Affairs

The story humorously concludes with: "The medal weighs about half a pound, and will certainly add considerably to the weight of Hoo-Ke-Op's dignity."

 Why do certain Mexican dollars show the name of one king and the picture of another?

In the sixteenth, seventeenth, and eighteenth centuries, when Mexico was merely a colony of Spain, the Mexican dollar was the eight-real coin (piece of eight). From 1772 these large silver pieces bore the bust of the Spanish ruler.

When Charles III died in December, 1788, news of his death did not reach Mexico until March, 1789. Since it took considerable time to prepare new dies the colonial government authorized that an extra "I" be cut into the existing dies, thus changing the wording from "Carolus III" to "Carolus IIII." Later other dies were altered to read "Carolus IV."

Thus coins of Charles IV exist that bear his father's picture instead of his own. And more than that, Charles IV was a fine-looking man, while his father was extremely homely.

By 1791 proper dies with the handsome bust of Charles IV had arrived from Spain, so for only two years did the dollars of Mexico incorrectly picture her ruler.

❧ What is a "Sprinkle dollar"?

Back in the 1830's a Kentuckian by the name of Josiah Sprinkle gained some notoriety when arrested by the federal government for manufacturing silver dollars of his own making. These "Sprinkle dollars" were well-nigh forgotten until a story appeared in the Wheeling (W. Va.) *Register* in 1895 and was passed on to numismatists by the *American Journal of Numismatics* in its issue of January, 1896. We quote from the *Register:*

Not long ago a man living in Grayson, Carter County, Ky., received in payment for a horse sold to an old farmer living near the Lewis County line, $46, among which were three of the famous Sprinkle Dollars of the early '30s. It has been more than twenty years since any of these particular coins have been found in that section, and the production of these will recall a story character who flourished in the early part of the century, Josiah Sprinkle, who lived in one of the roughest sections of Lewis County. One day he appeared in Washington, the county seat, with a buckskin pouch full of silver dollars of his own make. In every respect they appeared the equal of the national coin. The weight was more, and the quality and ring of the metal were all that could be asked.

He spent them freely, and they were taken upon the assurance of Sprinkle that there was nothing wrong with them beyond the fact that he, and not the United States mint, had coined them. When asked where he got the silver, he laughed and shook his head.

The inscriptions on the coins were crudely outlined, and no attempt was made at imitation of the legal coin. Unevenly outlined on one side was an owl, while a six-cornered star showed with more accuracy upon the other. The coins were considerably larger than the regulation article, and thicker as well. Upon various occasions Sprinkle afterward visited town, and spent more and more freely. At one time he volunteered the fact that he had a silver mine in the hills, but no one ever succeeded in inducing the old man to reveal his secret.

Finally, the Government agents came to investigate. Sprinkle was arrested and brought into court, but the dollars were proved to be pure silver, without alloy, worth, in fact, a trifle more than a dollar each, and he was acquitted. After the exciting trial he reached down in a cavernous pocket and drew out a bag of fifty of the coins and promptly paid his attorney in the presence of the astonished officials. Sprinkle was never afterward bothered, and continued until his death to make the dollars, how and where no one ever knew.

Could some still exist in the Kentucky hills, near the Ohio–West Virginia border?

🕮 *What is a "Beard Tax token"?*

Czar Peter I (1682–1725) of Russia, after a visit to western Europe, attempted to westernize his country through a series of reforms, beginning in about 1699. One order was that the Russian men should shave off their beards.

This arbitrary order on the part of the Czar was resented by most Russians, who took great pride in their beards. Some were religious fanatics who believed it irreligious to shave. Others felt that the Czar only issued the order because he himself did not have the ability to grow a manly beard.

Male members of his court were required to remove their beards, as well as anyone seeking an audience with him. As to the rest of his subjects, they resisted. His next move was to  place an annual tax on beards, the amount being from thirty to one hundred rubles, depending on the individual's social and economic position.

Evidence of payment of the tax was a receipt in the form of a round token that pictured a mustache and beard and the words in Russian translating to "BEARD MONEY" on one side, and the date with a two-headed Russian eagle on the reverse. Specimens are known dated 1699 and 1705. A later token, dated 1724 or 1725, is also known. It is rectangular in shape, uniface, with inscriptions that read in Russian, "A tax for the beard" and "The beard is an unnecessary burden."

It is stated that the Czar derived a large revenue from this source until the tax was rescinded at the time of his death in 1725.

✍ Why were early United States notes privately printed?

Before the Civil War the only paper money in the United States was that of state-chartered banks and other private corporations. In 1861 Congress authorized demand notes, our first "greenbacks." Since the government had no facilities to print them, contracts were let to bank-note companies.

The need for a government-owned and -controlled printing department was immediately apparent and in November, 1862, a department was set up for the purpose of engraving plates. Initially this branch of the Treasury Department was called the National Currency Bureau.

Although in 1864 a request was made to the Secretary of the

Treasury that an "Engraving and Printing Bureau" be established, congressional approval along with an adequate appropriation was not received until August 15, 1876. As a result, by October 1, 1877, all government securities finally were engraved and printed by this new bureau, now known as the Bureau of Engraving and Printing.

The notes that were privately printed before 1877 all had the name of the manufacturer on either the front or back. The Demand Notes of 1861 were all printed by the American Bank Note Co. The Series of 1862 Legal Tender one- and two-dollar notes were printed by the National Bank Note Co. The Series of 1869 Legal Tender five-, ten-, and twenty dollar notes were the first engraved by the new Bureau. After private firms were no longer used, the small block used to designate the manufacturer was dropped, even that of the Bureau, which had read "Bureau, Engraving & Printing."

What is a Treasure Trove?

This is an English term that defines any newly discovered gold or silver, in whatever form, which was intentionally concealed and whose ownership cannot be determined. Under British law Treasure Trove belongs to the Crown.

In ancient times the rulers of England added this precious metal, whether in the form of coins, art objects, or bullion, to their personal fortune. In this modern day the finder is reimbursed for the actual value of the find or allowed to keep it. This latter is allowed only if the British Museum determines that there is nothing that is needed to improve the collection in its custody, or needed by other museums. Either way, the finder is adequately compensated.

When a treasure is first uncovered, the finder is required to report the fact to the county Coroner. A court of inquest, called a Coroner's Court, is convened. This court makes the determination as to whether the items found are Treasure Trove.

The court has no problem in determining the metallic content of the treasure. But there is always the question as to whether the precious metal was intentionally concealed.

An excellent example of the problem was the Sutton Hoo treasure, discovered in Suffolk in 1939. There was unearthed a Viking galley of about the seventh century A.D., which was the tomb of a Norseman. With him was a treasure in gold and silver in the form of armor, ornaments, and coins. Since this was not intentionally concealed, the Coroner's Court decided that it was not Treasure Trove. Only because the owner of the land where the grave was found, a Mrs. Pretty, generously gave the treasure to the British Museum is this great find intact. Mrs. Pretty could have melted down the gold and silver for her own use had she been so inclined.

 When was the first United States silver dollar made?

If we do not take the words "United States" too literally, and are willing to include that period in American history when the formal name was United Colonies, then certainly the Continental Currency dollar of 1776 was the first silver dollar struck.

Little is known of the origin of the Continental dollar. Some say that it was probably struck in Birmingham, England, where many of the coins of colonial America were minted. The pieces in

silver are exceedingly rare. Copies in brass are also rare, while the common pewter varieties today are still considered scarce.

On the obverse is a chain of thirteen rings. Each ring bears the name of one of the thirteen original states. Within the ring are the words "American Congress" and "We Are One." On the reverse is "Continental Currency 1776" forming a circle. Within the circle is a sundial and below it the words "Mind Your Business."

Students of numismatics generally agree that this piece was struck as a pattern coin, to suggest a possible design for the future coinage. This belief has much merit since the "Fugio" cents of 1787 followed the obverse and reverse designs of this dollar quite closely. These designs were not original with the Continental dollar. They also appeared on paper currency of the Continental Congress dated February 17, 1776.

Two varieties are known in silver, one with currency spelled "CURENCY" and the other with the word properly spelled. On some of the latter type also appears the statement "EG FECIT" (EG made it). In almost two centuries no one has been able to discover the identity of EG. Either he was a better speller than the die sinker who made the one-"R" variety, or possibly EG made both types, with someone correcting his poor spelling.

How do you determine the date of a Moroccan coin?

Most countries that reckon according to the Mohammedan calendar do not number as we do. If such is the case you will have to first learn the Arabic-Turkish equivalents to Arabic numerals. Morocco is one of the few countries using our type numerals, but dating according to the Mohammedan era.

The formula to convert is relatively simple. Add 622 to 97 per cent of the date. For example, suppose we translate 1370 (written A.H. 1370) to our dating system: $1370 \times .97 = 1328.90$ and then $1329 + 622 = 1951$. The reason for this formula is quite logical. The Mohammedan calendar is dated from A.D. 622, the year the Prophet fled from Mecca. And the Mohammedans use a lunar year of 354 days instead of a solar year of 365.25 days, or about 3 per cent fewer days in a year according to their calendar.

Many uninformed collectors mistakenly get excited when they find a coin dated 1347, failing to realize it is an issue of 1929 and not a three-hundred-year-old piece. Remember too, most coins were not dated prior to the sixteenth century.

✇ What is a Lesher dollar?

Using the word "dollar" is improper when referring to "Leshers," although it must be admitted that most people do refer to them that way. Properly they should be called "Joseph Lesher referendum souvenir pieces."

According to Farran Zerbe, who wrote about "The Lesher or Referendum Pieces" in *Mehl's Numismatic Monthly* in May, 1919, Joseph Lesher was born near Toledo about 1840, moved to Colorado as a young man, returned to Toledo after "some years," engaged in the livery business and later in farming. About 1890 he and his wife returned to Colorado, settling in the town of Victor, a short distance from Colorado Springs. Here he engaged in mining and real estate.

Lesher conceived the idea for a money substitute to bring more silver into circulation. By designing an octagonal piece he made sure that it could not possibly be considered a counterfeit of

United States money. The first issue, dated 1900, all contained one ounce of silver. He believed silver to be worth $1.25 an ounce although it only sold for 65¢.

The first type, consecutively numbered from 1 to 100 read: "JOS LESHERS REFERENDUM SOUVENIR ONE OZ. OF COIN SILVER PRICE $1.25 MFGD VICTOR COLO. 1900" on its face, and "A COMMODITY WILL GIVE IN EXCHANGE CURRENCY COIN OR MERCHANDISE AT FACE VALUE NO____" on the reverse. He called the pieces "referendum" coins because (quoting Zerbe) "they are to be referred to the people for acceptance or rejection." It was Lesher's idea that local merchants would buy the pieces from him for $1 and be willing to give $1.25 in merchandise for each one tendered.

For the first merchant who agreed to use the coins he changed the reverse to read: "A COMMODITY WILL GIVE IN EXCHANGE MERCHANDISE AT A. B. BUMSTEAD." No other merchant tried these "coins" in 1900.

The following year Lesher reduced the size and value of his pieces. The weight was made 412.5 grains, equal to the United States silver dollar and the value was made $1. The wording was also changed. The face now read: "IN THE PEOPLE WE TRUST. A COMMODITY. WILL GIVE IN EXCHANGE MERCHANDISE AT (space for name and city of merchant)." The back was changed to read: "JOS LESHERS REFERENDUM SILVER SOUVENIR MEDAL." Pieces of this type are known for J. M. Slusher of Cripple Creek, Sam Cohen of Victor, D. W. Klein & Co. of Pueblo, Geo. Mullen of Victor, Boyd Park of Denver, W. L. Alexander of Salida, Goodspeeds & Co. of Colorado Springs, J. E. Nelson & Co. of Holorege (Nebr.), W. F. White Merc. Co. of Grand Jct. and H. Stein (no city given). Zerbe reports others, but none are extant.

In all, some three thousand pieces were struck of these most unusual money substitutes. Today, even the commonest varieties, in very fine condition, sell for about $150 each. Men like Joseph Lesher make the study of numismatics truly fascinating.

✄ὄ What is Mexican soap money?

Farran Zerbe, the enterprising numismatist whose collection forms the foundation stones upon which was built the fine Money Museum of the Chase Manhattan Bank, wrote in 1933 about his discovery of the fact that soap was used as money in Mexico.

He made his discovery when reading a book called *Narrative of the Texan Santa Fe Expedition* which was published by Harpers, New York, in 1844. The author, George Wilkin Kendall, told of his experiences in Mexico between May, 1841 and May, 1842.

Entering an unfriendly country where all "gringos" had been held suspect ever since the Texas Revolution, which began in 1836, he and his fellow travelers were arrested as enemy aliens. While prisoners of the Mexicans, he and a friend were given parole to wander about the town where they were held captive. His friend sought to purchase some fresh fruit from a vendor and offered to pay with a U.S. dollar. Since the seller did not have sufficient change, a soldier who was guarding them was asked to obtain change. He returned with sixty-four bars of soap.

It seems that the soap, properly stamped with the name of the town, was legal tender for about a cent and a half a bar. The town government actually authorized certain citizens to manufacture the soap and impress the name of the town upon each bar. Some towns had reciprocal agreements with other towns concerning the legal status of the bars of soap. Then again other communities refused to accept the soap as money.

Many of the bars were partially used, but the author explained that as long as the name of the town was visible, the soap was still worth one and a half cents to the holder.

Why were there no silver dollars struck from 1804 to 1840?

French and Spanish coins were legal tender in the United States during this period. These foreign coins had a lower metallic content than their American counterparts. This allowed speculators to profit by exporting large quantities of United States silver dollars previously purchased with foreign coins. These were in turn sold in Europe as bullion, and the speculators received a greater amount in foreign coins than they had originally paid. Since the end result was that no silver dollars got into circulation, President Jefferson ordered his Secretary of State to send the following directive to the Director of the Mint:

Department of State May 1, 1806

Sir: In consequence of a representation from the director of the Bank of the United States that considerable purchases have been made of silver dollars coined at the mint for the purpose of exporting them, and as it is probable that further purchase and exportation will be made, the President directs that all the silver to be coined at the mint shall be of small denominations, so that the value of the largest pieces shall not exceed half a dollar.

James Madison

Mint records indicate that 19,570 dollars were struck in 1804 and 321 in 1805, but all authorities agree that this is incorrect and that none were struck either year. And not until 1836 was it felt that a need for silver dollars existed.

Patterns for a proposed new silver dollar appeared in 1836, 1838, and 1839. In 1840 a modified design of the obverse of the patterns was used and continued until the silver dollars were again discontinued in 1873. But this time only four years elapsed before the series was continued.

What are "Bingles"?

At the height of the depression, in 1935, the United States government established a program to relocate farmers of droughtstricken areas of the Continental United States in the Matanuska Valley of Alaska. This rich farm land was purchased by the Alaska Rural Rehabilitation Corporation, a government agency. The agency in turn "sold" parcels to the settlers, but retained title until the newly settled pioneers could pay for them out of profits derived from the sale of surplus products.

These farmer colonists were brought to Alaska at government expense and were guaranteed a subsistance allowance until they could support themselves on the land. Initially, in March, 1936, they received tokens for this purpose, issued by the Alaska Rural Rehabilitation Corporation. They were struck in aluminum for one, five, ten, twenty-five and fifty cents, and one dollar, and in brass for five and ten dollars. Both sides showed similar designs, with the amount expressed in numerals in the center, while around the edge were the words "GOOD FOR (Amount) IN TRADE ARRC."

These tokens were called "Bingles" by the natives, and were accepted at face value at the local trading post in Palmer established by the ARRC to supply all the necessities of life until the farmers became self-sufficient. This money substitute in the form of tokens was distastful to the settlers. As a result, the Alaska Rural Rehabilitation Corporation recalled them in January, 1937, replacing them with United States coin and currency, and advising the settlers that they would not be redeemed after December 31, 1938. Today the eight-piece set is rare, and sells for more than $200.

Over the years notes of the Confederate States of America have become widely dispersed. More collectors have turned to this field of collecting, especially since the days of various Civil War centennial celebrations, which introduced these notes to a new generation.

Because of these factors, along with the introduction of an excellent catalog on Confederate notes by Grover and Clarence Criswell, all of the notes have increased in price. Certain notes have always commanded a large premium, especially the first series issued in Montgomery, Alabama, in 1861. But the more common types that formerly sold by the pound now bring a dollar or more apiece.

A word of warning—many counterfeit notes exist.

 When was a murder commemorated on a coin?

Every boy and girl has read of the life of Julius Caesar, which ended with his assassination in the Roman Senate by his two friends, Brutus and Cassius. This event took place on March 15 (the Ides of March), in the year 44 B.C.

But what most people do not
know is that in the following
year Cestianus, a soldier under
Brutus, had denarii (silver pennies) struck to commemorate the
event. To their followers, Brutus
and Cassius were not murderers, but saviors.

The face of the coin shows the bust of Brutus. The reverse
shows a Liberty Cap or pileus in the center. On each side are
daggers. And below these objects are the words "EID MAR."

This coin ranks as one of the rarities of the Roman series. And
beware—many counterfeits exist.

How many of the rare 1804 silver dollars are there?

It is doubtful if the whole story has been told or ever
will be told. But the most authoritative book on the subject is *The
Fantastic 1804 Dollar*, by Eric P. Newman and Kenneth E.
Bressett, with Walter H. Breen and Lynn Glaser as Associates in
Research, published by Whitman Publishing Company. They list
fifteen pieces, giving their pedigree and history as known.

Nos. 1 and 2 are in the U.S. Mint Collection at the Smithsonian
Institution. No. 3 is the Stickney Specimen now owned by Louis
Eliasberg of Baltimore. No. 4 is the Cohen Specimen now owned
by the Lammot Du Pont family. No. 5 is the Mickley Specimen

now owned by the Massachusetts Historical Society in Boston. No. 6 is the Parmalee Specimen owned by the City of Omaha. No. 7 is the Dexter Specimen now owned by Harold Bareford. No. 8 is the Watters Specimen now owned by the C. F. Childs family. No. 9 is the Siam Specimen, first seen in 1962, with ownership undisclosed. No. 10 is the Berg Specimen owned by Johns Hopkins University. No. 11 is the Adams Specimen now owned by Amon Carter of Fort Worth. No. 12 is the Davis Specimen now owned by Samuel Wolfson of Jacksonville, Florida. No. 13 is the Linderman Specimen also owned by the Lammot Du Pont family. No. 14 is the Rosenthal Specimen owned by the Chase Manhattan Bank. No. 15 is the Idler Specimen, which was sold in 1961 to an undisclosed purchaser.

All of the 1804 silver dollars are considered to be restrikes, that is, not minted in the year which date they bear. They were first mentioned in a publication in 1842. Each one could tell a story.

Some, such as the No. 9, the Siam Specimen, were struck as gifts from the United States to rulers of other nations. This No. 9 was discovered in 1962 in a proof set of 1834 coins, boxed in a yellow leather case that bore the American eagle on the cover. The design of this case is similar to one ordered in 1834 for the King of Siam. Others showed up after 1842 and were of two types. The first type were believed struck in 1834 or 1835. The second type were believed coined in 1858.

Except for the few that may have been struck for presentation to a foreign dignitary, probably the remainder were the result of chicanery at the Mint. If your appetite is whetted, read the book mentioned in the first paragraph. It might even stimulate you to start your own research project on the subject.

✒ *Is there a list of Lafayette Medals?*

The Marquis de Lafayette is the most revered of the foreigners who helped America achieve her independence. He is equally as well loved in his native land. Because of this, literally hundreds of medals have been struck in his honor.

The most complete listing in the English language was prepared by Melvin and George Fuld for presentation at the 1957 American Numismatic Association convention and then published in the September, 1957, issue of *The Numismatist*. A further supplement with additional listings appeared in the December, 1958, issue of the same publication.

The question recalls one medal, mentioned in an 1876 publication that this writer has yet to see described or pictured. It was a gold medal presented to Lafayette by the Seventh Regiment of the New York National Guard. It was described thus:

Its front was embellished with emblems of the friendship existing between France and the United States surrounding raised medallions of Lafayette and Washington. On the reverse was the following inscription:
"THE NATIONAL GUARD, TWENTY-SEVENTH REGIMENT, N.Y.S. ARTILLERY, TO LAFAYETTE, CENTENNIAL ANNIVERSARY OF THE BIRTHDAY OF WASHINGTON, NEW YORK, FEBRUARY 22, 1832."

After being exhibited to the members of the Regiment who had purchased the gold with their own funds, the medal was forwarded to James Fenimore Cooper, the American Consul at Lyons, who made the formal presentation to General Lafayette.

Let us hope that this medal is still intact and can be someday viewed by all who love freedom.

What is a Janauschek taler?

Franziska Magdalena Janauschek (1830–1904) was a Bohemian actress. She became the toast of Prague, then moved into Germany with her talents. Finally in 1867 she made a brief tour of the United States, playing her parts in German. She returned to the United States in 1873, having learned English well enough to play Shakespeare and other great dramas of the day.

Probably as a publicity stunt, she let it be known that she was the model that posed for the shooting festival taler of the free city of Frankfurt in 1862 (Davenport No. 653). As a result this silver dollar-size coin for a time became known as the Janauschek taler.

Mr. S. K. Harzfeld of Philadelphia, a resident of Frankfurt in 1862, advised the numismatic world in 1877 that the story was a fabrication, and that he intended to prove it. And prove it he did.

Being unable to contact the designer of the coin, Herr von Nordheim, who had recently suffered a serious injury, he had his good friend, Adolph Hess, contact Dr. Edward Ruppell, the director of the Mint Cabinet at Frankfurt. The reply stated that the female figure was merely a personification of Germania presenting a wreath of victory. In indignation Dr. Ruppell stated:

I must say that it is altogether incomprehensible to me, how an actress dares fancy that the municipal authorities ordered the representation of a statue, bearing her features, in recognition of her performances. . . .

Regardless of the truth, "Fanny" Janauschek gained from the

publicity that she started in 1867. She won fame and fortune in the United States.

A coin could not have been named for a more accomplished actress!

🐭 What is Mickey Mouse money?

Practically every G.I. who saw service in the Pacific Theatre during World War II brought back with him notes issued by the Japanese government, payable in centavos or peso, the monetary units used in the Philippine Islands.

This paper money had been printed in Japan in advance of the invasion of the Philippine Islands and the attack on Pearl Harbor. After gaining control in the Philippines, the Japanese ordered all of the population to turn in whatever money they had and gave the people in return this new currency.

Initially it traded at par, but as the tide turned against Japan, inflation set in. In a derogatory manner this highly devalued currency became jokingly called "Mickey Mouse" money.

The first G.I.s returning from the Philippines brought back quantities, mistakenly believing that it would be valuable. But the printing presses of Japan must have been very busy, because bundles of these bills in unused condition reached the United States at war's end. It is doubtful whether they will ever be worth more than a very nominal premium.

🐚 Why did Canada print a twenty-five-dollar note?

To honor George V, King of England and Emperor of India, on the twenty-fifth anniversary of his reign, Canada outdid herself. A special series of postage stamps were issued (this was common practice throughout the British Empire), struck her first silver dollar and issued a twenty-five-dollar bill.

For this silver jubilee, this Bank of Canada note pictured King George and Queen Mary in their ermine coronation robes and wearing their coronation crowns. The dates 1910–1935 appear at the top of the note

Records state that only $2,215,950 worth of these unique notes were printed and that by 1956 only $46,350, or 1,854 notes, were still outstanding. None circulate today because they are very high-premium collectors' items.

Why is a she-wolf nursing two children shown on a coin of Romania?

This is a controversial piece. According to *A Catalog of Modern World Coins* by R. S. Yeoman, it is a gold medal. Vernon L. Brown, writing in the *Coin Collector's Journal* of August, 1940, refers to it as a twelve-ducat or one-hundred-twenty-five-lei gold coin. It is dated 1939 and pictures King Carol II on horseback on its face. I class it as a coin.

Romanians claim kinship with Rome through the introduction of Roman colonists by the Emperor Trajan between A.D. 101 and 103 after defeating the Dacians, who lived there at that time.

According to legend, twin sons of the god Mars were cast adrift in a basket on the river Tiber. They were saved by a she-wolf who nursed them until they were strong enough to fend for themselves. The boys, Romulus and Remus, subsequently quarreled and Romulus killed his brother. Later he founded the city that bears his name.

Ancient Roman coins often used a design showing the she-wolf nursing the two infants. Modern Romania, proud of its Roman heritage, followed suit in 1939 on this large gold coin.

Does United States currency have to be signed to be valid?

No, it does not. With reference to the currency in circulation today, the notes are not hand signed, but are printed. But the printing of the signatures, seal, and numbers, all of which appear on the face, is a second run through the presses. Exhibits of freak notes have included some where this second step in the printing of the notes has been missing. Nevertheless, the bill is still legal tender.

Before 1929, when U.S. currency was of a larger size, national banks had the privilege of issuing their own notes. These were printed by the Bureau of Engraving and Printing and sent to the individual banks as uncut sheets. The notes were then supposed to be signed by the President and Cashier of the issuing bank before being passed out over the counter. But sometimes there was a slip-up and unsigned notes were released. In spite of being unsigned the notes were still legal obligations of the government and the issuing bank.

What is an Arnprior Variety dollar?

This term is used only when referring to Canadian silver dollars. The normal silver dollar of Canada pictures on its reverse two voyagers paddling a canoe. To give the illusion of water, lines representing waves appear in front and in back of the canoe. On a perfect or unimpaired die three water lines appear both in front and in back.

In December, 1955, a firm in Arnprior, Ontario, special-ordered 2,000 silver dollars from the Ottawa Mint, after the normal run of silver dollars had been completed for the year. These particular dollars came through with one and a half water lines in front of the canoe, creating a variety for that year. This coin type took the name of the town where the variety first appeared.

It was then discovered that some of the 1950 silver dollars also came through with only one and a half water lines. These, too, took the name of Arnprior Variety. With the increased interest in this series other varieties were also noted. There is the 1952 silver dollar with no water lines in evidence either in front of or behind the canoe and the 1957 variety with one water line in front of the canoe.

These water line types exist because in the process of maintaining clean dies, the lines became buffed off in the polishing process.

Why is the word "WAITANGI" on the 1935 New Zealand crown?

The Commonwealth of New Zealand became a Dominion in 1907 and a member of the British Commonwealth of Nations when that body was formed in 1931. But not until 1933 did she issue her first coins. These were the three pence, six pence, shilling, two shilling (florin), and half crown.

The first crown or five-shilling piece was struck in 1935 to commemorate the twenty-fifth year of the reign of George V. New Zealand also wished to honor the signing of the Waitangi Treaty, which had taken place ninety-five years earlier. Thus this coin was to serve a double purpose. The obverse, with the crowned bust of the king, honored him. The reverse, with a Maori warrior and a British sailor, Captain Hobson, shaking hands, and the word "WAITANGI" directly under their feet, honored the treaty made in 1840.

These fierce, warlike Polynesians, known as Maoris, resisted colonization by the British. The Treaty of Waitangi was signed to guarantee the tribesmen their land provided they in turn allowed British settlers to acquire property in this vast territory. The signing of the treaty by no means stopped the fighting. The ten years from 1854 to 1864 saw the worst of the bloodshed.

In 1935 there were 364 proof sets struck, plus an additional 764 crowns, also proof-struck. With a total mintage of only 1,128 pieces, the Waitangi crown is a modern rarity.

Why was Fractional Currency issued?

In normal times the currency of a nation is backed by gold or silver. The nation's paper currency can be redeemed for the valuable metal on demand. When a nation finds itself in a position where it can no longer redeem its paper money we say that it has suspended specie payment.

After the start of the Civil War, the United States government found itself in the position of being unable to redeem its notes for gold or silver. The result was that people panicked and started to hoard their metal money—gold, silver, copper, and copper-nickel.

Merchants, finding that banks could no longer supply them with enough small change, started to improvise. Some issued their own I.O.U.'s in lieu of small change. Others pasted postage stamps on cardboard and these circulated for the value of the attached stamps.

Finally, on July 17, 1862, President Lincoln signed into law the first bill authorizing postage currency. The idea had come from General F. E. Spinner, Treasurer of the United States, who had earlier issued postage stamps on cardboard and had arranged for the Post Office Department to redeem worn-out stamps for new ones, without charge.

This first issue called for five-, ten-, twenty-five-, and fifty-cent notes. The five-cent note showed a reproduction of the current five-cent stamp with the picture of Thomas Jefferson. The ten-

241

cent note pictured the ten-cent stamp with Washington's portrait. The twenty-five-cent note showed five five-cent stamps, while the fifty-cent note showed five ten-cent stamps. The inscription on this first series read: "Postage Currency furnished only by the Assistant Treasurers and designated Depositaries of the U.S. Receivable for Postage Stamps at any Post Office."

After the first issue, it was decided that the issuing of the notes should be a function of the Treasury Department and not the Post Office Department. Therefore beginning with the second series, authorized March 3, 1863, the notes were designated Fractional Currency instead of Postage Currency. These now became "exchangeable for U.S. notes . . ." and took on legal-tender status.

✣ Why did Liberia issue only one- and two-cent pieces until 1896?

The Republic of Liberia has always had a close relationship with the United States. Her history is most interesting.

A group of New Yorkers, sympathetic to the problems of the freed Negro slaves in the United States, in 1816 organized the American Colonization Society. They were not an abolition group, trying to free the slaves of the South, but an organization of compassionate people who felt that the free Negros in America wished to return to Africa, the home of their forebears.

In 1820, they obtained title to land that we now know as Liberia. In 1822 colonization began and by 1847 the Republic of Liberia formally adopted a constitution. To show her sovereign power she had one- and two-cent pieces struck that same year.

With a small population, Liberia had no need of ever establishing her own mint. Her currency was on a par with the United States, and a good part of her economy was supported by gifts from America. Therefore United States currency and coin was used to a large extent. Only in 1896 were dimes, quarters, and halves struck for Liberia. The first nickel did not make its appearance until 1960 and the first silver dollar not until 1961.

We can in truth say that national pride made this young republic issue the one- and two-cent coins, and a desire to assert her independence more fully led to the issuing of the other denominations, beginning in 1896.

✑ *What is so unusual about the Lafayette dollar?*

First, it is the only commemorative dollar-size silver coin struck by the Mint. Second, although dated 1900, it was struck in 1899, contrary to Treasury Department regulations. Third, it reads "Lafayette Dollar" instead of "One Dollar" as required by law. Fourth, the U.S. government donated the silver used, which was never done before or after with a commemorative issue. Fifth, it was the first U.S. coin to bear the portrait of an ex-President (Washington). Sixth, its reverse design, showing the equestrian statue of Lafayette, is almost identical to the 1953 British Coronation Crown of Elizabeth II. Seventh, whereas all the events honored on other issues took place in America, this coin was struck for the French International Exposition of 1900 and honored the placing of a statue of General Lafayette in Paris. And eighth, even though the issue was limited to 50,000 pieces and sold initially at $2 per coin, the whole issue was never sold and 14,000 coins were remelted because of the lack of demand.

But conditions change. An uncirculated specimen cost $15 in 1947. Ten years later the price had jumped to $37.50. In 1966 the coin is considered a good buy at $150.

Why was the Jenny Lind Medal struck?

Blame (or credit) can go to Phineas T. Barnum, one of the greatest showmen of all times.

Jenny Lind (1820–1887) was born in Sweden. She studied opera, making her debut in 1838. By 1847 she had gained international recognition as the greatest soprano of her day. When she decided to abandon opera for the concert stage in 1849, Barnum offered to manage an American tour.

Dubbing her the "Swedish Nightingale," Barnum arranged a bit of fanfare for her opening American concert, to be held on September 11, 1850. This included a triumphal parade from the ship to her hotel, along well-decorated streets with floral arches and flags of many nations. Then he offered a two-hundred-dollar prize to the party who composed the best "ode of welcome." With the scene set and the excitement created, he announced that for opening night seats would be auctioned off. The winner paid $225 for the privilege of having first choice in selecting his seat. Even the regular seats sold for $5, an extremely high price in 1850, equal to a week's wages for skilled workers.

After the opening concert, Barnum announced that Miss Lind had donated her entire share of the receipts to charity. To make sure that this generous act would be remembered, he had a small medal struck that pictured the head of Jenny Lind on one side, while the other side had the inscription "FIRST CONCERT IN AMERICA/ AT CASTLE GARDEN N.Y. SEP. 11, 1850/ ATTENDED BY 7,000 PEOPLE/ PROCEEDS 35,000 DOLLARS/

12,500 DOLLARS GIVEN BY MISS LIND TO CHARITABLE INSTITUTIONS." Copies are known in bronze and white metal.

Jenny Lind's American tour was a tremendous success, owing to the great showmanship of P. T. Barnum. The public may have laughed at his tricks, but it paid good money to see his artists.

An interesting poem, said to have circulated in 1850, appeared in the November, 1896, issue of the *Ladies' Home Journal*. Mr. Barnum is supposed to be the speaker:

So Jenny come along: you're just the card for me,
And quit those kings and queens for the country of the free;
Folks'll welcome you with speeches and serenades and rockets,
And you shall touch their hearts and I shall tap their pockets;
And if between us both the public isn't skinned
Why my name isn't Barnum, nor your name Jenny Lind.

✍ *Why is the 1895 silver dollar listed only in "proof" condition?*

Although the *Mint Reports on Coins Manufactured by Mints of the United States* record 12,880 silver dollars struck at the Philadelphia Mint in 1895, the only specimens known are those struck for the proof sets of that year.

Mint records indicate 880 proofs stuck that year of dimes, quarters, halves, and silver dollars and a larger number of minor coins. Until recently it was assumed that the 12,000 regular strikes might exist.

In November, 1954, the Bureau of the Mint reported more than 271,000,000 silver dollars in government depositories. The majority of such coins would be mint-sealed new coins of various dates up to 1935, the last year of coinage.

Each Christmastime some two or three thousand bags from the stockpile would be released because of public demand for silver dollars for yuletide gifts. And almost each year some previously rare or scarce date became less rare or scarce because of an increase in the "supply" of that year. By 1964, less than 3,000,000 silver dollars remained in the government vaults and the dates of these were spot checked. Result: no 1895 coins were discovered.

This coin, with each passing year, has enjoyed greater and greater popularity, reflected by the increase in catalog value. In 1940 it cataloged at $6, in 1949 at $75, in 1958 at $550, and in 1966 at $4,500.

Note: Silver dollars were also minted at New Orleans and San Francisco in 1895. These pieces can be identified by the mintmark "O" or "S" on the reverse side at the bottom of the coin under the wreath. They are scarce, but not rare. Counterfeits exist where a mintmark has been removed.

✒ Did Cellini design coins?

The famous Florentine jeweler, sculptor, and medalist Benvenuto Cellini (1500–1571) had a few coins attributed to him, although his fame came from designing other art objects and not coins.

Cellini moved to Rome in 1524, where he became well known as an ornamental jeweler. He executed medals for Pope Clement VII, and in 1530 was appointed Engraver of Coins at the Papal Mint. The doppia or double scudo of Clement VII is said to be his work. The early doppia of Pope Paul III (1534–1549) is also attributed to him.

Paul III and Cellini soon had a falling out and the artist had to flee Rome. He sought the protection of Alessandro de' Medici, Duke of Florence, who welcomed the artist. For his new patron he designed a silver forty-soldi piece.

Many beautiful medals were engraved by this master craftsman, but the three coins mentioned are believed to be the only coins that he designed.

Why would there be a Kirtland Safety Society Anti-Banking Company?

The Mormons left New York State in 1831 and moved to Kirtland, Ohio. Here, some twenty miles east of Cleveland, they developed a rural community of some 4,000 God-fearing souls. By 1833 they had started to construct their first temple, a fine building that still stands to this day.

In 1836 they decided to start a bank to be known as the Kirtland Safety Society Bank. In anticipation of being granted a charter they ordered notes printed in Philadelphia. When the Ohio legislature refused to grant the group a charter, they decided to organize regardless.

Since they already had printed notes, they decided to call themselves the "Kirtland Safety Society Anti-Banking Company." Thus they could add "Anti" in front of "Bank" and "ing Company" after it. In so doing they did not need to go to the expense of having new notes printed.

The company was established in January, 1837. The Panic of 1837 led to its failure in August of the same year. The organizers were accused of perpetrating a swindle, which accusation was completely unfounded. In time it became meaningless because the Mormons as a group redeemed all notes on demand, even though legally not required to do so. As a result these notes are very rare.

In 1914, Waldo C. Moore, an Ohio banker and numismatist,

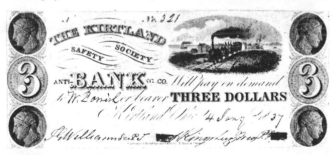

wrote an article about these notes in *The Numismatist.* At this late date he reported that he had yet to locate a twenty-dollar or fifty-dollar note, even though various publications had referred to notes for one, two, three, five, ten, twenty, fifty, and one hundred dollars.

To illustrate how these rarities turn up, Mr. Moore quoted an April, 1890, issue of the *Willoughby Independent,* which said in part:

In Chardon, Ohio, on April 19, there was found in an old desk in a secret drawer between the leaves of an old account book, ninety-five dollars in Kirtland bank notes, thirty-one in number, consisting of $1, $2, $3, $5, $10 and $20 bills. How long they had remained in hiding no one now can tell. The desk once belonged to the grandfather of the finder. How he obtained them and why he laid them by, can only be imagined. The bank officers' names, as they appear on the bills are J. Smith, Cashier and S. Rigdon, President, and sometimes the signatures of J. Smith, Jr., O. Pratt, S. G. Williams, N. R. Whitney, W. Parrish, Omo O. Hyde, and S. Smith appear, but only as holding minor offices. The engravers were Underwood, Bald, Spencer & Hufty, New York and Philadelphia.

More often than not, the bills appear without the added printing of "anti" and "ing Company," making those known with the correct name as the scarcer variety.

What is a Peale's Museum token?

One hundred and fifty years ago the name Peale was as well known as Ringling Bros., Barnum and Bailey is today.

It all started with Charles Willson Peale (1741–1827) of Maryland, the most famous portrait painter of his day. Besides being an artist he was also a good businessman. He settled in Philadelphia after the Revolutionary War and with his son Rembrandt (all his sons were named after famous painters) opened the first Peale's Museum in Independence Hall. In 1821 it was incorporated as The Philadelphia Museum. Tokens of this Philadelphia enterprise are known.

In 1825 his son Rubin Peale opened a similar museum in New York. This one had the name of "Peale's New York Museum of Fine Arts." Both museums had galleries of fine paintings, many executed by members of the Peale family, since three of Charles's sons were fine painters. But the museums also attracted considerable attention because they included unique natural history displays of snakes, lizards, stuffed animals, and birds, and many other seldom-seen *objets d'art.*

Edgar H. Adams, numismatist, researched the New York Peale's Museum tokens in 1912. Among his discoveries was an advertisement in a New York City newspaper in 1831 that announced in part: "Tickets for a whole family for one year, $10; ticket for a gentleman with the privilege of a lady each time with him, for one year, $5; single admission, as usual, 25 cents; children, half price." (Yes, the half cent circulated at that time.) This would indicate at least three types of tokens, although but one type is currently known.

Mr. Adams stated in 1912 that the museum "seems to have been conducted until some time in 1842." He was probably unaware that in 1842 that master showman, Phineas T. Barnum, purchased Peale's Museum and another one in New York and reopened them under the name of the American Museum.

Peale's Museum tokens are therefore slightly related to "The Greatest Show on Earth." And Charles Willson Peale and P. T. Barnum were each in his way the super showmen of their day.

Who was "Hog Mouth"?

Probably more coins of the seventeenth century exist today that show the profile of Leopold I, Holy Roman Emperor, King of Germany, Hungary and Bohemia, Archduke of Austria, Duke of Burgundy and Count of Tyrol, than of any other ruler of that century. He ruled from 1657 to 1705.

Leopold was a Hapsburg, a member of the Germanic royal family that ruled the Holy Roman Empire almost continually from 1438. A characteristic of this noble family was a protruding lower jaw and a thick lower lip. This feature can be noted on coins of Charles V (1500–1558) and on Alfonso XIII (1886–1941), the last Spanish king.

Emperor Leopold seemed to be proud of this mark of Hapsburg royalty. Instead of attempting to conceal his large hanging underlip, he insisted in being pictured in profile with this deformity prominently displayed.

For this reason he justly earned the nickname "Hog Mouth."

What is unusual about the medal given Zachary Taylor for the Battle of Palo Alto?

After you hear the story, you might agree that General Zachary Taylor's place in American history was assured by his friend and political rival, Winfield Scott.

Scott abandoned a law career in 1808 to accept an Army commission. By 1841 he had risen to the position of supreme commander of the United States Army, holding that position for twenty years. When the United States went to war with Mexico in 1846, General Scott picked Zachary Taylor to command the troops for the "northern campaign," while he personally directed the "southern campaign."

General Taylor's victory at Palo Alto, against great odds, was so decisive that on July 16, 1846, Congress by resolution authorized the striking of a gold medal to be presented to the newest American hero. This act inspired his commander-in-chief to address the following request:

HEADQUARTERS OF THE ARMY
WASHINGTON, JULY 25, 1846
HON. W. L. MARCY, Secretary of War:

As medals are among the surest monuments of history, as well as muniments of individual distinction, there should be given to them, besides intrinsic value and durability of material the utmost grace of design, with the highest finish in mechanical execution. All this is necessary to give the greater or adventitious value; as in the present instance, the medal is to be, at once, an historical record and a reward of distinguished merit. The credit of the donor thus becomes even more than that of the receiver interested in obtaining a perfect specimen of the fine arts.

The within resolution prescribes *gold* as the material of the medal. The general form (circular) may be considered as equally settled by our own practice, and that of most nations, ancient and modern. There is, however, some little diversity in *diameter* and *thickness* in the medals heretofore ordered by Congress at different periods, as may be seen in the cabinets of the War and Navy Departments. Diversity in dimensions is even greater in other countries.

The specific character of the medal is shown by its two faces, or the *face* and the *reverse*. The within resolution directs "appropriate devices and inscriptions thereon." For the *face*, a bust likeness is needed, to give, with the name and the rank of the donor, *individuality*. To obtain the likeness, a first rate miniature painter should, of course, be employed.

The reverse receives the device, appropriate to the event commemorated. To obtain this, it is suggested that the resolutions and

despatches belonging to the subject, be transmitted to a master in the art of design—say Prof. Weir, at West Point—for a drawing, including, if practicable, this inscription:

PALO ALTO
RESACA DE LA PALMA
MAY 8 AND 9, 1846

A third artist—all to be well paid—is next to be employed—a die sinker. The mint of the U.S. will do the coinage. Copies in cheaper metal of all our gold medals should be given to libraries of the Federal and State Governments, to those of colleges, etc.

The medals voted by the Revolutionary Congress were executed—designs and dies—under the superintendence of Mr. Jefferson in Paris about the year 1786. Those struck in honor of victories in our war of 1812 were all—at least so far as it respected the land service—done at home, and not one of them presented, I think, earlier than the end of Mr. Monroe's administration (1825). The delay principally resulted from the want of good die sinkers. There was only one of mediocre merit (and he a foreigner) found for the army. What the state of this art may now be in the U.S. I know not. But I beg leave again to suggest that the honor of the country requires that medals voted by Congress should always exhibit the art involved in their highest state of perfection *wherever* found; for letters, science, and the fine arts, constitute but *one* republic, embracing the world. So thought our early Government and Mr. Jefferson, a distinguished member of that general republic.

All of which is respectfully submitted to the Secretary of War.

General Winfield Scott's recommendation led to bronze copies that were sold at reasonable prices to an admiring public. This recommendation could have also been a contributing factor that led to Taylor's election as President in 1849.

Identical bronze copies may still be purchased from the Superintendent of the Mint at Philadelphia.

Where did the term "wildcat" note come from?

In the 1830's, many banks were started in Michigan with fraudulent intent. A loophole in that state's law allowed them to receive charters. Within two years 38 of 40 such banks failed, and their notes became worthless.

These banks all were said to have used a wildcat as part of their design. Thus, the worthless notes were called "wildcat" notes. Shortly all notes of dubious value were referred to as "wildcat" notes.

The Michigan legislators should have been more wary, for, according to an article that appeared in *The Numismatist* of July, 1912, Detroit citizens had been duped as early as 1806 by a remarkable "wildcat" scheme.

The story goes that two eastern slickers came to Detroit in 1806, put up an impressive fortresslike building, then displayed $19,000 in gold coin in the "bank" window. Next they sold shares to investors at $25 per share. After selling some $10,000 worth they printed $150,000 worth of beautifully engraved bank notes. Immediately thereafter they packed up their gold and their bank notes and headed back East, passing off their worthless notes all over New England.

The tale concludes that "so far as human knowledge goes only $500 of it was ever redeemed, and that under dire threats."

Why did Canada issue more copper tokens than the United States?

The pieces referred to were undoubtedly substitutes for pennies (cents) and half pennies. The United States Mint has struck one-cent pieces each and every year (except 1815) since 1793, whereas Canada had no coinage of her own until 1858.

Most of the tokens of Canada that one finds were manufactured before that date. They were privately made because there was a dearth of small change. By far the largest number were made for Canadian banks. The most common seem to be the tokens of the Bank of Montreal, the City Bank, the Quebec Bank, and La Banque de Peuple. These were issued from about 1837 to 1844. In the period from 1850 to 1857 the country was flooded with the tokens of the Bank of Upper Canada.

Private firms also issued tokens. There were those of retail stores, hotels, and a whole series of the Hudson's Bay Company. Many of this group were redeemable for a specific item, such as "one drink" or "one shave." The Hudson's Bay tokens were given in payment of furs and redeemable for merchandise in one of their own stores.

The Canadian copper tokens filled a great need, at a time when Canada was growing rapidly. They make an interesting study, with well over a thousand varieties. And the nicest part is that they are relatively inexpensive.

 Why was the design on the back of the one-cent piece (U.S.) changed in 1959?

The Treasury Department felt that a design change would help point up the observance of the sesquicentennial of the birth of Abraham Lincoln in 1809. The approval of President Eisenhower was needed for this move. His approval was received on December 20, 1958.

For the first time in United States coinage a major change was made on one side of a coin while the other side remained unchanged. It was felt that Victor Brenner's head of Lincoln, on the face of the coin, could not be improved. Therefore only the reverse would be changed.

The design for the reverse had as its central feature a picture of the Lincoln Memorial. This most impressive building, standing in Potomac Park, across from the Washington Monument, looks like a temple of ancient Greece. It was designed by Henry Bacon. Within its marble columns is a gigantic statue of Lincoln seated. This awe-inspiring statue was the work of Daniel Chester French. The Memorial was dedicated in 1922.

The new one-cent piece was simultaneously released all over the nation on February 22, 1959, the one-hundred-fiftieth anniversary of the birth of this great American.

 Why did Mexico switch from a silver to a copper-nickel five-centavo piece in 1882?

This is the story of a fiasco supreme. In 1882 the Mexican legislature authorized the minting of one-, two-, and five-centavo pieces of copper-nickel, 75 per cent copper and 25 per cent nickel. This combination of metals is identical to that used in the United States nickel five-cent pieces from 1866.

The one centavo replaced the large copper centavo, the two centavos was a new coin denomination, and the five centavos replaced a like silver coin. Naturally the seigniorage (profit from producing coins whose metallic content is less than exchange value) was far greater by using copper-nickel rather than silver in the five-centavo pieces.

To insure maximum use of the new coins, laws were passed making these coins legal tender up to twenty-five pesos, and making one third of all customs payable in these coins. Further, the army was paid entirely with these new pieces. Finally, the government allowed a 30 per cent discount to quantity purchasers. This meant that many employers bought these coins at seventy centavos on the peso and literally paid their workers with bags of money.

Naturally public resentment ran high and rioting and bloodshed was reported in Mexico City and Vera Cruz. Regardless of the law, storekeepers refused to take these small coins; soldiers and workers found that they could not use them to make their normal retail purchases.

Finally the legislators admitted defeat, with a public announcement on December 11, 1883:

The last nickel coin has been struck. The contract for the coinage of nickel was made about two years ago with Messrs. Wexel & DeGress. The late Major DeGress with the energy for which he was so widely known, immediately went abroad to purchase the machinery and dies. He also ordered an ample supply of blank nickel pieces from which the coins were made. The coinage began last winter and continued almost without interruption until Friday last (Dec. 7th), when the massive machine left its impress on the nickel for the last time.

No records were kept as to the number minted in 1882 and 1883 by year, only by total mintage. In 1884 the Mexican government reported that 100,000,000 one centavos, 50,000,000 two centavos, and 40,000,000 five centavos were struck. Today we know that the 1882 one-centavo and two-centavo pieces are scarce, and that the 1883 five-centavo coin is rare.

Why is a "broken bank" note more valuable in one state than in another?

The term "broken bank" refers to those banks which issued their own notes, subsequently failed, and as a result could not redeem their own legal obligations. Between 1793 and 1861 these banks sprang up all over the United States. They were state-chartered banks given the privilege of issuing their own notes. Regulations controlling the amount of notes a bank could issue were inadequate. Often the officers, directors, and stockholders were dishonest. But whether because of poor management, the unstable economy of the country, or dishonesty, these banks failed and their notes became worthless.

Their value today is that they have historical significance, are often beautifully engraved, and were generally hand-dated and signed. Most are collected by states. So it naturally follows that collectors who are residents of Ohio are more likely to wish to form a collection of Ohio "broken bank" notes, while New York collectors would prefer those of their own state.

Further, most states and many cities have their own historical societies. These cultural institutions often have a "coin and paper money" room devoted to numismatic items that refer to their area. And still further, descendants of the signers of these notes help create a demand even among noncollectors for notes that bear the signature of one of their ancestors.

What modern American has been the recipient of the greatest number of medals?

That man has to be Charles A. Lindbergh. This young aviator won the hearts of both Americans and foreigners with his New York-to-Paris flight on May 20–21, 1927. His youth, good looks, modesty, and ability won plaudits from all over the world. One way of expressing praise and extending an honor is by issuing a medal to the hero. Some of the more interesting ones are worthy of mention.

Probably the first one struck was by the businessmen of St. Louis who backed Lindbergh financially. The inscription read: "COMMEMORATING THE FIRST NEW YORK–PARIS FLIGHT BY CAPT. CHARLES A. LINDBERGH 'SPIRIT OF ST. LOUIS' NEW YORK MAY 20TH PARIS MAY 21ST 1927." Three were struck in gold and presented to Lucky Lindy, his mother, and President Calvin Coolidge. Twenty-five, in silver, were presented to Ambassador to France Myron T. Herrick, King George V of England, King Albert I of Belgium, the President of France, and other high public officials. Finally, two thousand in bronze were struck for presentation to museums around the world.

The French government announced, a month after the flight, a "Lindbergh Medal" reading "ALARUM REMIGO VINCTA PRIMUM OCEANI LITTORA" (the birds fly, for the first time are the boundaries of the ocean conquered by flight).

The National Geographic Society awarded its Hubbard Medal to the "Lone Eagle." This rare honor had only previously been bestowed upon Rear Admiral Robert E. Peary, Roald Amundsen, Capt. Robert A. Bartlett, Grove Carl Gilbert, Sir Ernest H. Shackleton, Vilhjalmur Stefansson, and Admiral Richard E. Byrd.

The Smithsonian Institution followed suit with its Langley Medal, previously only presented to the Wright Brothers, Glenn H. Curtis, and Gustav Eiffel.

The United States Army elevated Captain Lindbergh to the rank of Colonel and presented him with the Distinguished Flying

Cross. The French gave him the Legion of Honor, the Belgians the Order of Leopold, and the British the Royal Air Force Cross. Other foreign governments made similar presentations, as did many cities in the United States, all saying "well done" medallicly.

Probably the one that meant the most to Lindbergh was the Congressional Medal, authorized by a joint resolution of the United States Congress on May 4, 1928. This resolution called for a gold medal, suitably inscribed "in recognition of the achievements of Col. Charles A. Lindbergh," and authorized an appropriation of $1,500 for that purpose. (Copies of this medal may still be obtained from the Philadelphia Mint.)

✍ *Who was "Old Coppernose"?*

To most of us Henry VIII, King of England (1509–1547), is known because of his many wives. To the numismatist he is better known because he earned the nickname of "Old Coppernose."

One way of "cheating the public" is for the government to debase its coins. Debasing means reducing the intrinsic value of the metal at a time when metal is supposed to be worth the amount stamped on it.

Henry VIII reduced the silver content of the coins struck during his reign from better than 90 per cent to less than 40 per cent silver. The difference was made up of copper.

When such debased coins showed wear, the color changed from silver to dirty copper. Henry VIII's coins showed him full face, with the nose, naturally, in high relief.

Therefore, when the coin started to wear, the first part to discolor was the nose. Hence the nickname "Old Coppernose."

Who is the lady pictured on the hundred-dollar Confederate note of April 6, 1863?

She is Lucy Holcombe Pickens. Her picture also appears on the C.S.A. one-dollar note of June 2, 1862. She has the distinction of being the only woman, other than allegorical figures, to appear on the currency of the Confederate States of America.

Her name will not be found in an encyclopedia today, but will always be remembered by students of the Confederacy. She was born Lucy Petway Holcombe in Amelia County, Virginia, changing it to Mrs. Francis Wilkinson Pickens in 1858.

Her husband served, with her at his side, as Minister to Russia from 1858 to 1860. While in St. Petersburg, Mr. Pickens was elected Governor of South Carolina, which position he accepted. He is best known as the man who directed that Fort Sumter be attacked and captured.

Mrs. Pickens was used as a symbol of Confederate womanhood. She is said to have sold her jewelry and advanced the Southern cause by using the funds obtained to outfit a regiment. There is some question as to the authenticity of the story, but it is believed that she contributed large funds to that group which honored her by calling themselves "The Holcombe Legion." The legion was made up of seven infantry companies and one cavalry company. They fought at Manassas, Stony Creek, Kingston, and Goldsboro.

One author compared her sacrifice to that of Queen Isabella of Spain, who also gave up her jewelry for a cause.

ᘏᕒ What is a U.S. one-cent piece, 1922 Plain?

It is well known that in 1922 all U.S. one-cent pieces were struck at the Denver Mint with the mintmark "D." The Philadelphia Mint struck no one-cent pieces that year. The "Plain" refers to certain of these Denver Mint coins that do not show the "D."

This is the result of a die becoming clogged with dirt or other matter. When we remember that the raised part of a coin is the part countersunk on the die, we can then realize that a clogged or filled die will prevent the striking up of the raised portion. We can consider that a 1922 "Plain" cent is a defective coin, the result of poor workmanship and control.

Nevertheless, it is a recognized variety in the recognized coin catalogs, and as such brings, in new condition, more than ten times the price of the normal uncirculated 1922-D. In fact, today it is the highest price coin of the Lincoln cent series and sells for over $700 in new condition.

ᘏᕒ Why do coins of England have much of the wording on them in Latin?

Many countries have used Latin on their coinage as well as on heraldic devices. Latin has been the language of the Church. Spoken and written knowledge of it was required, not only of the clergy, but also of the nobleman and scholar. Most of the European languages had their origin in Latin, gradually changing through the use of slang, corruptions of words, and the introduction of other tongues from conquerors from time to time (but this is another study).

Further, the first coinage was introduced into England about the first century B.C., and it was composed of crude copies of Greek and Roman coins. With the Roman invasion of A.D. 43, Roman coins replaced the crude native coins. These coins, naturally, had all inscriptions in Latin. From then on, all English coins used the language of the Romans.

There is one notable exception. That was when British royalty was overthrown in 1649 and the Commonwealth of England issued her own coins. From 1649 to 1653 the coins of England used only English. But even under the Commonwealth, when Oliver Cromwell became Lord Protector of England in 1653, he allowed Latin to be used again on English coins.

Certainly, it has a noble ring, considering that it was the language of only the highly educated, which in earlier years meant only the clergy and the nobility.

Does the United States Treasury wash and reissue paper money?

Not at present, but it used to. The New York *Sun* reported in 1916 that dirty paper money, sent to Washington for redemption, was examined, and if found usable, was washed, ironed, and reissued. It was stated that some banks preferred the washed money since it was softer and easier to handle. Thirty-five thousand bills could be washed daily and a savings of about $350 a day was possible since it cost 30 cents to wash one hundred dirty bills and $1.30 to print the same number.

In an earlier report, in 1912, an article in *The Numismatist* stated that the laundering of paper money added three months to the life of a bill which only had a life expectancy of thirteen months. Here the cost of printing one hundred new bills was stated as $3.52½, not $1.30, while the cost of washing and ironing was estimated to be 50 cents per one hundred.

Conclusion: more efficient techniques for both printing and washing bills were developed between 1912 and 1916.

✍ *How was Tiffany & Co. associated with numismatics?*

Probably most American numismatists associate Tiffany & Co. with the Bryan satirical tokens that were struck during the Bryan-McKinley presidential campaign. The medals known as Zerbe No. 1, 2, 3, and 4 were all struck by this firm.

Spink's Numismatic Circular of September, 1912, lists this company in its series of articles of "Biographical Notices of Medallists," which reads in part:

TIFFANY & CO. (Amer.) A famous firm of Silversmiths of New York with branch houses in London and Paris. The founder, Charles Lewis Tiffany, a Goldsmith, was born at Killingly (Connecticut) and died in 1902. First employed in his father's manufactory, he founded in 1837 a business of fancy goods, Bohemian crystal ware, porcelain and diamonds. The firm became renowned for the sale of plate.

C. L. Tiffany's son, Lewis Comfort Tiffany, who was born in New York in 1848, devoted himself to painting. He also distinguished himself in decorative art and has executed numerous designs for the Glass Works which he founded in 1879.

Messrs Tiffany has edited a number of medals. . . .

The article concludes with a listing of some of the outstanding medals struck by this internationally known firm. They include gold medals presented by the New York Chamber of Commerce and Citizens in 1858 to individuals for service rendered in laying the telegraph cable between Europe and America, medals struck to honor the four-hundredth anniversary of the discovery of America by Christopher Columbus (1893), a Grant Monument Medal in 1897, a Greater New York Medal in 1898, the Edgar

Allan Poe Centenary Medal in 1909, and the Commander Robert Edwin Peary Medal in 1909.

Every once in a while copies of Tiffany & Co. medals show up at antique shows. Be alert, and you might find one of these beautiful medallic art objects.

🔊 *What is the history of the Confederate States of America one-cent piece?*

On order from a local jeweler who was in contact with representatives from the seceding States, Robert Lovett, Jr., a Philadelphia die cutter, designed and cut dies for a Confederate one-cent piece. He struck twelve pieces in copper-nickel and then, out of fear of prosecution by the United States government for assisting the enemy, he hid the coins and dies.

In 1873, by accident he passed one of the coins, which eventually came to the attention of Captain J. W. Haseltine, a well-known Philadelphia coin dealer. The captain recognized the obverse as being similar in design to Mr. Lovett's "store card" of 1860.

After some persuasion, Mr. Lovett sold Captain Haseltine the remaining eleven pieces and the dies.

The following circular continues the story:

CIRCULAR TO COLLECTORS

Philadelphia, April 2, 1874

Having succeeded in discovering and purchasing the dies of the Confederate Cent, we, the undersigned, have concluded to strike for the benefit of Collectors a limited number, and in order to protect those gentlemen who had the nickel pieces, originally struck in 1861, we determined to strike none in that metal. Our intention was to strike five hundred in copper, but after the fifty-fifth impression the collar burst and the dies were badly broken. They are now in the possession of Mr. Haseltine, and may be seen at any time at his store, No. 1343 Chestnut Street, Philadelphia.

The history of this piece is probably known to most Collectors, but, for the information of those who are ignorant of the facts, we will state that the dies were made by Mr. Lovett, of Philadelphia, in 1861, who says that they were ordered in that year for the South, and that he struck but twelve pieces, but probably thinking that he might have some difficulty in reference to them (having made the dies for the South), he mentioned the matter to no one until a few months since, when he parted with ten pieces, struck in nickel, which he stated were all he had, having lost two pieces. One of the lost pieces was the means of the die and pieces being traced. Although the Southern Confederacy did not adopt this piece, it will always be considered interesting as the only coinage for the said Confederacy.

Description—Obverse, 1861; head of Liberty; inscription, "Confederate States of America"; reverse, a wreath of corn and wheat, with a bale of cotton at the bottom; in the centre, the words "1Cent." The restrikes were struck by Peter L. Krider, No. 618 Chestnut Street, and we now offer them at the following prices:

Gold, only seven struck, each $30.00
Silver, only twelve struck, each 15.00
Copper, only fifty-five struck, each 4.00
Nickel, originals struck in 1861, only four left, each 20.00

All orders to be addressed to J. W. Haseltine, No. 1343 Chestnut Street, Philadelphia.

Respectfully,   J. COLVIN RANDALL
                   JOHN W. HASELTINE

Philadelphia, April 2, 1874

We, the undersigned, do hereby certify that the following is the exact number of pieces restruck from the dies of the Confederate Cent mentioned in the forgoing circular, and that the dies are now broken.

Seven in Gold
Twelve in Silver
Fifty-five in Copper

J. COLVIN RANDALL
JOHN W. HASELTINE
PETER L. KRIDER

These pieces seldom come on the market today, but when they do, are highly sought after, and bring prices in four figures.

Who is J. Brooke, Rajah?

Still fairly common are minor copper coins of Sarawak dated 1863. On the reverse is shown the denomination (¼ cent, ½ cent, 1 cent), the date 1863, and the word "SARAWAK." On the obverse is the head of a handsome Englishman and the words "J. BROOKE, RAJAH." The story of how an Englishman became ruler of part of the Island of Borneo reads like a fairy tale.

James Brooke was an adventurer who had worked for the East India Co. and had made his fortune. After retirement he journeyed to Borneo for a dual purpose. One was to stop piracy in this part of the world and the other was to help make life better for the Borneo natives.

Upon arriving in Sarawak he found the country torn by civil war being waged by the native Dyaks and the Malays. The country was nominally ruled by a Rajah Hassim, acting on behalf of his uncle, the Sultan of Brunei, who held sovereignty. Hassim appealed to Brooke to help end the war. This was accomplished by a small group of Europeans whom Brooke was able to mold into a strong fighting force.

Brooke's reward was to be given a residence in Sarawak and permission to trade with the natives. In time he endeared himself to both the Dyaks and the Malays. Seeing that he had the ability to maintain peace, the Sultan offered him the governorship, which carried with it the title of Rajah. A few years later the Sultan gave Brooke and his heirs this area in perpetuity. In 1843 he was knighted by Queen Victoria and in 1863, the date of his coins, the British government recognized Sarawak as an independent state.

Rajah Sir James Brooke was succeeded, upon his death in 1868, by his nephew, Sir Charles Johnson Brooke, who was succeeded by his son, Sir Charles Vyner Brooke in 1917. In July, 1946, the Brocke dynasty ended when Sarawak became a British Colony. Today, of course, it is part of Malaysia.

 Does the word "LIBERTY" appear on every United States one-cent coin?

In the whole one-cent series, only on the flying eagle cents, issued in 1857 and 1858, does the word "LIBERTY" not appear. On the early cents until 1808, the word appeared in large, bold letters above the goddesslike head of Miss Liberty. Thereafter, on the large cents it appears on her diadem or head band. With the introduction of the "Indian Head" cents in 1859, it appeared on the head band of the Indian warbonnet. Here the letters were raised and extremely small in size. As a result, on all normally circulated coins of this type, the lettering became obliterated. With the introduction of the Lincoln cent in 1909, "LIBERTY" can be plainly seen in the field to the left of Lincoln's bust.

Why are so many coins of Ceylon in shapes other than round?

In a country where a large part of the population is illiterate, there is an advantage to having square coins, or coins with fluted edges. It makes for easier identification.

Egypt, also a country with a problem of illiteracy, has made coins with holes, six-sided and with fluted edge, no doubt for the same reason. India, too, has done likewise.

But then we find that Canada, with no illiteracy problem, found it expedient to make her five-cent piece twelve-sided instead of round in 1942. Her reason was that the 1942 (and 1943) issue was made of an alloy of 88 per cent copper and 12 per cent zinc. This metal, called tombac, had a tendency to discolor to a dirty brown, and so was often mistaken for a one-cent piece. This only proves that people may look at a coin, be able to read, but rely merely on color or shape to make identification.

What are "Feuchtwanger's Composition" coins?

These are coins made of a "German silver" composition. This alloy was said to have been introduced in the United States by Dr. Lewis Feuchtwanger. This learned scientist, a graduate of Heidelberg University, was a German. He migrated to the United States in about 1830.

The metal, German silver, that he introduced looked like silver, but was an alloy of about 50 per cent copper, 20 per cent zinc, and 30 per cent nickel, although each part could vary as much as 10 per cent and the metal would still have a silvery appearance. Dr.

Feuchtwanger executed pattern coins of one- and three-cent denominations, using German silver, which is called "Feutch-wanger's Composition." These coins showed an eagle on one side and the date 1837. The other side said "Feutchwanger's Composition" around the perimeter, with a wreath inside the inscription and with the denomination spelled out within the wreath.

To further his cause he sent a petition to Congress in September, 1837, requesting that the government consider his composition in place of the present pure-copper minor coins that were being struck.

The good doctor's appeal was rejected, but bore some fruit later. If Dr. Feuchtwanger had not suggested his alloy, the Mint would not have started its own experiments to find an alloy with better wearing qualities than pure copper. These experiments eventually led to the introduction of the copper-nickel cent in 1857 and the copper-nickel three-cent piece in 1865.

🏵 Why were there three types of United States one-cent pieces in 1864?

From 1793 until 1857, the one cent was made of pure bronze and only slightly smaller than the half dollar. When it was decided in 1857 to reduce the size of the coin to its present size the metallic content was changed to 88 per cent copper and 12 per cent nickel. This alloy was used in 1857 and 1858 in the "flying eagle" cents and from 1859 to 1864 in the "Indian Head" cents.

There was public disapproval of this copper-nickel alloy. When first struck the coins had a silvery appearance, but with age this changed to a dirty light brown or bronze. Therefore, early in 1864 it was decided to change the alloy to 95 per cent copper and 5 per cent tin and zinc (which continued to be used until 1962).

Later in the year, J. B. Longacre, the designer of the "Indian Head" cents, decided to place his initial on the coin. This was subtly done by placing a small "L" on the bonnet ribbon of the Indian headdress.

Why Mr. Longacre did not place his initial on the cents of 1859, 1860, 1861, 1862, or 1863 is anyone's guess. Trial pieces in bronze and other metals were struck in 1863 using both the regular die of 1863 (without the "L" on the ribbon) and using another die identical to it, but with the "L."

Of the three varieties of 1864 one-cent pieces, the bronze without "L" is the commonest and the bronze with the "L" is the scarcest.

How did England happen to name a gold coin a "guinea"?

In the middle of the seventeenth century most of England's gold came from the mines of the "Company of Royal Adventurers of England Trading in Africa," also known as the African Company. This firm operated mines on the west coast of Africa in the territory known as Guinea.

Earlier English gold coins were known as the unite, the broad, the angel, and at times the pound. In 1663 the coins minted from gold mined by the African Company was given the name of guinea. This coin was to be made of 22 carat gold, weigh 13½ grains, and have a value of twenty shillings. Later the weight was reduced and at times the value changed, sometimes being in excess of 21 shillings.

Pieces with a value of five, two, one, and one-half guineas were struck during the next 150 years. Most of these pieces showed an elephant or elephant and castle as a means of identifying them as being struck from gold mined by the African Company.

Later, although the gold no longer came from West Africa, the coins kept the name of guinea, until the reign of George IV (1820–1830). With this monarch the gold pound of twenty shillings was reborn, although the term guinea continued to be used. Even today, when a price of 21 shillings is indicated the term guinea is most likely used.

✣ Which United States note is the most picturesque?

There was a series of Silver Certificates issued in 1896 of one-, two-, and five-dollar notes. As a series, no other can match its artistry. In the series, my vote goes to the one-dollar bill, which is known as the "Educational Note."

The face of the note shows a seated woman in Grecian robes with her right hand around the waist of a standing boy and with her left hand pointing toward an open book. The background shows the Potomac River with the Washington Monument and the Capitol in the distance. To the right is the book, with its pages open to the Constitution of the United States. This scene is captioned "History Instructing Youth."

The border has the names of famous Americans, each enclosed in a wreath. Those named are Longfellow, Sherman, Lincoln, Irving, Cooper, Fulton, Calhoun, Clay, Jackson, Adams, Jefferson, Washington, Franklin, Hamilton, Perry, Marshall, Webster, Morse, Hawthorne, Bancroft, Grant, Farragut, and Emerson.

Even the reverse is most attractive, with an ornate "one" in the center separating busts of Martha and George Washington.

✍️ Bibliography

Altz, C. G. and Barton, E. H. *Foreign Coins Struck at United States Mints*. Racine, Wisconsin: Whitman Publishing Co., 1965.

American Journal of Numismatics. American Numismatic Society, Vol. 1–49 (1866–1915).

Ancient and Medieval Coins: Selections from The Numismatist. Whitman Publishing Co., 1960.

Becker, T. W. *Pageant of World Commemorative Coins*. Whitman Publishing Co., 1962.

Breen, W. *Dies and Coinage*. Chicago: Hewitt Bros., 1965.

———. *Major Varieties of the United States Three-Dollar Gold Pieces*. Hewitt Bros., n.d.

———. *Varieties of United States Quarter Eagles*. Hewitt Bros., n.d.

Bressett, K. E. *A Guide Book of English Coins—19th & 20th Centuries*. (19th ed.). Whitman Publishing Co., 1965.

Brown, M. R. and Dunn, J. W. *A Guide to the Grading of United States Coins*. Whitman Publishing Co., 1964.

Buttrey, T. V. *A Guide Book of Mexican Decimal Coins 1863–1963*. Whitman Publishing Co., 1963.

Canadian Numismatic Journal. Canadian Numismatic Association, Vol. 1–10.

Charlton, J. E. *1966 Standard Catalogue of Canadian Coins, Tokens and Paper Money*. Whitman Publishing Co., 1965.

Carson, R. A. G. *Coins of the World*. New York: Harper & Brothers, 1962.

Coin Collector's Journal. New York: Scott & Co., Vol. 1–10 (1875–1885).

Coin Collector's Journal. Raymond, W. (ed.). Vol. 1–21 (1934–1954).

Criswell, G. C. and C. L. *Confederate and Southern States Currency*. Pass-A-Grille, Florida: Criswell's, 1957.

Dodson, O. H. *Money Tells the Story*. Whitman Publishing Co., 1962.

Donlon, W. P. *Donlon Catalog of United States Small Size Paper Money*. (2nd ed.). Hewitt Bros., 1966.

Davenport, J. S. *European Crowns 1700–1800*. Hewitt Bros., 1961.

————. *European Crowns Since 1800*. Foster & Stewart Publishing Corp., 1947.

————. *German Talers 1700–1800*. Hewitt Bros., 1958.

————. *German Talers Since 1800*. Published by the author, 1949.

Friedberg, R. *Coins of the British World*. New York: Coin and Currency Institute, Inc., 1962.

————. *Gold Coins of the World* (2nd ed.). Coin and Currency Institute, Inc., 1965.

————. *Paper Money of the United States* (5th ed.). Coin and Currency Institute, Inc., 1964.

Fuld, G. and M. *A Guide to Civil War Store Card Tokens*. Whitman Publishing Co., 1962.

————. *Patriotic Civil War Tokens*. Whitman Publishing Co., 1960.

Gould, M. M., Bressett, K. E., and Dothridge, K. and N. *Alaska's Coinage Through the Years*. Whitman Publishing Co., 1965.

Gould, M. M. and Higgie, L. W. *The Money of Puerto Rico*. Whitman Publishing Co., 1962.

Harris, R. P. *A Guide Book of Modern European Coins*. Whitman Publishing Co., 1965.

Higgie, L. W. *The Colonial Coinage of the U.S. Virgin Islands*. Whitman Publishing Co., 1962.

Judd, J. H. *United States Pattern, Experimental and Trial Pieces* (2nd ed.). Whitman Publishing Co., 1962.

Kadman, L. *Israel's Money*. Tel-Aviv, Israel: Schocken Publishing House, 1963.

Kolman, M. *The Numismatic Lincoln Cent Error*. Published by the author, 1961.

Kovel, R. M. and T. H. *A Directory of American Silver, Pewter and Silver Plate*. New York: Crown Publishers, Inc., 1961.

Krause, D. R. *Swiss Shooting Talers and Medals*. Whitman Publishing Co., 1965.

Linecar, H. W. A. *Coins*. London: Ernest Benn Ltd., 1962.

Mehl, B. M. "The Star Rare," in *Encyclopedia and Premium Catalog*. Published by the author, 1932.

Mehl's Numismatic Monthly. Mehl, B. M. (ed.) Vol. 1–8 (1908–1917).

Modern Foreign Currency: Selections from The Numismatist. Whitman Publishing Co., 1961.

Newman, E. P. and Bressett, K. E. *The Fantastic 1804 Dollar*. Whitman Publishing Co., 1962.

Numismatic Scrapbook Magazine. Vol. 17–31, Hewitt Bros.

Numismatist, The. American Numismatic Association, Vol. 14–78.

Pennington, P. *How to Read Greek Coins*. Hewitt Bros., n.d.

Raymond, O. E. *The Standard Catalogue of United States Coins*. New York: Wayte Raymond, Inc., 1957.

Raymond, W. *Coins of the World—Nineteenth Century Issues*. Wayte Raymond, Inc., 1947.

———. *Coins of the World—Twentieth Century Issues*. Wayte Raymond, Inc., 1945.

———. *The Silver Dollars of North and South America*. Whitman Publishing Co., 1964.

———. *The Standard Catalogue of United States Coins*. (16th ed.) Wayte Raymond, Inc., 1952.

———. *The Standard Catalogue of United States Coins*. (13th ed.) Wayte Raymond, Inc., 1948.

———. *The Standard Catalogue of United States Coins*. (12th ed.) Wayte Raymond, Inc., 1946.

———. *The Standard Catalogue of United States Coins—1940 ed*. Wayte Raymond, Inc., 1939.

Rothert, M. *A Guide Book of United States Fractional Currency*. Whitman Publishing Co., 1963.

Schilke, O. G. and Solomon, R. E. *America's Foreign Coins*. Coin and Currency Institute, Inc., 1964.

Seaby, H. A. and P. J. A. *Catalogue of the Copper Coins and Tokens of the British Isles*. London: B. A. Seaby, Ltd., 1949.

———. *Standard Catalogue of the Coins of Great Britain and Ireland*. B. A. Seaby, Ltd., 1954.

Shafer, N. *A Guide Book of Modern United States Currency*. Whitman Publishing Co., 1965.

———. *A Guide Book of Philippine Paper Money*. Whitman Publishing Co., 1964.

———. *United States Territorial Coinage for the Philippine Islands*. Whitman Publishing Co., 1961.

Sheldon, W. H. *Penny Whimsy*. New York: Harper & Brothers, 1958.

Skinner, D. H. *Renniks Australian Commonwealth Coinage Guide*. Utley, South Australia: Renniks & Co., 1964.

Slabaugh, A. R. *Confederate States Paper Money*. Whitman Publishing Co., 1961.

———. *Japanese Invasion Money*. Hewitt Bros., 1963.

———. *Prisoner of War Monies and Medals.* Hewitt Bros., 1965.

———. *United States Commemorative Coinage.* Whitman Publishing Co., 1962.

Spink's Numismatic Journal. Vol. 7–38 (1899–1930), London: Spink & Son.

United States Coins: Selections from The Numismatist. Whitman Publishing Co., 1960.

United States Paper Money and Miscellaneous: Selections from The Numismatist. Whitman Publishing Co., 1960.

Taxay, D. *Counterfeit, Mis-struck and Unofficial U.S. Coins.* New York: Arco Publishing Co., 1963.

Utberg, N. S. *The Coins of Mexico 1536–1963.* Published by the author, n.d.

Weissbuch, T. N. and Hoober, R. T. *Price Catalogue of U.S. Colonial and Continental Currency.* Hewitt Bros., 1965.

Willem, J. M. *The United States Trade Dollar.* Whitman Publishing Co., 1965.

Yeoman, R. S. *A Catalog of Modern World Coins.* (6th ed.) Whitman Publishing Co., 1965.

———. *A Guide Book of United States Coins.* (19th ed.) Whitman Publishing Co., 1965.

———. *Handbook of United States Coins.* (23rd ed.) Whitman Publishing Co., 1965.

———. *Moneys of the Bible.* Whitman Publishing Co., 1961.

✍️ Index